OUR PRINCE OF SCRIBES

OUR PRINCE

OF SCRIBES

Writers Remember Pat Conroy

EDITED BY Nicole Seitz AND Jonathan Haupt

FOREWORD BY Barbra Streisand

AFTERWORD BY Cassandra King Conroy

The University of Georgia Press ⁓ Athens

Published with the generous support of the
Georgia Writers Hall of Fame

Published by the University of Georgia Press
Athens, Georgia 30602
www.ugapress.org
© 2018 by Nicole Seitz and Jonathan Haupt
All rights reserved
Designed by Erin Kirk New
Set in 10.7 on 15 Minion Pro
Printed and bound by Thomson-Shore, Inc.
The paper in this book meets the guidelines for
permanence and durability of the Committee on
Production Guidelines for Book Longevity of the
Council on Library Resources.

Most University of Georgia Press titles are
available from popular e-book vendors.

Printed in the United States of America
22 21 20 19 18 C 5 4 3 2 1

Library of Congress Control Number: 2018018091
ISBN: 9780820354484 (hardcover: alk. paper)
ISBN: 9780820354491 (ebook)

Contents

Foreword

~ BARBRA STREISAND

Pat Conroy was a force for good in our world. With courage and grace, he brought the gifts of the devastating beauty of his writing and his transcendent vision of the human heart to the lives of the readers he touched and the writers he inspired. Long after his days in the classroom had ended, Pat continued to teach all of us through his generous example of how an artist can live in service and gratitude to others. In bravely telling his story, as only he could, Pat emboldened others to see the difficult truths of their own lives, but he also welcomed us to glimpse the possibility of transformation and salvation through love and loss. In October 2015, just before Pat's seventieth birthday, what would tragically be his last, I wrote him the following letter, sent from my heart to his. The words still ring true. As writers gather in these pages to honor Pat with our collective remembrances of him and of the lessons he passed on to us, I am delighted for this opportunity to share my letter to Pat once more—in recognition of my teacher, my student, my dear friend, our prince of tides.

~

October 1, 2015

Dear Pat,

First, I fell in love with your book, and then I fell in love with you.

I started reading *The Prince of Tides* and couldn't put it down. I'm always drawn to stories about transformation—love and loss—and the secrets that can destroy you until you bring them into the light. I responded to the theme of forgiveness—being able to accept people with all their flaws. And I personally believe in the healing power of therapy.

As soon as I finished the book, I started to visualize it as a movie.

I wanted to know everything about the characters. I wanted to know Tom. How could I know Tom? By getting to know the man who created him.

So I invited you to come see me in New York, and we spent two wonderful weeks together. I just wanted to hear your stories—about your father, your mother, your family, your whole life. I was greedy for any detail that would help me flesh out the characters and understand the world of the movie. I'm far from a southerner, but one of your wives was Jewish, from Brooklyn, so I took that as a good sign. I knew you'd understand me.

From the first moment we started talking, you were so generous and kind, humble and loving. I vividly remember you teaching me how to do the Shag. It's a dance that was mentioned in the book, so I said, "Could you show me how to do it?"

Well, talk about transformation! Suddenly this rather shy, courtly southern gentleman turned into a hip-shaking hepcat. Loose as a goose. Boy, you could really fling that tush around! I'm shy, too—another reason we got along—and I rarely get up and dance. But we had such fun, dancing the Shag in my office. I don't think I was even doing the right steps but it didn't matter because you were *so good.* You took my hand and swung me in and out and I just followed you. I was so impressed with your footwork!

You were such a joy to work with, Pat. I was so honored that you entrusted your beautiful book to me. And besides the book, you gave me another gift.

My son Jason wanted to play Bernard but I thought that might be complicated. Could he take direction from me, his mom? So I had hired someone else. But then you saw a photograph of Jason in a crystal frame on the piano in my den and you looked at it and said, "That's Bernard." Dark, curly hair, expressive eyes, full lips, and prominent nose (like his mother), just as you describe him in the book. It says Bernard weighs 140 pounds. I called Jason up and asked, "How much do you weigh?"

Jason said, "One hundred forty pounds. Why?"

I said, "You're hired."

Because of your encouragement, I got to work with my son. It was you, Pat, who made that happen. And Jason was wonderful in the role. He *was* Bernard, in a way. And he learned how to play that very difficult violin piece in the middle of Grand Central Station. I was so proud. Thank you.

I once read an interview where you were quoted as saying that working with me was like working with the goddess Athena. That was extremely generous of you.

Well, if I'm Athena, you're my Apollo—the god of poetry, truth, and music. Your natural language is poetry. You write sentences that are like an incantation. You observe every nuance of human behavior and dig deep down to the truth, presenting it in all its glorious and stubborn complexity. And as far as music goes, let's just say you can come back and dance with me any time!

I'm sending you all my love and gratitude,

Barbra Streisand

P.S. Happy Birthday!

Preface

〜 NICOLE SEITZ

> My wound is geography. It is also my anchorage, my port of call.
> —Pat Conroy, *The Prince of Tides*

To say Pat Conroy has impacted the southern literary landscape is an understatement. The "Prince of Tides" himself created lasting ripples that impacted writers and readers not only in the South but also throughout our country. As we edited this anthology, structuring this varied web of memorials and tributes proved no easy task; in the end we decided to order the essays loosely by Pat's own chronology, each of them winding along his story river, stopping at important ports of call. Cities he called home and longed to visit, along with each book he birthed, became characters as equally important as the people he touched and loved along the way. Pat, the undeniable hero in this story, was a complex man, often becoming his worst antagonist. His relationships weren't always easy, and people and places he thought he'd left behind often circled back in his life at crucial moments.

Each author in this collection of essays knew a slightly different facet of Pat. Through many voices, a portrait of him seems to be spoken to life in a vibrant, multifaceted way that sheds new light on the writer and man so revered. He was a fellow student to some, a teacher or mentor to others, and he became family or friend to many. They connected with Pat through the love of words or food, or through the shared sufferings of childhood or existential questioning.

Pat wasn't a hermit as some brilliant writers become. His was a messy fellowship of people from all walks of life. A person didn't meet Pat and stay the same before and after. He became a port of call himself. Perhaps even more than his seventy years with us and the multitude of books he left, Pat's most important work is to come. His legacy lives on in each of us who knew him. He taught each something different: how to be a generous writer, a lifelong learner and voracious reader, or how to be fallible, utterly human, and yet brave—to stand up for those who have no voice. Pat left us a lifetime of words and tales to savor, but his true legacy is the seed he planted in each person who shook his hand. In this way his story river continues, and perhaps the best is yet to come.

Mount Pleasant, South Carolina

OUR PRINCE OF SCRIBES

Introduction

⁓ JONATHAN HAUPT

Writers of the world, if you've got a story, I want to hear it.
I promise it will follow me to my last breath.
—Pat Conroy, *My Reading Life*

Pat Conroy (1945–2016) was arguably the most beloved American writer of his generation. Indeed, we may need to look all the way back to Charles Dickens to find another writer of any nation or era who was as appreciated in his lifetime by his throngs of devoted readers. Long before he wrote the dozen volumes of fiction and memoir that established his literary legacy, Pat had dedicated himself to teaching, first for two years at Beaufort High School (his own alma mater) and then for his storied year as the first white schoolteacher on remote Daufuskie Island, the experience that became the catalyst for *The Water Is Wide* and thus the fuse that ignited his writing career. After Pat was fired from his position on Daufuskie he was never again a full-time professional educator in any school. But as those of us can attest who were fortunate enough to find our way into Pat's circle of friends, he never truly stopped being a teacher. Over the course of a writing career that spanned six decades, Pat continued to mentor writers—dozens upon dozens of us—some over the arc of their own impressive careers and others simply by offering the right advice, or connection, or a hand extended in earnest friendship, or by being a courageous model of what a writer and an artist can mean to her or his community.

Pat died on March 4, 2016, less than five months after hundreds had gathered alongside him in his adopted hometown of Beaufort, South Carolina, in celebration of his seventieth birthday. In the unplanned, unscripted, and wholly unforgettable final five minutes of the historic Pat Conroy at 70 festival, Pat took center stage before an audience of some five hundred people to thank his readers, his family, his friends, his teachers, and his fellow writers for giving him the writing life he had dreamed of as a young man in Gene Norris's English classroom. He concluded his off-the-cuff remarks with a heartfelt promise to write "as well as I can for as long as I can" in honor of all those who had brought him to that time and that place, a monumental moment in his career. Robbing both Pat and the world of that promise was an aggressive pancreatic cancer that even the self-proclaimed "son of a warrior" could not defeat, although he tried valiantly to do so. Surrounded by family and close friends, in the caring embrace of his wife, Cassandra King Conroy, and looking out over his cherished Battery Creek, Donald Patrick Conroy voyaged on ahead at sunset on March 4th.

March forth. It was Cassandra who first recognized the significance of that date as a final directive from Pat telling us that others would now need to continue in his stead. Pat's marching orders have since taken the form of the Pat Conroy Literary Center, a nonprofit museum and teaching institution in Beaufort that continues Pat's legacy as a teacher, mentor, advocate, and friend to readers and writers alike through an inclusive approach to literary community building. Thousands of pilgrims from around the country and around the globe are now making their way to beautiful Beaufort by the sea to visit the Conroy Center and participate in its programming and annual literary festival. In recognition of the Conroy Center's quick rise in significance as an educational and interpretive site, in its first year of operation the Center was named South Carolina's first affiliate of the American Writers Museum and the state's second American Library Association United for Libraries Literary Landmark—both national distinctions. Within and beyond the Conroy Center, Pat's legacy reverberates in the writing lives of those he inspired, both through his instructive example in person and his powerfully honest words on the page.

Because of the abuses of his childhood, Pat found it impossible to foster sustained joy in his own success, but he could experience tremendous vicarious bliss in the successes of others. Serving as the sage tribal elder in the mentoring of other writers brought Pat a happiness that even international literary fame could not. Teaching, in this sense, was not only life affirming for Pat, it was life saving. One need only look at the absolute devotion Pat showed to his ragtag band of Story River Books writers, the authors, editors, foreword writers, and contributors to the impressive twenty-two books Pat championed as editor at large for his original southern fiction imprint at the University of South Carolina Press. The enterprise was a source of well-earned pride for Pat in his final years. When he described Story River in an interview as "a gift to writers and to readers," he didn't mean just the Story River writers or the readers of those books, but ALL readers and writers. Story River was Pat's way of boldly illustrating the quality of novels and story collections that were still possible to find, foster, and publish amid the ever-changing landscape of modern literary publishing. That "gift to writers and to readers" continues now as the Pat Conroy Literary Center, a growing haven for a chorus of emerging voices and myriad literary interests and passions.

As another chorus of emerging and established voices representing a broad, inclusive definition of the mantle of "writer," dozens of the members of Pat's tribe of writers have contributed their personal remembrances of him to this volume. The contributors range from writers who have known Pat for all (or nearly all) of their lives—like his brother Tim, daughter Melissa, goddaughter Maggie Schein, students Valerie Sayers and Sallie Ann Robinson—to those who knew Pat primarily if not exclusively through his books—like Janis Ian, Anthony Grooms, and Mark Powell. Falling in between those extremes is a veritable pantheon of exceptional storytellers including *New York Times* best-selling writers, stars of stage and screen, Pulitzer Prize–winning journalists, the defining voices of twentieth- and twenty-first-century southern literature, and writers largely unheralded outside their regional spheres but exceptional enough at their craft to have drawn Pat's nurturing interest. Pat's orbit, like his mischievous smile, was wide and welcoming.

What emerges in these pages, made possible by the range and depth of vantage points included, is a robust portrait of Pat Conroy as artist and teacher, honoring the generosity for which the self-effacing writer could never give himself full credit. While it would have been an easy task to assemble a cultish love-letter collection in celebration of Pat, that is not this book. Pat was a complicated and occasionally contradictory man, which is to say he was human, he was flawed, and he was still in the act of self-discovery, of becoming. The richly mosaic nature of this collection honors that complexity, because death has not simplified our Mr. Conroy in the least.

~

I first came to know Pat by way of a well-intentioned if also rambling voice-mail I left on his Fripp Island answering machine as a university press marketing manager, newly arrived in the Palmetto State in 2004, seeking an endorsement for an author's forthcoming Charleston novel and having little hope of getting a return call. But Pat did call, the very next day, and chatted at length with an absolute stranger. And so began our ritual of call-and-response, for seven years, before I caught Pat's full attention as interim director of University of South Carolina Press. When I told Pat I wanted to establish an original fiction imprint under the auspices of the press, one open to undiscovered new writers as well as those with a career's worth of acclaim, he was intrigued and supportive. When I was named director of USC Press, bolstered by a stalwart and comical letter of recommendation from Pat, he invited me to visit him in Beaufort for a celebratory lunch. This turned out to be one of his legendary Thursday lunches with the boys wherein he put me through the gauntlet of an exquisite meal with his longtime best friend and muse, the incomparable Bernie Schein (whose essay is included in this collection). This, I would learn, was the trial by fire that one must pass for admittance into Pat's innermost circle. And pass I did. Afterward, as Pat made a point of driving me back to my car at Beaufort's downtown marina, he extended his big lion's paw of a hand and said, as a solemn oath, "We're going to be friends." From that moment forward we were.

Pat's interest in the fiction imprint took hold of his desire to teach and to mentor writers. At another Thursday lunch, and to the absolute shock of everyone gathered at the table, Pat volunteered to serve as editor for what would soon become Story River Books, with only two requirements: (1) that he not be paid any royalties, wanting all proceeds to support the writers and the imprint, and (2) that we open the doors widely to southern writers.

Pat had two in mind, Katherine Clark, whose first novel, *The Headmaster's Darlings*, became the first university press book ever to win the Willie Morris Award for Southern Fiction, and Mary Hood, who became the only writer to ever twice win the Townsend Prize for Fiction, the latter honor for her story collection *A Clear View of the Southern Sky*. Pat could pick winners, spotting their untapped or unrecognized potential as his teachers had done for him. He wrote lavish forewords to both of those Story River Books, and their writers are included herein. Pat was head cheerleader for Story River as well as its editor in chief, as evidenced by the many forewords and blurbs he wrote in support of those books and in the time he devoted to appearing at book festivals and special events with his writers as "crowd insurance," as his friend and Story River writer John Warley called it, and to introducing his loyal readers to his new Story River family.

Following a particularly lively Evening with Story River Books event in front of an audience of several hundred at Furman University (the sports rival of Pat's alma mater, The Citadel), Pat and I settled at a table in front of a long line of fans eager for his autograph. Pat signed for three hours that night, always striving to carry on meaningful conversations with each reader in the line, letting them know how much he treasured his audience. While the majority of books put in front of him were his own, he was delighted whenever a Story River Book by another writer was extended to him to inscribe. At the end of the night, when all the other writers had left and only Pat, the venue staff, my wife, and I remained, Pat rose at last from the table and bellowed, "Haupt, I have never worked so fucking hard in my life selling books by other writers."

"*Your* writers," I corrected him.

"*Our* writers," he corrected me, ever the good teacher.

"And do you love it?" I asked him.

He paused for a moment, just long enough for a twinkle, a chuckle, and a dropping of his curmudgeonly façade. Then came the truth teller's honest answer: "Yes. Yes, I do."

Our Prince of Scribes is our collective return of Pat Conroy's faith in other writers, a giving back of the great love Pat entrusted in each of us represented in this collection and in so many others whose lives he touched and whose hearts he opened with the overarching message of his timeless body of work: you are not alone. Pat's legacy is still growing; his star is still ascending through his beloved books, through our remembrances of his instructive example, through the brilliant writings of the Story River Books family he forged and the even larger tribe of writers he inspired, and through the yeoman's work of the new Conroy Center established in his honor and his stead. This collection is our gift to writers and to readers; we honor Pat by sharing his stories and our own—our truths as we know them to be. "Tell me a story," Pat would say. These are the stories writers tell of Pat Conroy, our friend, our teacher, our Prince of Scribes.

Beaufort, South Carolina

I

Headwaters

∼ *The Early Years as Student and Teacher*

(Beaufort, Charleston, and The Citadel)

A Boy, a Girl, and a Train

~ ALEXIA JONES HELSLEY

A sleeping boy, a pillowed blow—and the world changed.

The year was 1962. On a cool October day, Beaufort High School seniors and their families gathered at the depot in Yemassee, South Carolina. The class of '63 was embarking on its much anticipated senior trip to the magical mecca of New York.

The students and their chaperones boarded the train—anticipation tempered with frissons of uncertainty. Beaufort was a small town, and for many, a train trip was a radical departure and being part of the "herd" was a socializing challenge.

On the rails, the car gently rocking, students sat in their seats reading, talking, or sleeping. Others wandered from car to car relishing the freedom and the unexplored possibilities.

Gene Norris, our beloved English teacher, was one of the trip chaperones. The pied piper of BHS, he would lead several of us on unscheduled adventures. On a memorable side trip to the National Gallery of Art, Gene led us on a mad race to catch the departing bus. Also, we sneaked into Ford Theatre in Washington, D.C. He not only wanted us to experience more of the world than the tour covered, but he also cared about the whole student. And at times, he facilitated social interactions, especially for shy students like me.

At that moment, this revered authority figure handed me a pillow, pointed to a sleeping boy, and said, "Hit him!" Ever obedient, I did. The sleeper jumped up and stared at me in disbelief. Pat Conroy was the boy, and that was the beginning of a lifelong friendship. Pat and his seatmate tore the cover from an *Esquire* magazine and penned the first "Ode to Sexy Lexy." Obviously, it would not have been nearly as entertaining if, in fact, I had been sexy. With my permed hair and academic bent, I wasn't. But even then Pat loved words and loved playing with them. So my parents gave me the perfect name for the situation. That evening in Washington, D.C., Pat and friend composed an ode on toilet paper, scented the epistle with English Leather, and, unfortunately, pushed it under the wrong door. He was funny and sweet. Now we were friends, or as Pat wrote, "And the happiest moments of my life—starting with a pillowed blow."

The trip had other adventures. One evening, the intrepid chaperones led the naïve students on an expedition to Greenwich Village. En route we boarded subway cars, but unfortunately, everyone could not fit on the same one. Consequently, Pat and some of us were on a separate car. The train stopped, and as we began to disembark we realized it was not our stop. The altruistic Conroy threw his body between the closing door and the jamb, and we clambered safely back aboard. In the Village, we visited a nightclub where Pat and the Mexican Hat Dance were part of the entertainment. The grand finale saw an older comedienne concluding her set by bending over: "The end" was printed on her white bloomers.

Pat was now a hero because he had "saved" us from being left in the bowels of NYC. On another occasion he faced the wrath of our principal, Bill Dufford. We were dining in one of the ubiquitous Tad's Steakhouses, and Pat and his friend were late. I looked out the window, and there was Dufford "dressing down" the miscreants in the middle of an NYC boulevard. Having survived Dufford's reprimand, Pat's street cred was high. Later, on the bus trip back to the train station, I lost a contact lens on the dirty bus, in the dark, seated on the backseat. But no challenge was too demanding for our hero. Against long odds, Pat found the contact on the floor under the seat in front of me, and I made the rest of the trip clutching that contact between two fingers.

From that senior trip we launched the ill-fated revolt. We were enrolled in Advanced Composition, and the teacher of the course spent most of class time talking about "Thus Spake Zarathustra" and sacrificing oneself to feed tiger cubs in India. So in one class, several of us protested. We wanted more focus on the literature we were reading and more feedback on our compositions. But to no avail. As Pat noted, "Our beaten bodies were strewn the length and breadth of second period." While unsuccessful, the "revolt" did show a capacity for unified action that helped cement our friendship.

We also worked together on the school newspaper, *The Tidal Wave*. I was the editor, and Pat was a feature writer. Consequently, as my husband likes to joke, I was Pat's first editor. He was an editor's dream because he could take any situation and produce a lively, even nail-biting narrative. My favorite Conroy column concerned a track meet between BHS and our lowcountry rival, Ridgeland. Written from Pat's unique worldview, a prosaic race between two high school boys symbolized not only youthful dreams but also the ultimate conflict between good and evil. Of course, the BHS runner was on the side of the angels.

Another memory that I think encapsulates the raw talent of the young Conroy occurred during a spring assembly in 1963, our senior year. The entire student body was gathering in the gym when Principal Bill Dufford stopped Pat in the doorway and asked him to make a few remarks about the recent Powder Puff football game between junior and senior women—an annual ritual that I trust has long since been abandoned. But at the time it was a matter of honor, and the women of the class of 1963 had unexpectedly won. As senior class president, Pat was responsible for sharing the news and assuaging egos on both sides. Rather than an "aw shucks, we won," Pat grabbed a napkin and wrote an elegant ode—including graphic depictions of the bloodied bodies of a high school Armageddon. His muse, apparently, was always on call.

The next challenge we shared was more personal. Dealing with a massive retinal detachment, I spent weeks in Chatham Memorial in Savannah, Georgia, and additional time at home recuperating. Pat and other classmates visited, and Pat called before basketball games. "This one's for you," he would say, and while I was in the hospital the BHS Tidal Wave did not lose a basketball game.

When I finally returned to school, our connections were awkward. As Pat later said, he needed to feel needed, and I don't think that imperative ever changed. He lived to assist others, encourage friends, mentor aspiring authors, and launch careers, and he rarely said no. Just as he once walked the halls of BHS—with his distinctive rolling gait—saying, "Hi ya, babe" to everyone he met, he spent hours at book signings. He spoke to all comers, remembered old acquaintances, and persevered until the last patron walked through the line.

Our senior year drew to an end. We faced our futures uncertainly, and there was a last high school outing. Bruce Harper, Julie Zachowski, Pat, and I went out for dinner. Then we sat in the car in Julie's driveway and one-upped each other with television trivia. We did not want the evening to end.

While three of us stayed in Beaufort, the Marine Corps transferred Pat's family to Nebraska. We made plans to meet. My father had accepted a revival in La Mirada (a suburb of Los Angeles), California, so we embarked on a cross-country car trip with the idea that we would see Pat in Nebraska on the return trip. Yet the fates intervened. A wreck in Albuquerque totaled our car and cost us several days, so the return trip did not include a Nebraska stop. Still, we corresponded. My sister, Martha, was Pat's date for our senior prom. Consequently, when we arrived in California there was a large envelope filled with mail that Dad's secretary had forwarded from Beaufort. Dad tore open the envelope and dumped out the mail on the other pastor's desk. There, before him and the other minister, was our mail—a neat mountain with a postcard on top, just an ordinary postcard from the post office, no photograph, no cartoon, but in his own hand, Pat had carefully printed "sex, sex, sex . . ." over every square inch of that postcard. I will never forget the looks on the faces of those two ministers! Despite his inner pain, Pat enjoyed the overt and subtle humor of even the smallest events. Who can forget the bathroom scene from *The Water Is Wide?*

In the fall, Pat enrolled at The Citadel and I entered Furman University. We still corresponded, and when The Citadel played Furman in Greenville, I saw him play. Later, my sister was his date for Citadel's graduation festivities, and I accompanied a friend of his. But after college graduation we took different paths.

In the ensuing years Pat wrote prodigiously—fiction, nonfiction, and even a cookbook. Movies based on several of his books graced the big screen. Yet

Pat still connected with his past compatriots, and he kindly wrote a blurb for one of my Beaufort books. Together, we shared the sad duty of saying good-bye to our beloved Gene, the glue that brought these musketeers together and bound them tightly in a grip that even death could not destroy.

Best All Around

~ STEPHANIE AUSTIN EDWARDS

Pat Conroy and I had at least three essential things in common: we went to Beaufort High School together in an era of BHS history defined by a remarkable group of educators (many of whom Pat immortalized); we were both military brats whose lives led us to entrances and exits from multiple schools and friendships over the course of our education; and we both found ourselves such admirers of the written word that we became authors.

At BHS, Pat and I learned about literature and the larger world from our English teachers Gene Norris (Pat's storied mentor) and Millen Ellis, homeroom teacher Grace Dennis, and principal Bill Dufford. In addition, Pat and I were in French class together, we were section editors of the *Breakers* literary magazine, and I frequently watched as Pat and my brother Chris played one-on-one basketball after school and on weekends. Changing schools often was something we talked about years later. I went to five elementary schools, three junior highs, and two high schools. Pat changed schools every year until coming to Beaufort for his junior and senior years. In our later conversations, we shared that we felt arriving at the haven of Beaufort High School was a supreme gift in our lives. We got to stay in one place long enough to forge genuine friendships and glimpse the literary possibilities that would take shape in our adult lives.

Many say that all of Pat's books center on his conflicted relationship with his father in one way or another. But to look at Pat's senior year annual you'd never know he had a care in the world. Besides being a star athlete in baseball, basketball, and football (and captain and MVP of the basketball team),

Pat was a member of the National Honor Society, and he was voted senior class president, Best All Around, May King, and Mr. Congeniality.

As a docent at the Pat Conroy Literary Center, I am often asked by our visitors if I (or any other BHS classmates) recognized early on that Pat was destined for greatness. Of course not. We were all just awkwardly making our way through our teenage years. But when I look back in my 1963 annual, Pat's senior (and my sophomore) year, I see a clue to the person he became. While most of our BHS classmates were scribbling generic phrases like "stay your sweet and cute self," Pat wrote these words to me: "Dearest Stephanie: Good Frenching, the language that is . . . Pat." I blushed and laughed then, just as I did almost every time we talked in the ensuing years.

For a kid who had only come to Beaufort in his junior year, Pat Conroy was something else. And that wry personality combined with the originality of his literary voice made certain he would be something else the rest of his life.

As a writer who also returned to make my home in Pat's beloved Beaufort, I've seen firsthand what the literary center established in Pat's honor has come to mean to so many so quickly. More than 2,500 people from 38 states and 8 countries made the pilgrimage to the center during our first year. After listening to our tour, many guests have offered their own stories of meeting Pat and of how he influenced their lives as readers, as writers, or simply as good citizens of the realm. Each story is distinctive, personal, and poignant. Sometimes it feels as though Pat is there with us, soaking up the love and guiding the experience for all of us here in Beaufort—Pat's home, his muse, and the town that first gave him what he needed to become the Best All Around.

Pat Conroy's First Novelist and Final Homecoming

⌒ DAVID LAUDERDALE

Beaufort novelist Ann Head (born Anne Wales Christensen) thought it was cheating to write fiction based on her own life. Perhaps she should have reconsidered. Her most famous protégé certainly held a different opinion. Ann Head was the first novelist Pat Conroy ever met, and she left an imprint on him like the slap of a typewriter key.

Conroy lit up when I asked him about Ann Head in what would turn out to be our last conversation. It was in October 2015, and I was writing about this often-overlooked local influence as Beaufort celebrated Pat's seventieth birthday with a three-day literary festival.

Several of us came full circle that night in Conroy's magical world of words.

But first, you need to meet Ann Head.

In 1962, Conroy was a senior at Beaufort High School, a Marine Corps dependent still new to town. Ann Head was a divorced mother whose stories had to sell if she was to make rent. English teacher Gene Norris (whom Conroy immortalized in fiction and memoir) cajoled her into teaching a creative writing class to six promising students. Conroy took the class in secret and in defiance of his father, who thought it a useless course for a fighter pilot's son.

Ann Head was a Beaufort native who published four novels and scores of novellas and magazine articles in the 1940s, '50s and '60s. When Conroy wrote about her in *The Pat Conroy Cookbook*, he called her "my first novelist."

Portions of this essay originally appeared in the *Beaufort Gazette*, October 24, 2015.

She advised Conroy never to use the word "poignant." She tried to get him into Antioch College in Ohio, where some of her own free thinking evolved. She did battle with his father, Col. Donald Conroy, and told young Conroy that someday he needed to write about that guy. Her home became an escape for Pat, and her mentoring influence became a model for how Pat would commit himself to supporting other writers.

In our interview, Pat shared with me that Ann Head had exchanged letters with him during his college years. "She wrote me all during The Citadel years, wonderful, loving, fabulous letters. She sent me books, like Ernest Hemingway's *A Moveable Feast*. She had me read Ingmar Bergman's screenplays, and she told me I needed to know more of the darkness of the world.

"She told me she could not write about things because she was a native of Beaufort and she would hurt too many people in Beaufort, but I was lucky because I was a military brat and it didn't make any difference who I hurt."

Ann Head sat at the typewriter at least six hours a day whether anything came out or not. Her idol was Daphne du Maurier. In the early years, she forced herself to produce one story a month, on the theory that if she sold three per year she could survive. But at times she had to move in with family. Her novels *Fair with Rain* and *Always in August* sold well, followed by a mystery, *Everybody Adored Cara*. But her biggest hit was *Mr. and Mrs. Bo Jo Jones*, a story of teen pregnancy that was made into a TV movie and stayed in print and on school reading lists for half a century.

Ann Head never got to see the success of her young protégé, Pat Conroy. She died unexpectedly in his first year of teaching at Beaufort High School after Pat's graduation from The Citadel. She was only fifty-two. Conroy said that every time he published a new book, he placed a rose on Ann Head's grave at the Parish Church of St. Helena. "She said, 'One day I'll take you to Paris, or if you make it as a writer you can take me to Paris,'" he told me.

It was a trip Conroy never got to take with his former high school creative writing teacher and the first novelist he ever met in person. But Ann Head's good influence on Pat—and that of so many of the teachers who had shaped his writing life—was easy to see in how Pat treated his readers and fellow writers.

I was fortunate to get to interview Pat many times over our years in Beaufort. He was so giving. I treasure his lavish words when he signed his foreword in Maggie Schein's collection of fables, *Lost Cantos of the Ouroborus Caves*. "For the love of words and story of the Lowcountry—you're the writer of my Beaufort life."

In our last conversation he really didn't have time for me, but he stopped everything to help. It happened during one of his final book signings—but it wasn't a signing held in Pat's honor. It was for one of his own protégés, the poet, teacher, and novelist Ellen Malphrus, now writer-in-residence at the University of South Carolina Beaufort. Then, in October 2015, Malphrus was proud author of a newly released first novel, *Untying the Moon*, published by Conroy's Story River Books imprint and introduced by Conroy's foreword. Conroy signed books with Malphrus at Old Town Bluffton's historic Heyward House, the line stretching on for hours as Conroy—Malphrus's mentor if not also her "first novelist"—turned hundreds of his loyal readers into hers. Teacher and student, side by side.

It closed a circle for me as well. This circle also started in a high school. This one was in nearby Ridgeland where Malphrus was editor of the school newspaper and I was her adviser, pleased that she took words seriously.

Ann Head also would have been proud of her student. Conroy had not only made it as a writer, as she had hoped for him, he brought other writers along with him, Ellen Malphrus being just one of many. In his way, Pat brought all of Beaufort (the subject Ann Head could not write about) along with him too. His lyrical novels painted harsh pictures of inadequate schools, an abusive father, and South Carolina's military college, The Citadel. He tackled threats to the lowcountry environment with equal vigor. But he loved each of his subjects, and the town he adopted after twenty-three moves in sixteen years loved him back—and loves him still.

The Brutal Truth of It, Liberated at Last

~ BERNIE SCHEIN

As the world would eventually learn, throughout Pat's childhood Peg Conroy, early the mornings after, before school, would obscure Pat's night visits to the emergency room with deftly, subtly applied makeup. If there was a bandage, well, back then, as now, he'd fallen on the sidewalk practicing his dribbling or run into a door, the usual excuses. Back then, no one knew about child abuse. Reports of it were at most vague whispers, the statistics as closeted as the abuse itself. In the time of Billboard families, when you were taught that if you couldn't say anything nice about anybody you shouldn't say anything at all, when appearances were everything, when divorce was a scandal and homes for unwed mothers unmentioned, when displays of emotion were considered unmanly in men and a form of infantile hysteria in women—"It's okay, baby, it's okay"—no one talked about it.

In our early twenties, when we were teaching in Beaufort, Pat hinted and hinted and hinted, but every kid grows up thinking that every family is like his own, and I just didn't get it. A psychiatrist who'd met Pat socially back when we were teaching in Beaufort once asked me why Pat was so angry.

Naïve as I was, I didn't know what he was talking about. "Angry? Pat? No, he's just joking. It's his humor; he exaggerates everything. Actually," I explained, "Pat speaks in opposites. If he tells you he hates you, it means he loves you." That was actually true. Pat did speak in opposites, but that was only to people he loved. His hatred, his anger, even when misplaced, was real. What did I know?

This essay is excerpted and adapted from the author's forthcoming memoir *Santini's Hero.*

I'm neurotic as hell, obsessive, compulsive. Yes, the Jewish disease. But there was no fear of violence in my family. My concern, back in the forties and fifties, was that we were "abnormal" because Mom and Dad were unlike Ozzie and Harriet. "Maybe," Mom offered, "if you behaved yourself and acted more like David and Ricky, then your dad and I could act more like Ozzie and Harriet." Then she looked at my dad. "What do you think, Morris?"

"Maybe," he said. "Anything's possible, I suppose."

I registered that as less than a commitment.

So, like with the psychiatrist, when Pat began going on and on about his father I told everyone he was just exaggerating. "You know Pat," I'd tell them. And when he began writing fiction: "Hell, he lies for a living." Which he did.

But he's also the greatest truth teller I've ever known. He opened me to a world of suffering, of hatred, of self-hatred, of depression and despair I had never even imagined, and consequently he shared that with my students at Paideia—the school in our Atlanta neighborhood where I taught at the time—letting them know, as he would let his readers know, that they were not alone.

I was at the time reading his first draft of *The Great Santini*. He had used the same typist my wife and I had used for our book about teaching. Other than the typist, of course, no one else had looked at Pat's draft yet, not even Anne Barrett, his editor at Houghton Mifflin. I came across a particular scene that, over my objection—for good reason, I think—he left in the manuscript unchanged.

That scene was a lie, fare made palatable for people like me. If you've read *The Great Santini*, you might remember it. Pat's father's alter ego is Col. Bull Meechum, his mother is Lillian Meechum, and Pat is Ben Meechum. Ben's father brutally attacks his mother one night after dinner. He's drunk, threatening the whole family. But in this first draft Ben Meechum is a man now, a married man with a family. For the first and only time in his life, Ben Meechum picks up his drunken father and throws him out of their house, all the way down the steps onto the front lawn on the Point in Beaufort, a neighborhood of old money, much of it gone, of stately antebellum homes, many in need of repair, and interior gardens dominated by thousand-year-old oak trees dripping Spanish moss. After this, Bull stumbles drunkenly down the street onto the Green, a park-like quadrangle of grass and oak trees. Ben follows him relentlessly, his father awkwardly stumbling about, Ben chasing him all over the Green bombarding him with, "I love you, Dad, I love you. I love you, Dad. I love you." His dad just can't take it, running away from him, stumbling, weaving awkwardly this way and that as if evading tacklers, tripping over himself, until finally, exhausted, he collapses under an oak tree and passes out.

Fascinating, I thought. Disturbing, yet hopeful. Love wielded as weapon, yet no less real for it.

But I was a teacher. And a teacher is always looking for what is not said, for what is hidden, perhaps between the lines, perhaps absent from the page, and this particular scene was written in Pat's hand above the originally typed passage, which had been crossed out.

Here's the real scene I managed to decipher, the true one, the typed one that had been crossed out.

All is the same: Colonel Meechum's brutal assault on Ben's mom and their family, Ben's throwing him out of his house, down the steps onto the front lawn. But afterward, Ben goes back into the house, guilty and ashamed of having become, in his mind, the man he so loathed and despised, and after taking care of his family, walks around the neighborhood looking for his father.

As before, he finds him on the Green. Only in this scene Colonel Meechum has already fallen and passed out, lying there under an oak, harmless. Defenseless. There is no "I love you, Dad, I love you."

Instead, what I see on the page with a magnifying glass shocks me forever out of my ignorance, shatters my own world, and submerges me into Pat's, into the world of more than a quarter of the families in America, into a world of approximately a quarter of the kids in my classroom every year whom I knew I was failing, regardless of how socially polite and academically successful they might have appeared—a world, in a few words, of shame, self-loathing, and vengeful hatred, all of which Ben through my magnifying glass is unleashing on his father.

Ben straddles him, turns his father's face toward him, and completely unharnesses and unleashes such fury and hatred and brutality that I could never have imagined was inside him. He beats him in the face, over and over, pummels him, fist over fist over fist, his father's face black and blue and already swollen, a bloody mess, until Ben Meechum exhausts himself and collapses on top of his father, after which he carries him home.

"Leave it in," I told Pat. "Leave it in."

"No one will believe it, Bernie," Pat said. "Anne Barrett won't believe it. No one will."

~

Perhaps he was right. I just don't know. I hadn't believed him, and he'd tried to tell me over and over again. But I do now. And my students do. He came to my class at Paideia, as he often did. Teaching is listening, and he listened so sensitively, so attentively, so carefully to my students' stories, those stories until then sadly beyond my reach, that they understood for the first time in their lives they were no longer alone. Their classmates now knew, they understood. The tiny world of our classroom became more intimate, more openhearted, more opened-minded, as would the greater world. Not just me, not just my students, but the entire world now knows, understands.

And the reason is none other than my best and dearest and most loving friend Pat Conroy.

Pat Conroy.

Pat Conroy.

I love you, Bubba.

Wearing the Ring

~ SCOTT GRABER

It is Saturday, July 30, 2016, five months since Pat Conroy's death, and I'm still dealing with a chronic, low-grade melancholy. Sometimes I think this persisting sadness is attached to my advancing age and a growing cynicism, but I'm certain that Pat's abrupt departure is the real pathogen that has dulled and saddened my life.

Pat and I met at The Citadel sometime in the fall of 1964. I didn't know him when I was a "knob." I was too stunned, too distracted to know anyone other than the upperclassmen who were trying to run me out of the Corps. Because of his writing and our later-in-life friendship I know he was profoundly unhappy that first year. He was, like me, doing his best to survive a system designed to degrade, humiliate, and then rebuild every boy who came through Lesesne Gate.

But we were trapped.

I was trapped because my grades were so bad that I could not transfer. He was trapped because he had a basketball scholarship and a father who would not pay tuition at Carolina or Clemson.

Both of us stayed, and our lives eventually intersected. Neither of us got rank, both of us wrote poetry, and I would defend cadets in front of the Honor Court where Pat was a "judge." We weren't the best of friends—I was in Third Battalion and he was in Fourth—but there was a continuing, burgeoning friendship based on a mutual loathing of what we had endured as freshmen.

Those of us who had no stripes on our sleeves and wore no sabre sometimes wondered why. How, we wondered, could our classmates overlook our leadership skills? This lack of rank was most obvious when there was a dance, a parade, a big weekend when our out-of-town dates lined the parade ground. But lack of rank was also a badge of honor. We "senior privates"—like it or not—were a legion of lepers who took pride in being unwashed, untouchable misfits.

Then, in the middle of my fourth and final year at The Citadel, I was summoned to the president's office in Bond Hall and told I was now an officer. In the course of several confusing minutes I was summarily removed from the ranks of the senior privates—from Pat—and put on Regimental Staff. My portfolio would be public relations.

Within a few weeks of my promotion a company commander at Friday parade, thinking he was being mocked by an underclassmen, stabbed that cadet with his sabre. It was not a fatal wound, but there was enough blood on his white duck trousers to attract comment from those who had gathered around the parade ground. As regimental public relations officer I was told that word of this incident should not make its way off campus. This was an internal problem, and names, body parts, weaponry, and any corrective action would remain internal.

Pat Conroy had other ideas.

Pat wrote up a broadside condemning the "cover up," and then he (and some confederates) put copies on every table in the mess hall.

That night when the Corps sat down to eat and found unexpected reading material—Pat's words—there was a sustained roar from the outraged cadets.

Now the task changed. Now it was necessary to find the author of this unauthorized report and remove him from the Corps. I wasn't the leader of this posse, but as the regimental public relations officer I was in the room.

The most important thing was finding a witness. There had to be an African American server who would identify the tall, well-spoken, joke-telling basketball star who put the fliers on the tables. But none of the ubiquitous women seemed to remember who placed the single-sheet indictment on the tables. Then something happened that diverted everyone's attention.

In the middle of the investigation, three cadets who followed a shrimp boat out of Charleston Harbor did not return. As the days passed and the

Coast Guard widened its search, everyone on campus assumed they were dead.

This was the end of my senior year, when everyone was looking forward to graduation and—even though most were headed for a rifle platoon in Vietnam—feeling a sense of accomplishment. But in April 1967 there was only a sense of tragedy and the certainty of a collective funeral service in Summeral Chapel. Then came word that the cadets, all three of them alive and well, had washed ashore on Daufuskie Island.

I remember a second sustained uproar in the mess hall. But this time it was joyous.

As a side effect of the news that the three cadets had survived, the administration apparently decided that the public had heard enough news from The Citadel that year and that further pursuit of the "writer of the underground newspaper" should end. The investigation, the incident, was over. Pat Conroy would graduate with the class of 1967.

In March 2016, as I sat in the vast interior of St. Peter's Catholic Church on Lady's Island, my eyes were drawn to a tall, ribbon-wearing officer with stars on his collar. General John Rosa, president of The Citadel. With him were a hundred Citadel graduates from the class of 2001.

As we waited for the Catholic hierarchy to reclaim its wandering son, I could not help but wonder what might have happened if Pat had not written that memo in April 1967. What if he had chickened out or weighed the consequences and had not put his protest on the mess tables that night? And what about *The Lords of Discipline* and *My Losing Season*? What would have happened if Pat had not questioned the foundational traditions of The Citadel?

But fortunately he did write about the hazing, the late-night violence, the belief that tradition trumps self-examination and change. He did champion Shannon Faulkner and an old, exiled officer called Boo.

Somewhere along the way Pat Conroy forgave The Citadel and The Citadel forgave him. That reconciliation was cemented when Pat gave the now famous "I Wear the Ring" speech to the class of 2001.

In that speech he recounted his long roller-coaster relationship with The Citadel. He finished up with the following: "So I'm going to tell you how to get to my funeral. You walk up . . . you find the usher waiting outside, and here's your ticket . . . you put up your Citadel ring. Let them check for the 2001, and each of you, I want you to say this before you enter the church at which I'm going to be buried. You tell them, 'I wear the ring.'"

And they did. For Pat.

One Cadet's Lamentations

～ JOHN WARLEY

"In the winter of 1965, I retrieved a thrownaway baseball glove from the trash can in the Romeo section of Fourth Battalion at The Citadel." So began Pat Conroy's generous eight-page preface to my first novel, *Bethesda's Child*, in which he detailed "a friendship that has flourished over long distances and many late night conversations." Though more than fifty years have passed, I still see him crossing the floor of the mess hall in that trademark jaunty stride, sitting down at my left elbow, and extending his right hand. "Pat Conroy," he said, though like me he wore a nametag, and I'd known who he was for three years.

The Citadel was funny that way. You saw guys every day in the barracks, their faces and nametags registering as a matched set, so that if one day Jones wore Smith's nametag, you'd know instantly something was amiss without knowing either Smith or Jones personally. Until that spring of our junior year, when Pat and I went out for the baseball team, I knew him by sight, by nametag. His major was English, mine Political Science; he belonged to R Company, I was in T; he played basketball, I played football; so the usual intersection of activities that would allow you to get to know someone simply wasn't there.

Because I'd watched him for three years play basketball like a man possessed, I counted myself a fan. He lacked exceptional speed, memorable leaping ability, or Jordanesque control of the ball, but he played to win every second he was on the floor, and he measured up against boys with twice his talent. A relentless defender, he relished the chance to shut down a big ego wearing the opposite side's jersey. On offense he drove the lane like his personal salvation lay just over the rim. Our opponents left McAlister Field House knowing Pat was a warrior, as The Citadel would one day learn, too.

After we shook hands at training mess that spring evening, he began his observations: about the food, the service, the guys at the table, the uniforms, the skimpy second helpings brought by the "waitees." He seemed to hold an opinion on just about everything, and I went from smiling to chuckling to laughing. His sarcasm bit hard, but I loved it. He held up to humorous ridicule everything I had taken seriously for almost three years. And he showed just enough self-deprecation to reveal a genuine human being behind all the bluster. Where had this guy been?

As many college baseball teams do, ours took a southern swing where the weather tended to be warmer. Even a few degrees made a difference with your hands wrapped around a wooden bat (yes, they were all wooden then) and you connected with a fastball off the trademark, sending a shiver up your arms to your shoulders. We played Valdosta State in Georgia. Trips like that reminded us of how the other half lived, though that other half was more like the 99 percent, the guys our age who didn't attend military colleges. Springtime, azaleas in bloom, aromas from tea olives and Confederate jasmine that lifted you two inches off the ground, greens being manicured up the road for the Masters, coeds in summer silks passing in front of us as if guys and girls on the same campus was the most normal thing in the world.

The team stayed in a nearby one-story motel. We finished practice, showered, and headed back to the room. I can't remember whether Pat or I suggested that a cold beer would taste mighty damn good, but we bought a six-pack at a convenience store. Back at the room, we opened the door to admit the perfect springtime weather. We each opened a beer, and we probably nodded our agreement that yes, this was living. At that moment Coach Chal Port walked by. He looked at us, kept walking, then suddenly filled the doorframe.

"What in hell do you guys think you're doing?"

"Having a beer, Coach. Want one?"

It was clear he did not. "Beer is a violation of training rules," he said. "If I catch you with beer again, you can kiss your athletic scholarships good-bye."

What had tasted like liquid ambrosia moments before now turned sour, like rancid milk. He did not need to repeat his warning that season, nor did he catch us again.

We traveled to away games in station wagons with "The Citadel" stenciled in blue letters on the doors. Those were long trips, made less tedious by Pat's prolific observations about the towns we passed through, the condition of the highways, random pedestrians we observed at forty miles per hour. Not everyone appreciated his sarcasm, and it took me awhile to realize they simply didn't get it. He always brought books with him on those road trips, a habit that made him suspect to several.

"What do you do with all those books, Conroy?" Coach Port asked.

"I read them, Coach."

Port, driving, looked in the rearview mirror to select another occupant. "Look at Webster there. He doesn't bring any books."

Pat said, "That is because Webster is a dimwit who has an IQ of fifty-one."

From the back came Webster's rejoinder. "Fuck you, Conroy."

And so the season went.

Pat spent most of the following summer as a counselor at Camp Wahoo, a basketball sweatshop outside Charlottesville. He planned to be at the top of his game for his last college season. I, on the other hand, answered Uncle Sam's summons to scenic Fort Bragg, North Carolina, for six weeks of ROTC summer camp. Shortly before my report date, I received this letter from Pat.

Camp Wahoo is as detestable an experience as man ever endured. My muscles scream in pain; my skin peels off in pelts from the heat of the sun; my feet are gnarled, twisted fragments, remnants of a medieval past, when torture was the method and the vogue. Campers, little carbuncles on my sensitive behind, pimples that defy remedies. The lamentations that arise from my room rival those of Jeremiah on that old Wahoosian desert.

But when I think of you living in that tent, singing army hymns, covered with forest scum, and seasoning your wormridden food with hog manure, I get a feeling of patriotism far inside my anal passage.

I remember lingering over the word "lamentations," thinking it must be extraordinary to be corresponding with someone in college who actually used it. That may have been the point at which I realized Pat would fulfill his dream to be a writer. He had read every book I'd ever heard of. I kept his letters thereafter.

In the spring of our senior year we decided to forgo baseball. We'd each spent four years at our scholarship sport and craved one last, leisurely waltz with that lovely lady named Charleston. We drove around in my 1958 MGB, bought off cinder blocks from the back of a used car dealership for $400. We spoke often and freely about "getting lucky," but math was against us because most of the city's girls were off at distant colleges. If either of us did get lucky, he kept it to himself. We debated fiction versus nonfiction (you can guess which side of that argument Pat was on) and Vietnam (Pat was an early and vocal critic of the war, and time proved him right for all the reasons he gave me in 1967).

He worshipped Thomas Wolfe. He spoke so reverently of Ben's death scene in *Look Homeward Angel* that I felt compelled to read it.

"What did you think?" Pat asked.

"It took Ben a lot of pages to die," I said. On the day Pat died, I recalled that exchange. I stood at the foot of the hospice bed as he breathed his last. Real death carries a power no writer can match, even Thomas Wolfe.

At Pat's funeral I remembered one of his letters for what it said in the last paragraph. We had graduated from The Citadel weeks before, getting ready to "start life," the real thing.

"The night is changing into morning. Thanks again for your letter, John. I emerged from college with no better friend than you. I am tenacious about keeping friends. I plan to go through life with you somewhere within reach. Mawkishly and shamelessly, good luck next year. If you need any help financially, morally, physically, spiritually or anything else, call me."

He was good to his word. For fifty years we shared a friendship that must be rare in this world. It was marred by only one tiff that we patched up without much discussion. And so as the survivor let me say, mawkishly and shamelessly, how much I will miss him and how many are the lamentations at his passing.

Golden

⌒ VALERIE SAYERS

1969

We must have called him Mr. Conroy, but that's hard to imagine. Outside class, if we thought we were cool, we referred to him as Pat. When we gossiped, we called him Patconroy, one word on one breath, a movie star's name. When he paced our high school psychology classroom, he was all performer, good-looking in a Paul-Newman-*Cool-Hand-Luke* kind of way, only taller, younger, cooler. He was master of the sudden pause, the beat, the punch line. He told us funny, self-deprecating stories—his fears, his gaffes— and we didn't believe a word. Two years out of The Citadel, he was only six or seven years older than we were, but he was Robert Kennedy, Wilt Chamberlain, and the Beatles rolled into one.

We were a collective unit, juniors and seniors in a rare elective, hanging onto every word. Patconroy quoted Shakespeare, called us yahoos, and wisecracked through the class hour. He knew everything. My father was a psychologist who liked to check our quizzes and proclaim them "the real thing. He's teaching a serious course." We knew that already! He taught us Freud (thrilling and embarrassing), Jung (mystic and mysterious), Maslow (cheerful and possible). He asked us to consider thorny issues: abortion, disability, mental hospitals. He coached baseball and advised the Afro-American Society. He spoke sarcastically about the powers that be. In other classes I was dreamy, in Patconroy's class, wide awake.

One day he told us his parents would visit and begged us to shine—or at least not to laugh. He proclaimed his own nerves, which made us all giggle (as if Patconroy ever doubted himself). His parents swept in, golden as he was, movie stars too: his mother breezy, his father supremely sure. They smiled graciously, as if they interrupted class every day, and took two desks at the far side of the room.

In my memory I always have Pat lecturing on the Oedipus complex for his parents, but that surely can't have been. The lecture part I'm certain of, though; at the start of every class, chalk in hand, he gave us concepts. That day we took notes more diligently than usual and sneaked peeks at the beautiful people who had produced Patconroy. The three of them made perfect genetic sense. Pat cracked jokes as usual, unfazed behind his desk, or so we thought.

After a short while, his parents swept out again and he stood for a moment at the door, watching them down the hall. When he turned to face us, he said: "I thought I would die." It was only then that we saw how damp his forehead was, how red his cheeks. Had his voice been quavering like that all along?

We already worshipped him, but we liked him in that moment more than we could say. He let a roomful of raucous teenagers see what it cost him— the object of our adoration—to perform for us, to act the perfect son. Some of us would hold that red-faced picture of him for the rest of our lives.

1986

My editor mused on the phone which writers to ask for blurbs for my first novel. "You don't know Pat Conroy, do you?" I gulped. It had been a long time. In the year after college when I taught in Beaufort, I was even crankier than I'd been in high school. Pat was newly married to a war widow, and I sat in their lovely old house emanating silent disapproval of just about everything, dying to show him what a counterculture rebel I'd become. I winced at the memory of how full of myself I'd been. Now he was famous, and we'd fallen out of touch.

But Pat produced a beautiful blurb in record time and sent me an even more beautiful letter suggesting we'd spoken only yesterday. When he wrote again from Rome about what it was like to grow up Irish Catholic in Beaufort, I went time traveling with him. He was coming to New York—*The*

Prince of Tides was just out—and he invited me to the publication party. I spent the next six weeks fussing over the right shoes to wear.

Even before the publication date, *The Prince of Tides* had hit the best-seller list, my golden teacher the golden writer now. The party was as fancy as New York pub parties come—on a pier overlooking the harbor, the big room crowded with familiar writers and publishing bigwigs, glamorous waiters bustling about with stylish hors d'oeuvres. Pat had imported half the South—old neighbors from Atlanta were the first folks he introduced to me—and after a minute I tried to pull away, to make room for others to greet him. He wouldn't have it. He had to hear the story of my last dozen years in granular detail. My husband was a Chilean? He let the neighbors know. Two children—*What? When?*

"Oh, Pat," I said. "So many folks are trying to shake your hand."

And sure enough, a publicist was coming to pry Pat away, but he had me by the hand. We followed the publicist to a corner of the room where a slew of well-wishers waited to approach him one by one: it was a receiving line of sorts. He hung on tight to me, and after he said hello to each fan, each friend, each editorial assistant, he said my name and the name of my book: "You have to meet this writer. You have to buy this book." He said it over and over and over, my name, my book, at his own publication party.

I blushed redder than he'd reddened in his parents' presence, but I was grinning too, and boy was I learning something about what it means to have another writer, a golden godfather, stretching out his hand. Over the years, I would hear how often he stretched out that famous hand and to how many writers. But that night I hadn't been around publishing long, only long enough to know how precious his generosity was.

That's another picture—his hand clutching mine, holding me captive, repeating my name—another picture to hang onto.

2014

After I moved to the Midwest, I savored Pat's notes and e-mails, his approximate typing an art form from a man who wrote all his manuscripts by hand. About those high school psychology days, he wrote: "i soothed my own great loneliness by throwing my unkempt life into the middle of yours."

About the death of one of my classmates: "I had a mass said for the repose of sweet cindys soul." About Story River Books, his labor of publishing love: "im going to bother you for a manuscript for the rest of my ill lived life." And maybe my favorite: "say hi to your handsome husband. bernie and i love the way he looks. great love, pat conroy." You couldn't get better than a closing that combined his notorious friend-for-life Bernie Schein, a handsome husband, and his signature sign-off, "great love."

Out of town the weekend I signed copies of a new book at Red Piano Too, Pat rushed in from a long drive, bought up copies for every member of his large family, and squeezed my shoulder the way he'd squeezed my hand all those years and books before. *So proud, so proud*, he said, over and over and over. He posed for pictures with the old gang from high school psychology and strangers who popped over to beg a snap. I sensed, even in his posing, a new centered calm.

Soon after, Pat finally let my husband and me buy him the meal we'd been trying to buy him for years, small payback for all the meals he'd bought, all the kindness. It wasn't the last time I saw him—I'd get to thank him from a stage and hug him at his seventieth birthday bash—but it's the picture I hold now: Pat sitting across from me, framed against Beaufort Bay, centered and peaceful. His beloved wife Cassandra, surely the bearer of that new calm into his life, was there, and so was Julie Zachowski, who graduated with him from Beaufort High.

By then the whole world knew of Pat's long struggles and sorrows and crack-ups. But sitting next to graceful Sandra and laughing with Julie about high school days, his hard-bought, quiet calm stretched out through the meal. He seemed content to talk at a slow pace, to name the books he treasured, the students he held dear. We shook our heads over politics, but he never failed to brighten speaking of a friend. His excessive, unearned praise had not been diluted one drop over the years. He fairly beamed at me. I hold that picture dear.

"Great love." He had that sign-off right. His was a great, golden love, and when I step into a classroom or write a blurb for a young writer and remember how much Pat Conroy gave of himself, I'm basking in it still.

Pat Conroy, My Teacher and My Friend

～ SALLIE ANN ROBINSON

I still remember the first time I ever saw him. It was day one of the 1969–70 school year at Mary Fields School on South Carolina's Daufuskie Island, just north of Savannah. Eighteen of us native kids—the island's fifth- through eighth-graders—sat restless and then shocked as a young white male teacher entered our classroom with his big smile and long sideburns. He was the first white teacher we'd ever had. He was also the first male teacher we'd ever had. We just stared as he said, "Good morning" to us while writing his name on the blackboard:

Pat Conroy.

Then he asked us to tell him our names. When it was my cousin's turn, Pat interrupted him and said playfully, "That's not your name! Your name is Jack."

In an instant my cousin snapped back, "Your name's not Pat Conroy—your name's *Conrack*." And that's how Pat got the nickname that would eventually become the title of the first movie to be made from one of his books.

That school year was unforgettable for me. Pat was patient and generous. He made every day an adventure while teaching us about history, math, spelling, reading, music. You name it, he taught it. And all the while, he was preparing us for the wide world we were going to face once we left our island. He could take the words in a book and bring them to life for us, and we were amazed. We learned about things we had not been taught before— the planets, the Great Lakes, the Sahara, U.S. history, and current events that were changing our world.

Pat had a way of making it seem easy to learn something hard, like it was a game. He taught us to appreciate classical music, which we had never heard—Beethoven, Brahms, Tchaikovsky. He gave us his undivided attention in the classroom and at play. It was so different from how we had been taught before Pat. Everything about Pat was different.

I was a curious student, hungry for knowledge. I got up every morning wanting to go to school because this wonderful teacher would be there who could make learning fun while opening our eyes to a future we didn't know was ours. Pat taught me to be a go-getter. "Get out there and get it. It's all out there for you. Education is your freedom, and know that you can do anything you want if you want it bad enough."

Pat saw that our experiences had been limited, and he wanted us to have more. So he took us on class trips to show us the world beyond Daufuskie. We went to Camp St. Mary to learn how to swim. The boys knew how from jumping off the docks, but us girls didn't know. Can you imagine living somewhere surrounded by water, that you can get to only by boat, and not having been taught how to swim? But Pat took care of that! He also took us into Beaufort on Halloween to trick-or-treat—something we didn't do on Daufuskie. It was such fun.

Our biggest trip was to Washington, D.C., for a week! It might be hard to picture him carefully organizing a weeklong trip for more than a dozen curious schoolchildren who had never been that far from home in our young lives. It wasn't easy to convince our families to let us go, but Pat promised to take care of us—and he did. One of the places he took us was the Smithsonian Institute, and I'm proud to say that I've since been back as an adult, as an invited speaker on Gullah culture and foodways in 2010. It was my turn to teach others, as Pat had once taught me.

Pat showed me how to live in the service of your friends and your ideals. I learned so much from him, not just in the classroom or on field trips, but over the course of a lifelong friendship. He wrote the foreword to my first cookbook, *Gullah Home Cooking the Daufuskie Way*, and he went to book signings and talks with me. We had such fun together—especially when we'd come to a store that had my book and not any of his! "Well, look who's come up in the world, little Sallie Ann Robinson from Daufuskie Island," he'd joke with me, and I knew he was as proud of me as I was of him.

Pat had such a big heart, and I am so grateful to have known him as my teacher and my friend. I miss him dearly. Every time I learn something new—or teach something new to someone else—I think of Conrack.

When Pat Conroy Slept on Our Sofa

~ DOTTIE ASHLEY

Just as the poet and writer James Dickey, author of *Deliverance*, was starting to lecture to his graduate class in the Criticism of American Poetry, which I was taking in 1973 at the University of South Carolina, a young man slid into the desk next to me and whispered, "I hope I'm not too late! I had to drive all the way up from Beaufort."

"Oh no," I whispered back. Suddenly, I noticed the person looked slightly familiar. In fact, he resembled the writer who had been featured in an article in *Life* magazine that I had read the night before.

"Are you Pat Conroy, who wrote the book *The Water Is Wide* about teaching black children on Daufuskie Island?" I asked.

With a smile, he answered, "Yes, I am. But when my book comes out, I'm hoping to move my family out of South Carolina as soon as possible."

Because my husband, Dr. Franklin Ashley, three years Pat's senior, had been on the junior faculty of The Citadel during Pat's senior year, when Conroy was a basketball star, Pat and I began to talk before and after Dickey's class, which met three days a week. One day, near the end of the fall semester, Pat, who had learned Dickey and Franklin were friends, asked me if I would introduce him to the esteemed poet-in-residence, which I did. Dickey was polite but in a hurry.

Pat didn't return to the poetry criticism class for the spring semester because by then he was on tour promoting *The Water Is Wide*. Franklin and I were among only a handful of those in Pat's audience one evening,

Portions of this essay originally appeared in the *Charleston Mercury*, 2016.

because he was still relatively unknown at that time. Knowing he had a long ride ahead of him that night, and feeling his disappointment at the poor turnout, we invited him to stay on the sofa at our apartment, an offer he quickly accepted. We stopped for takeout and stayed up late reminiscing about The Citadel. Since Franklin, then a professor at USC, was also a poet who had published in *Harper's* magazine, the two became friends, and to such a degree that Pat decided to stay another night.

When I returned home from teaching twelfth-grade English that day, I was surprised to find Pat standing with our refrigerator door wide open, desperately searching for something edible, but with little success. The mood brightened when I opened some chips and dip. When Franklin came home, we popped open a bottle of cheap red wine, and after downing every drop, we took off for an early dinner at a nearby Italian restaurant.

We talked to Pat about the harassment he experienced by going against the conservative educational establishment in 1970s South Carolina, and how he felt driven to get away from Beaufort even though he had many supportive friends there.

As a fellow liberal who had pushed for integrated schools, Franklin was assigned by the chair of the English Department at The Citadel to serve in 1966 as the adviser to the first black cadet to enroll there. A year later, I was teaching in the first integrated high school in the state, Charleston's Rivers High School, formerly on upper King Street. We each vowed our determination to make equal rights prevail in South Carolina.

That was our dream. And since we were so young, and because it was in the spring of 1974, we had no doubt it would come true.

After dinner, at my urging, Pat called his first wife, Barbara, who had already moved with their three young daughters from Beaufort to Atlanta, to inform her he would be very late arriving home. We stood in the fading spring light watching our friend weave away in his rickety yellow VW; it was the last time we would see Pat before the flame of his almost instant fame would burn brightly and change his life forever.

We maintained our friendship with Pat and his family, visiting many times through the years. The final time we saw our old friend was October 2015 when a three-day event marking Pat's seventieth birthday was held in Beaufort, sponsored mainly by the University of South Carolina Press, which Pat had begun to work with on projects promoting new writers.

Pat seemed thrilled to see us and insisted that before traveling back to Charleston the next morning we stop by the Conroy home to visit with him and Cassandra. Sadly, we had obligations the next morning, a Sunday, and realized we had to leave town extremely early to fulfill them. Later, I called Cassandra and expressed our regrets.

However, I'm glad we went to the trouble to go to this important milestone. Before the official birthday party took place at the Beaufort Museum that evening, Pat, in a brief, private moment, said to me with an expression of disbelief in his blue eyes, "You all came, you really came. And just think how much has happened to us, and how long we've known each other all these years. Where did it somehow all go?"

"But don't worry," he added, in an upbeat tone, "we'll be getting together real soon—I promise!"

My Private Conroy

〜 JOSEPHINE HUMPHREYS

If I could send Pat an e-mail today, here's what it would say: "Thank you for the Italian cookbook you sent. And for everything else you gave me over the years—the phone calls, the blurbs, and, my God, so much laughter. Thank you for writing every single one of your books. And most of all—most of all, my dear friend—I thank you for your courage."

But if I had signed only my first name on this e-mail speeding toward writers' heaven, I'm not entirely sure he would know whom the message was from.

Pat Conroy's inner circle must have included hundreds of people, but I wasn't in it. Our time together during the thirty years I knew him would add up to maybe two hours, three if you count phone calls. I would place myself maybe in the inmost ring of his million-member outer circle. I was an acquaintance. However, that's not how it felt to me. It felt like a strange, private, long romance that only I was aware of.

In 1970 I came home to Charleston with my new husband after being away for college and graduate school. I was twenty-five. Pat was twenty-five then, too, and was in and out of Charleston from time to time, but I didn't know him. He had already written *The Boo*, a memoir that wasn't on my radar. I was reading novels, hoping someday to write one. I was also adjusting to a return to Charleston, not sure if I could fit in here, not sure if I could write here, and especially not sure if I could write and fit in at the same time. The Charleston of my childhood had been a frightened town, and I'd been raised by frightened parents. The big questions in our family were, "What will people think? What will people say?" As a teenager I understood that I was bound by three main rules: (1) Never speak out publicly, even in a letter to the newspaper. (2) Do not take to the stage. (3) Do not get pregnant. These were consistent with the general Charleston rules: behave, be quiet, stay hidden. Don't question anything. Don't cause trouble. Don't offend anyone. Don't take risks.

These are not good rules for writers.

I loved my Charleston and the lowcountry insanely, but I had things to say that my parents, and probably Charlestonians and maybe southerners in general, would not be comfortable with. And I wasn't a particularly brave person. I did tend to hide and stay out of trouble. Real writers don't do that.

And then in 1971 I heard about Pat. Not as a writer but as someone in the headlines for misbehavior. The Charleston newspaper carried a story about this former Citadel cadet working as a teacher on remote Daufuskie Island. He had been fired for disregard of instructions, insubordination, gross neglect of duty, and conduct unacceptable for a professional educator. He had sued to be reinstated, and his case was being heard in court. The judge was not sympathetic, predicting that chaos would follow if rules were not obeyed. Conroy, according to the judge, had "rebelled at any attempt at authority over him." Specifically, what he'd done wrong was to bring the twentieth century and American culture into the Daufuskie classroom. He had played music for the kids and showed them "motion pictures." He'd taken them to the mainland, and once, without first checking with his boss, he had asked someone to sub for him while he went to a conference. But the real sin was that he had challenged the authorities. He had spoken out, telling the school board that they were failing these children. His petition to be reinstated was denied.

I wonder, did they really think they could keep Pat Conroy quiet?

If so, they were surprised when a year later he published *The Water Is Wide*, revealing his story not just to a South Carolina courtroom and regional newspapers but to the world. I can remember Pat telling me many years later that a powerful motive for writers is revenge. *The Water Is Wide* actually is a revenge book, I think, a recounting of the young teacher's unfair dismissal—but it rises above that; it's more. It's about loving the South even as it harbors things we hate. It lays bare the extraordinary poverty and neglect that were shaping the lives of our African American children. At the same time it is a story of energy and hope combined with a stunning passion for the place and the people.

Pat once said that Charleston is not a good city for writers. In context he seemed to mean that the place is too overwhelming in its beauty and mystery to be captured in words; he said it needs painters and photographers. But I had a feeling that he meant something more than that, and my suspicion was confirmed a little later, after my first novel came out. We were at a party in Atlanta, and he asked me, "Do you think you can survive as a novelist in Charleston?"

That was the very question haunting me. I scrambled for a positive answer and said that Charleston had always valued its eccentrics, so maybe I could just get accepted as a crazy lady, and that would be fine with me.

"That should work well enough," he said. "But be a brave crazy lady."

And I knew courage was in my reach, because I had Pat as a model.

Pat never stopped passing his courage on to other writers, especially the beginners. He wrote blurbs and pushed the books of countless young writers. He was close friends with my close friend Ted Phillips, and he learned that Ted's eleven-year-old daughter, Alice, wanted to become a writer. She had in fact already tried her hand at a novel, staying up late at night to write eighty pages. One day she was home alone when the doorbell rang. "I did not recognize the pink-faced, white-haired figure through the peephole," she says. She called out, "Who is it?" and to her surprise the man answered, "It's Pat Conroy!" She opened the door, stunned, and started to say that her dad wasn't home, when Pat said, "I heard a rumor that someone in this house has written a novel. And I've come to read it."

He liked it. He told her not to quit. She's in law school now, but I won't be surprised some day to see a newly published novel with her name on it. The Conroy blurb will be invisible, but we'll know it's there.

For his generosity to an eleven-year-old burgeoning writer, for his empowering kindness to one of Charleston's crazy ladies, and for so many other reasons, I loved Pat Conroy and continued to love him for the rest of his life, and will for the rest of mine. The secret romance never faded.

My Painting Life with Pat Conroy

~ WENDELL MINOR

How does a kid from the heartland of Illinois connect with a son of the South who is so passionate about his adopted lowcountry home? It all began quite serendipitously more than forty years ago when I was a young freelance designer and illustrator in New York.

I received a phone call in 1975 from Louise Noble, the art director of Houghton Mifflin Company. "I have an interesting assignment for you that I think you're really going to love. I'm putting the manuscript in the mail today. It's called *The Great Santini* by Pat Conroy, and it's about the Meecham family, focusing on a father-son relationship. Read it and let me know what you think."

The Great Santini manuscript arrived two days later. The minute I started reading it I was hooked! I read it once, and then a second time, making notes in the margins about some cover thoughts running through my mind. I've always told Pat that his poetic prose paints pictures in words, and the Meecham family—Col. Bull Meecham, the Marine fighter pilot, and his eldest son, Ben—were proof positive as they lifted off the pages and came to life. I truly identified with their relationship, perhaps because mine with my own father had striking parallels. My dad served in one of General Patton's armored divisions in World War II and maintained a strong military-style discipline with me until I left home for art school. Feeling that you can never please your father and win his approval is painful, and I felt Ben's pain deeply. It became abundantly clear to me that the colonel's old leather flight jacket was the perfect iconic image for *The Great Santini* cover painting, symbolizing the strong bond between father and son despite their dysfunction.

I obtained a vintage leather flight jacket and hung it on a hook inside my open closet door. I used that jacket as a template for what became the painting, which to my mind said it all. To quote Pat: "The paintings [Wendell] has done for my books honor them with their elegance and simplicity.... By his artistry, he interprets each of my books with a single stunning image that always surprises me."

It is not easy to find the one singular image that can sum up thousands of words, but that has always been my greatest joy and challenge to achieve for Pat's covers. The cover of *The Great Santini* was the genesis of my bond with Pat. His friendship, loyalty, and respect for me and for my art made us kindred spirits from afar. *The Great Santini* remains a seminal work for me and perhaps my favorite Conroy novel. Pat's friend Jim Townsend, the editor of *Atlanta* magazine at the time, made arrangements to buy the original cover art for Pat. It became the first of many Minor originals included in the Conroy collection.

Next came *The Lords of Discipline* (1980), the story of a young cadet coming of age at the prestigious Carolina Military Institute in Charleston during the Vietnam War era. For me, there was only one symbol for the cover: it had to be the cadet class ring, that final bond of loyalty and honor. I was amazed that Pat was willing to send me his class ring to use as reference for a simple still life. The painting shows a ring that casts its circumference in a long shadow creating a symbolic open portal. Needless to say, I was honored by Pat's trust in sending me one of his treasured possessions.

Pat's next book, *The Prince of Tides*, was published six years after *The Lords of Discipline* and required a different direction from my previous covers. It was the first time I used watercolors rather than the more opaque medium of acrylic. Watercolor is so much more spontaneous in capturing the essence of a landscape; Winslow Homer always comes to mind in this regard. The South Carolina lowcountry setting for the darker side of the novel required an evocative and moody image with a true sense of place.

Having gone to art school in Florida and traveling up and down the Southeast coast on many occasions, I got to know the incredible beauty of the lowcountry. My watercolor for *The Prince of Tides* wraps around the jacket and shows a small house on the back cover, appearing very vulnerable alongside a tidal marsh, with an ominous skyscape overhead. Pat's commentary on this image best brings it into focus: "When I wrote *The Prince of Tides*, I did not know where the book was leading until I saw the secret Wendell had gleaned from it. It was about a damaged and magnificent family living in a small white house beside a breathtaking tidal marsh. Neither the family nor the novelist could see the black, roiled storm clouds forming in the Atlantic. In that invisible, gathering storm, in the loveliest island country in the world, in that threatened house, three children were trying to make sense and art out of their broken lives. That storm would follow them always."

I well remember Pat telling me of his elation on seeing the *Tides* cover art for the first time. I couldn't have been more pleased when he told me he wanted the original art. It is, I believe, one of my most successful watercolors, which was spontaneously executed. In fact, it was my first and only attempt for the cover art. I captured what I was looking for on the first try. When that happens, it is the closest feeling an artist can have to an out-of-body experience, and that is rare indeed. Everything clicks perfectly without the slightest hesitation!

Conroy fans had to wait nine long years after that for *Beach Music*. Because of Pat's loyalty to me, I had made the transition with him to join Nan Talese at Doubleday. *Beach Music* has a multifaceted plot spanning time and place with settings in Rome and South Carolina. My instinct was to stay in South Carolina. I remember doing three sketches: two variations were of evocative distant night views of the bridge in Charleston; the third sketch was a distant view of the old beach house on a moonlit night, teetering precariously at the edge of the ocean. A bonfire, tiny figures, and car headlights behind the house create just enough of a sense of mystery to set the stage for Pat's narrative to unfold. I've always believed that a good cover is all about creating a compelling visual atmosphere that invites every reader to open the book and join in.

When Pat and I discussed the cover for *South of Broad*, he mentioned that he would like me to try an elevated overview of that famous street. It was the only time I can recall Pat offering any thoughts on a cover. I knew it was important to him because he offered to send me some photo reference. The resulting wraparound jacket art, set at twilight with the hint of a coming storm, set the tone for the book. I hope the reader truly feels that sense of place with its mystery and sultry ocean warmth and air.

My Reading Life was published in 2010 as a small five-by-seven-inch hardcover, which gave the reader the feel of an intimate and personal object. That feeling matched so well Pat's very personal essays on his passion for books that give flight to the imagination, thus the essence of my cover: an open book with its pages taking flight.

The publication of *The Death of Santini* in 2013 brought the return of the colonel's flight jacket to the central cover image. This time, the jacket appears on the back of a chair on a veranda overlooking a beautiful low-country marsh at sunset. I felt this was the perfect symbol to provide closure and complete the circle for father and son.

Because of the geographical distance, our phone visits were more frequent than our times together in person, but when we did see each other, it was always a special event for me and my wife, Florence. We both remember fondly joining Pat and Sandra and Pat's close friend, Doug Marlette, and his wife, Melinda, for breakfast in New York. We were all celebrating the publication of *Beach Music*, and it was a glorious time with many toasts all around. Later that day, Pat invited me to join him for his television interview in Central Park. He was more than generous with his compliments about my covers being his talisman.

The last time we saw Pat and Sandra was at the South Carolina Book Festival in 2014. The long evening of tall southern tales with all of their best writer friends and the wonderful dinner that followed was something we will never forget as long as we live. Being Pat's friend and creating his covers has been one of the most extraordinary and rewarding highlights of my life. Very few people have had such an impact on me. Everyone who knew him was touched by his heart and soul, and his ever warm sign-off, "Great Love!" Great love to you, dear Pat. Your heart lives on in all of us.

Being Ben Meecham, Loving Pat Conroy

 ～ MICHAEL O'KEEFE

It would be impossible to overestimate the effect of Pat Conroy's work on both my professional and personal lives. Had Pat not made the journey from tortured yet loving son of a brutal Marine fighter pilot to author of *The Great Santini*, I never would have had the opportunity to portray his alter ego, Ben Meecham, in the film adaptation of his wonderful novel. I would like to think I might have had a career as an actor without that role, but it would have been so starkly different from what transpired, it gives me pause to imagine what the hell that would even look like. Which is to say, without Pat's journey into the arts I might not have had one at all.

The day before I screen-tested for *Santini* I went to the local bookstore, bought the novel, and read it in one sitting. It articulated every nuance I had lived as the son of a man like Pat's father, so tortured by his own inner demons that he made the tragic mistake of letting them loose on his family instead of protecting us at all costs from his own personal hell.

It was in the summer of 1978 that Pat and I first met on the shore of Charleston's harbor. By then I'd been cast in the film, was twenty-three look-ing seventeen, the required age of the character, and was eager to connect. We were on our way to meet "the Boo," Lt. Col. Thomas Nugent Courvoisie of The Citadel, which Pat had attended in the 1960s. The subject of Pat's first book, *The Boo*, the gruff yet loving colonel was a father figure for Pat. When we'd been together for a while the Boo remarked, "You didn't have it so bad, Conroy. Your father just knocked you around a little. Some of my boys really had problems."

I was struck not just by the man's underestimation of Pat's childhood trauma but also by the nonchalance of his tone. The Boo had no doubt seen worse, but at the time I thought, *Let us not compare suffering like oranges, one pale and tart and the other blood red.*

Pat said nothing but bent his head to one side, looked as if he couldn't recall something, scratched his already balding pate, and we moved on. But the specter of Pat's father had been invoked, and neither Pat nor I could shake it off.

A moment later I thought, *Just another military brat whose father knocked him around?* Well, no. Not *just* that. Not just that at all. Pat was one of the rarest of all artists; he had found a way to transmute grief into prose and pain into poetry. The burden Col. Don Conroy imposed on him might have killed not just his spirit but the entire man. Instead, Pat didn't just survive; he thrived.

We were alike in so many ways that it's hard not to list similarities without giving the impression of more importance to some and less to others. We resembled each other—due, no doubt, to our shared Irish heritage and to being the offspring of fair-haired mothers paired with dark fathers in both demeanor and nature. But there was another, more compelling connection, and we both felt it though we never spoke directly about it.

After meeting me and shaking my hand, Pat looked quite deeply into my eyes and said, "Where did they find you?" He was not asking me where I grew up, or whether I lived in New York or L.A. He was taken by a more innate, more mysterious connection. Yes, we were both the oldest of seven Irish Catholic kids, were both athletic, and had a similar impish humor combined with fervent intellect, but there was something else we shared. We were both terribly wounded by the injustice of our childhoods. Loving a father whose primary characteristic is brutality imbues one with a unique worldview. Boys like us longed for a way to save our fathers from themselves and our families from our fathers. And because that was impossible, boys like us devoted our adult lives to expressing our failures as heroes in the world through aspiring to be heroic in art. Everything we did creatively, even our failures, ensured that we would never be at a loss for inspiration. Our wound was not just our geography, as Pat once wrote, it was the unique spark of our hearts' engines, and therefore kept us alive. In a way, it would not be an overstatement to say we shared the same heart, because we were always in sync, always moved to the same beat, and for more than forty years, we picked up where we left off after last seeing each other, no matter how much time had passed between meetings.

It's a testament to Pat's inherently benevolent nature that he allowed his father a second chance as a grandfather and as a satellite to his own literary star, which afforded Don a stage to strut his Santini persona for all the world to see. I cannot imagine that Pat envisioned doing book signings with his dad after the initial shock and disgust Don's family displayed when the novel was published. Yet, when the movie had modest success, the tide turned, and Don began to come around. It was he who exclaimed to Pat after the announcement for Academy Awards that year, "Both you and I got nominated, son. Your mother didn't get squat!"

For the small part I played in bridging the gap between them I was always gratified to know that something I did affected Pat even a little, because everything he did for me is a debt I can never fully repay. I loved him immeasurably and unconditionally. Had he asked me to, I would have jumped at the chance to do something directly for him, but Pat never required any demonstration of my love for him. He was just that kind of guy.

I was invited to the tribute given Pat in October 2015 at USC Beaufort, Pat Conroy at 70, and there I finally had the chance to tell him flat out how I felt about him. It's a rare thing for men to share something like that, and I will always be grateful that the moment arose and I took the risk to say, "Pat, I love you," because now that he is gone I don't think I'd ever rest easily knowing I'd left that unsaid.

If I could, I would grab him in a bear hug and pour buckets of praise on him for a life well lived and a marvelous run as a writer and a man. One tiny thing, though; I might suggest he stop styling his hair in a comb-over and just admit he was bald. Let me tell you, when we meet up in the next world, because I am almost certain we will, I will do both with equal gravitas.

Pat's elegiac, spectacular prose, his insight and ribald humor, will not only live on in his many books but will endure in my heart and mind's eye like no other memory. I love Pat Conroy so much. I only hope he left knowing that I am not the only one who felt that way. Those of us who knew Pat were fortunate to call him friend, and those of us who admired his writing gave him the opportunity not only to redeem his childhood and family but also to articulate for all of us the confounding nature of familial love in all of its splendid confusion.

Thanks, Pat. I'm going to miss you, and to paraphrase what you wrote for the eulogy of Lt. Col. Bull Meecham, I will like the world a lot less without you in it.

A Few Corrections

Some Edited Memories of Pat

⌇ JONATHAN GALASSI

Tom Stoppard once wrote that it was hardly a distinction to have been in love with Deborah Mitford, the legendarily seductive Duchess of Devonshire, who died in 2014. Aristocrats and workingmen, artists and farmers—all were hopeless confronted with Debo's regal charm, the essential ingredient of which was the magic of her absolute attention. Once she fixed her agate eyes on you, you were a goner.

Much the same can be said for Pat Conroy, perhaps the most beloved writer the South has produced since his great model, Thomas Wolfe. As Pat wrote somewhere, "Wolfe provided me with a blueprint of how even a boy like me could prepare myself to live a writer's life. By following the lead of this gargantuan word-haunted man, I could force my way into a life of art." That hunger for vocation, and that apprenticeship, defined the course of Pat's life. And it determined, too, how he would see and make use of his own story, which was where his work began and ended.

Pat so mythologized himself in his books that it's hard to get a memory in edgewise. No doubt the truth will be sorted out in the fullness of time— or not. It hardly matters in the great scheme of things. But the points at which Pat's life and mine intersected were significant ones, especially for me, and I'd like them to be recorded as accurately as possible. So here are a few memories, and a few corrections, offered with enduring love and in the spirit of honest exchange that always characterized our friendship.

My time working with Pat was short, but it marked me indelibly, and we remained devoted to each other for life. In our last thirty years we met only infrequently, but every few months the phone would ring and a thick southern broth of a voice would ring out, "Editor of Genius!" It was Pat, calling for me, with a healthy dollop of derisive irony, by the subtitle of Scott Berg's biography of the great Maxwell Perkins. He had long ago decided this was going to be my epithet, and whoever was around at Farrar, Straus and Giroux, the house where I've worked for the last three decades, soon came to understand it was his or her job to find me when Pat started bellowing it over the phone.

You could never call Pat yourself, or call him back. He was so inundated by importunings of one kind or another that he never answered the phone or read his e-mail. In an absolute emergency you could get through to him with an SOS to his all-knowing, all-comprehending wife, Cassandra King. Generally, though, I waited to hear from Pat and hoped I'd be around when he called, because conversations with him were always wonderful.

I was assigned as Pat's second editor at Houghton Mifflin in the late 1970s when Anne Barrett retired. Anne, whose father had been secretary of commerce in the William Howard Taft administration, had had a long and illustrious editorial career. The authors she had worked with included J. R. R. Tolkien. She had shepherded *The Great Santini* into print in 1976, and Pat and I both revered her. He had been "discovered," as we say in publishing, by Shannon Ravenel, a gifted editor who hailed from Charleston and who responded strongly to his passionate storytelling about his year teaching on Daufuskie Island, which became *The Water Is Wide* (1972). It in turn became the movie *Conrack* (1974) starring Jon Voigt, the first of a list of movies based on Pat's books, which attest to his inborn narrative gifts and his uncanny ability to connect with his audience.

Pat was bemused and dismayed to be getting another editor, this one a shy, bookish Ivy Leaguer who was far less knowledgeable about the ways of publishing than he was. He and his friend the novelist Terry Kay compared notes lamenting whom they'd been assigned. Terry had been given Grant Ujifusa, a bright young editor whose main interest was in politics. Pat got me. Let's just say that neither author was happy.

I was a sheltered, rather uptight New Englander in those days, more than a little intimidated by this hulking ex-athlete who wore his feelings on his sleeve and traded on them with just about everyone he met to establish an immediate intimacy. That winter of 1978, Pat, who had recently been divorced from his first wife, Barbara, went to work on me, inviting me down to visit him in the ramshackle little house where he was staying on Folly Beach outside Charleston. He took me to have Charleston oysters, and we listened together to Keith Jarrett's ecstatic, improvisational *Köln Concert*, the compositional method of which I came to see had more than a little in common with Pat's own. I fell in love with Keith Jarrett and still listen to him today, and when I do I always think of Pat.

Pat was writing *The Lords of Discipline*, his novel about The Citadel. He was animated by a powerful sense of injustice at the school, which he saw as a microcosm of the hierarchical racist politics of the South in those days—themes that were central to the plot of the book. Pat showed me The Citadel and introduced me to Lt. Col. Thomas Courvoisie, the hero of Pat's first privately published book, *The Boo*, written while he was a student. And he showed me the mansions south of Broad Street that represented the establishment the book was written in protest against.

Later, I would visit him in Atlanta and get to know Cliff Graubart and the crowd that hung around the Old New York Book Shop, among them Norman Berg, the legendary Houghton Mifflin book traveler, who adored Pat; his oldest Beaufort friend, Bernie Schein; and Marshall Frady, then the Atlanta bureau chief for the *New York Times*. I met his suave, charming lawyer, Jim Landon; Lenore Fleischer, who would become Pat's second wife; and her children, Gregory and Emily. Last but not least, I got to know Pat's father, Don, the Great Santini himself. Far from being estranged, father and son seemed to be living out a continual "Who's on First" routine; in fact, they were more or less inseparable. The immortally abusive father of Pat's fiction had become his biggest fan and chief publicist.

Late in 1978 I received a grant to work on a translation and was generously allowed a six-month leave of absence by the powers at Houghton Mifflin. I and my then-wife, Susan, who was working on a dissertation on Picasso, planned to spend the first half of 1979 in Paris and Rome. When I told Pat the news, with some trepidation, he announced he was coming along—we did not, as he has written, invite him. In fact, we were quite apprehensive about this intrusion into our idyll. As it turned out, Pat almost immediately became a vital and beloved sharer in our Paris life and a lifelong friend to both of us. All that cold, raw winter—we were really poor because the dollar was worth only four francs at that moment—we worked through the day and gathered in the evenings. Pat has written memorably about his attic room in the not-so Grand Hotel des Balcons on the rue de l'Odéon; about visiting museums with Susan and learning to look at painting; about eating with us at Le Trumilou and other dollar-a-plate restaurants that were all that any of us could afford. And he has described how I received approval from Austin Olney at Houghton Mifflin to take him out to a now long-gone one-star restaurant, Dodin-Bouffant, for what seemed to us then like a Lucullan celebratory dinner before we left for Rome in April.

Pat has also written about how he and Cliff and Frank Smith eventually followed us to Rome; how they were robbed along the way; and how he fell deep in love with the Eternal City, where he later returned to live with Lenore. Da Fortunato, known then as the Trattoria del Pantheon, was our restaurant of choice (luckily the dollar went a lot further in Italy), and we'd walk down from our apartment above Trastevere night after night into the very heart of the city for simple, memorable meals. I particularly recall the grappa in an enormous jar of fruit that we drank night after night. Fortunato was young then, a handsome natural gentleman of great charm. He died recently, but his son, who resembles him, still runs what has since become a serious restaurant for movers and shakers, no longer the modest watering hole we couldn't get enough of.

Pat had come to Rome to deliver the manuscript of *The Lords of Discipline*. It was spellbinding and ungainly—in fact, a mess. We had a talk in which he said, "I just want to spew it all out and have you shape it into a book." "That's not how it works Pat," I countered, but in fact it was, to a greater or lesser degree, how writing worked for him. I remember a particularly baroque mixed metaphor involving a scapegoat performing a very ungoatlike act; I drew a goat in the margin of Pat's page to illustrate how over the top his metaphor was. He laughed and laughed, but according to his longtime editor Nan Talese, who worked with him on all his books after *The Lords of Discipline*, Pat's methods never really changed.

The Lords of Discipline was published in 1981 to great excitement, and it, too, became a movie in 1983. Being a typical young man in a hurry, frustrated with what I thought of as the stolid ways of Boston publishing, I left Houghton Mifflin the following year for Random House. Naturally, I dreamed of bringing Pat there, but it was not to be—due to the internal politics of that byzantine organization and, no doubt, to my own ineptitude in working its system.

Needless to say, Pat stayed at Houghton Mifflin, where they were eager to keep him, and Nan became his lifelong editor; in fact, he followed her to Doubleday, an arm of Random House, when she herself left Houghton Mifflin.

The reasons were many, but my failure to bring Pat to Random House was humiliating and enraging for both of us and a matter of great grief. For some time we didn't speak. But eventually our affection for each other won out, and our friendship resumed, especially after I was fired from Random House in 1986. (I often told myself I should have left after the Pat debacle.)

After I came to FSG, we occasionally saw Pat on Fripp Island, where he was then living, and he and Cassandra made a memorable visit to us in Connecticut one summer. We met only rarely in New York, but our phone talks continued. I saw him last at his seventieth birthday celebration in Beaufort in the fall of 2015. We had a joyous evening at his house there with his longtime pal and agent Marly Rusoff and her husband, Mihai Radulescu, and his friend Ron Rash, whom Pat insisted on calling "Mr. Big," referring to himself as "Mr. Small." Pat seemed healthy and balanced if preoccupied by the emotional vectors of the weekend. I hadn't seen him for years, yet to me it seemed we picked up right where we'd left off.

He became ill not long after that. In March I returned to Beaufort for Pat's funeral with Marly and Mihai and Nan and Gay. The cadets and alumni of The Citadel served as an honor guard.

Pat was a friend of my youth, and we love our young friends with an intensity time doesn't lessen because we knew each other when, as they say. He was already famous when we met, but in the room of friendship we built, we could be just ourselves. Somehow the lowcountry boy and the shy New Englander broke through to common ground that remained, and for me remains, fertile. And it takes nothing away from my feeling for Pat to know that thousands felt exactly the same way and will miss him, as I will, forever.

This past June I was in Paris and walked up the rue de l'Odéon. The not-so Grand Hotel des Balcons is still there, probably still housing young writers aspiring to follow in the footsteps of Hemingway or Fitzgerald or Thomas Wolfe and who believe that Paris is the place to do it. Paris was that place for Pat, a rich and deepening moment in his life—as were Charleston, Atlanta, Rome, San Francisco, and above all, Beaufort. Wherever Pat was, he reflected back all he saw and did and felt in relation to the myth he was living. It was the life he'd imagined for himself as a boy, the life he created— and which he lived for the rest of us as a gargantuan, word-haunted talent and a much-loved man. Even if the details aren't precisely accurate, Pat's story always somehow ends up being ours.

II

Flow and Floodplains

~ *Becoming the Best-Selling Author*

(Atlanta, Europe, San Francisco)

The Prince of Tides · 1986

Beach Music · 1995

The Eternal Protagonist

〜 TERRY KAY

I am fuzzy about the time—1985, I believe it was—but we were in the hills of North Carolina, not far from Highlands, and we were sitting outside on a twilight evening that had both summer and autumn in it. Sweet smell of pine forest and honeysuckle, fireflies blinking, song of a night bird—the sort of setting he might have written about with such exuberance the words could have posed for a portrait.

We had hiked the hills and had dinner and were drinking wine fit for the occasion. Good vintage but not extraordinary. The mood was melancholy, as it always was in the comedown from hours of merriment that marked the energy of those blissfully young days.

That is when he said it: "Boys, they're about to make me famous, and I don't know how to handle it."

The memory is not fuzzy on that.

Pat Conroy said it. He said it to me and to Cliff Graubart and to Bernie Schein and to Frank Smith and to Dan Sklar.

This essay was originally published in *Atlanta* magazine, May 2016.

The Boys, we called ourselves, the same simple stamp of comradeship used by millions of men, men grouping up for a poker night or a game on television or just a sit-around visit for no purpose other than being together. No rules to being one of The Boys, other than holding true to trust.

And so, there we were on that evening—The Boys, enjoying wine and a melancholy moment, and Pat Conroy announces he is about to become famous.

My memory tells me our response was mostly silence, though there might have been an obscene but gentle put-down about it, for that is the way of language among most men who call themselves The Boys. But if there was anything profound suggested, it was lost in the mood of the evening.

Still, none of us forgot it.

It was not a prediction. It was a proclamation. He was finishing *The Prince of Tides*, the book that would secure his reputation following the success of *The Water Is Wide* and *The Great Santini* and *The Lords of Discipline*.

Being famous was there for the taking for him, but it was more than a public relations gambit. Fame was in his blood, in his presence, in the enigmatic something that finds a nest in select people.

He had a natural onstage presence so huge it overwhelmed his audiences. A large, imposing man, he could enter a crowded room and clear a path with his Irish smile and his Irish blue eyes and his Irish bluster, one of those rare people full up to the brim with charisma.

And he knew how to use it.

Yes.

Everywhere he went—to live or to visit—he had something to say, something to do, something to leave that would be remembered. His presence was more responsible for bringing attention to Atlanta writers in the 1970s and 1980s than anything, or anyone, else. The New York publishers paid attention because he talked it up. When he settled in South Carolina, at his home in Fripp Island and, later, in Beaufort, he made the state a center of southern literature. (I do think his designation as an editor at the University of South Carolina Press was hilarious, however. Pat Conroy, Editor. For anyone who read one of his first-draft manuscripts, it is the definition of an oxymoron. I would have enjoyed seeing Nan Talese's expression when she first saw the line, Nan having been his longtime editor at Doubleday.)

We met in the spring of 1973 at a luncheon that had something to do with Jim Townsend, then-editor of *Georgia* magazine. Jim had commissioned me to do a piece on the filming of *The Water Is Wide*, which was in production on St. Simons Island under the title *Conrack*.

We would spend some time at St. Simons, Pat told me. Talking, he said. He wanted to ask about my experiences as a film and theater writer for the *Atlanta Journal-Constitution*. It all sounded interesting to him, he vowed. Seeing all those movies and plays, mingling with celebrities.

That was the beginning of the relationship. Pat had moved to Atlanta earlier in the year to make a place for himself as a writer, and after St. Simons there would be get-togethers at the Old New York Book Shop and impromptu drop-ins at his home on Briarcliff Road. A small core of writers grew out of the gatherings—nothing official, just friends. We had a lot in common. Youth. Energy. Promise.

And we had Pat. He was the catalyst.

In the forty-three years between 1973 and attending his funeral on March 8, 2016, a lot happened between us, especially in the first twenty years.

We discovered we were cousins through the Peek bloodline.

"Distant," I would explain.

"Remote," he would counter.

The oft-told story of his influence on my career as a writer of fiction was true. He did make a phone call to Anne Barrett of Houghton Mifflin, telling her he had read 150 pages of a manuscript that his friend Terry Kay was working on and urging her to have a look at it.

It was a grand lie. I had never written a sentence of true fiction. When the letter came from Anne Barrett asking for the pages Pat had raved about, I went to his house to confront him. I snapped at him, cursed him, told him I had no desire to write fiction, and I would be grateful if he would drop the issue. He listened to the ranting, then advised that I had two choices: I could tell Anne the truth, that I had nothing to share, or I could write 150 pages.

I wrote the 150 pages in one month. Out of it came my first novel.

He knew what I would do because he knew I had been reared in a family with a work ethic that said this: *If someone has faith in you, you have an obligation to try.*

Pat had faith.

And there was the other call.

It was in the early 1990s. He was living in San Francisco and had received news that I was suffering from depression following publication of my novel, *To Dance with the White Dog*. It should have been the grandest of times for me. Reviews were good. There was interest in foreign sales. A movie was in the planning. The hoopla of it all was like theme music. Still, I was depressed. When Pat learned of it he began to call with regularity, asking each time about my writing. Each time, I lied, telling him it was going well. Then one day, he said, "Why are you lying to me? You're not writing anything."

I began weeping, the kind of weeping made of desperation and self-pity.

I had nothing to write, I told him. Nothing. When I paused, he said to me, "Kay, you've bored us for years about your miserable life in the Catskills, but you've never written a word about it, so here's your story: Young plowboy from a Georgia farm ties his mules to a fencepost, packs his meager belongings in a pillowcase, stuffs what few dollars he has into the toe of a sock, and boards the Greyhound bus going north. He runs out of ticket money in the Catskills, takes a job as a busboy in a Jewish resort, and falls in love with a beautiful Jewish girl who's a guest in the hotel."

I laughed. I knew Pat. Knew he was being deliberately absurd in an effort to change my mood. I said, "Conroy, that might be the silliest plotline I've ever heard."

There was a pause, a silence stretching from San Francisco to Atlanta, and then he said, "You didn't read *The Prince of Tides*, did you?"

I thought: *My God. That's exactly what he did. Dumb southern coach/teacher makes his way to New York to rescue his fragile sister and there meets the Jewish psychiatrist Lowenstein, love of his life.*

And then I thought: *If he can get by with that, so can I.*

Shadow Song came out of it. *Shadow Song* built the house I live in.

The phone call that led to *Shadow Song* also revealed something to me about Pat I had not realized—his need to be heroic. Thinking of him now, in the freedom of imagination, I believe as the first child in the combative family of Don and Peggy Conroy, he must have pinned a bath towel around his neck and set out in make-believe to save the world—first the one of his family, and second the one called Earth.

His father, Don—the Great Santini—once told an interviewer that Pat was always the hero in his stories, and because heroes required villains, he, Don, had served that role for his son, which was why there were so many references about the contentious father-son relationship in the Santini stories. There are those who would question Don's take on it, for he was as prone to exaggeration as Pat, and I always believed he had a myopic view of his place in his son's angst. There were many things that angered Pat other than his father's temper.

Still, Don was not wrong about Pat's wish to be heroic. In his writing, the Pat characters—the protagonists—are always valiant. Gloriously so. They encounter threat, meanness, injustice, and misery, and they metaphorically leap tall buildings and throw their bodies on nuclear warheads, and in the end, the world is saved and they stand triumphant—especially in the imagination of the reader. It is precisely that quality that has endeared him to millions, especially those who subconsciously wish to be rescued from some dastardly wrongdoing in the dysfunctional world of their existence.

Pat, the hero, is near operatic in each of his novels, but for me, his best writing was in his essays and especially in his letters of anger and protest against such issues as censorship and inept education. In those explosions of righteousness, the language is riveting because he was far more effective at the short, intense expression than in his long passages of singing description, as good as they are.

Then, too, much of his presence was beyond language; it was in the mere force of his name: Pat Conroy. His name peppers the front and back of book jackets of countless writers, writers who took nourishment from his cheerleading endorsements, who memorized his words and slyly dropped them into their conversation. They were his congregants. His name was their blessing, their heroic rescue from doubt, their wished-for passage into literary acceptance. In book festival crowds they thrashed around him like smiling piranhas.

On the day of his funeral, at St. Peter's Catholic Church in Beaufort, South Carolina, I heard people calling him a complex man.

Unquestionably, he was that. It was part of his ascension to fame.

In the praise heaped upon his memory by mourners who gathered to celebrate his life, he was described as kind and giving and caring. And, yes, that was true. I am a beneficiary of that generosity. Countless others gratefully make the same claim.

Yet there are those who will tell you he could be a bully, a stubborn man with an addiction to being right, a man beset by demons, and a man who could find curious pleasure in unleashing his devastating wit against people who cherished him. I knew that side of him also. There were a few times when the sting of his surprising, unexpected swipe left scars. He was a master at it, for he leveled it in the disguise of charm and you did not know whether to fight him or to laugh with him. There was no blood, yet you knew you had been wounded. To say he harbored a warped sense of humor is understatement.

"Just Pat," people would say. "Just Pat."

Over time, in his odyssey to find a place of adventure—Rome (Italy), Fripp Island, San Francisco—he eased away from early-on friends in Atlanta, though apparently he had been making an effort to reconnect with many of them. There was talk of it in the milling crowd attending his funeral. The mending was a good thing, those reconnected early-on friends admitted, a little like old times.

In fairness, time had a lot to do with the fading of his Atlanta influence, and it wasn't just Pat's doing. It was all of us. Anne Rivers Siddons moved to Charleston. I found my way to Athens. Rosemary Daniell relocated to Savannah. Cliff Graubart's book parties at the Old New York Book Shop— the parties that gave emerging writers an identity—ended. The Boys drifted apart. Frank Smith moved to Maine. Bernie Schein went home to Beaufort. Dan Sklar went north to New York. Others died—Paul Darcy Boles, Paul Hemphill, Bill Diehl, Marshall Frady.

It is the way of life. Change. Slow and swift. People go from improvised dinners of watery oyster stew in chipped coffee cups (as Pat once served) to champagne in Waterford crystal (as he surely enjoyed). Friends and acquaintances are lost along the way; new friends and acquaintances take their place. Novels are written of such storylines.

In full disclosure—as the newspeople say—I had not been close to Pat for twenty years. He would call occasionally, always with the same blarney he used with many people: "It's up to me to keep this dying friendship alive." I enjoyed those calls, but I had long known I was mostly a touchstone to another time for him, a memory residing in his Rolodex, one of the early-on people. Still—and this is honest—I was never bothered by the sense that I had become an outsider in his life. I knew there was more to the calls than periodically touching base. He had either a need to assuage some gnawing sense of obligation, a need to keep up appearances, or a wish to find some comfort in an old moment, perhaps one founded in the North Carolina mountains when not so much was expected of him. To me, it was Pat being Pat. Just Pat. I followed his rise to fame with interest and pride, but I preferred him as one of The Boys, not as a celebrity. Still, the sweet moments were indescribably fine. The last visit was one of those moments.

I saw him on Tuesday, January 26, at Emory University Hospital. He was weak and in some pain, but he was also jovial. We shared a few stories, ragged at the edges from so much telling over so many years. I hugged him. Told him I loved him. I did not believe I would again see him alive. And I didn't. My last viewing of him was on March 7, in Anderson Funeral Home. In the casket, he did not look famous. But he was, as he had proclaimed he would be. Death did not rob him of that quest.

Still, getting there was not easy work for him, not with the speeches, the blurbs, the parties, the begging of dreamy writers, the requests for selfies, the never-ending demands of giddy fans. Hard doing, it was, but necessary. As Pat learned, you cannot outrun fame, even if you wanted to. He didn't want to. He had an ordination to accept it, much like the title of a Robert Frost poem I have long favored: "How Hard It Is to Keep from Being King When It's in You and in the Situation."

It's a line that fit Pat perfectly.

In 2001, his fame riding high, Pat returned to The Citadel, his alma mater, to give the commencement address, ending an estrangement of many years. On that day he invited Citadel graduates to attend his funeral when the time came. All they had to do to gain entrance was to announce, "I wear the ring," the opening line to *The Lords of Discipline*, the book that had caused the rift.

If Pat had shared this plan with The Boys in 1985, in the North Carolina mountains, we would have convulsed in laughter.

But that was before he became famous. Famous people have a pass when it comes to being highly dramatic.

The graduates remembered his invitation, of course, for on March 8, at St. Peter's Catholic Church in Beaufort, they appeared, forming a long human corridor from the hearse to the church. Inside, an entire section had been reserved for them. When they went forward for communion, I saw several of them weeping as they accepted the wafer.

Too, there was this: the priest called for a statue of Pat to be erected in Beaufort.

If it happens, I hope they make it life-sized from bronze. He should be holding a bronze journal pad in his left hand and the bronze replica of a Montblanc fountain pen in his right hand, because that's what passersby and fans and wistful writers would want to touch, to rub. For the magic, I mean. With the touching, the rubbing, the bronze will stay bright on the pad and the pen, and that would please Pat.

If it does happen, if a statue is erected, I want to attend the unveiling with The Boys—with Cliff and Frank and Bernie and Dan.

We were there at the beginning. We should see it to the end.

Raised by a Son of Santini

~ MELISSA CONROY

I don't remember the first time I met Pat Conroy. I was a month or two old, staring up at him while soaking in two inches of water, a quizzical, absolutely serious look on my face. This was the impression he retained of me from that point forward.

I was suspicious and humorless. But my disinterest didn't stop him from adopting me and my older sister, Jessica, the children of my beautiful mother, Barbara Blaine Jones, and Joseph Wester Jones, a recently deceased Marine fighter pilot. Pat had fallen in love with my mom and he was ready to be a dad. I was the perfect challenge for "the Big Dad" as we called him. He always wanted to entertain, to make people laugh, to be adored. He put people at ease, listened to them, praised them, made them laugh; and in return, people worshipped him. I guess I was a harder nut to crack. It had nothing to do with the fact that he was not my biological father. How would I know the difference? I was only a baby. I think it was simply a personality thing. For some reason, Dad liked his new supercilious child. He rose to the challenge of helping me find a sense of humor. He made fun of me mercilessly and constantly. My response was to look at him with barely veiled suspicion.

I would tell Mom, "Dad doesn't care if things are true, as long as they are funny." But I was wrong. With Dad there was a difference between actual facts and a storyteller's truth. Dad never took actual facts very seriously, but there was always a grain of truth in his teasing, and he was good at it. While many people discovered Dad's voice through his books, I grew up hearing his stories in person. He made fun of all of us. He'd watch his kids and then retell our experiences through his own eyes, always throwing in details that we bucked at but in the end accepted because his version was so damn funny. In the end, he successfully helped me find a sense of humor. Because of Dad's nonstop teasing, I think I learned not to take myself too seriously.

What I didn't realize as a child was that Dad was using humor to mask pain. I'd like to think that the humor worked sometimes as a salve as well. His humor certainly taught me to see light in the dark at times. When we gathered with my uncles and aunts they would tell stories of abuse and laugh until those round Conroy cheeks flamed bright pink. Humor was embedded in the ridiculousness of their father's abuse. Once, when Uncle Jim was a boy, Don Conroy was so upset at him for getting hurt that he responded by beating him up more. Don sounded like an animal, reacting without an ounce of self-reflection. Dad made a career out of writing about the abuse he suffered at his father's hands, and yet I have only recently begun to recognize the irreparable damage that was done. Don was "the Great Santini," a Marine fighter pilot who fought in three wars and beat his children mercilessly. I grew up with a different "Great Santini." He was not a threat to me or my siblings. His posturing was funny to us. He was huge and larger than life, but not nearly as large in personality as Dad was. Dad systematically sought out retribution against his father with his superior wit. When Don was interviewed on the radio about parenting, Dad started calling him "the Nazi Dr. Spock." When Dad and Don spoke together at an event, Dad would tell the audience that his father's "IQ is the temperature of this room." Don could not tell a story or make a comment without a much more succinct and hilarious reply from Dad. Don never admitted to abusing his kids, but he did soften a bit as a grandfather and father to grown kids. One of the things he did regularly was go to the commissary at the closest Marine base and buy groceries for Dad. He would show up with practically a pallet full of canned goods—half of which would be diet Shasta sodas and those thick vanilla-malty-tasting protein shakes. Don chose to live in Atlanta in a tiny one-bedroom apartment on the top floor of the sprawling Darlington apartment complex on Peachtree Street. He called it his penthouse. My main memory of that apartment was the plastic massage chair that took up considerable space in his living room. It looked like it was upholstered in bulletproof pink bubble wrap. My theory is that Don decided to settle in Atlanta to be close to Dad. Don was heartbroken when Peggy, my grandmother, divorced him. To add insult to injury, she brought a copy of *The Great Santini* to court as evidence.

As shocked as Don was by *The Great Santini*, it is now public knowledge that he came to embrace the character. Don and his huge ego soaked up all the attention he could get from being made into a literary icon. For Christmas one year I was given a photograph of Don making a "whatever" gesture with his shoulders shrugged, eyes rolling, and palms up. Collaged onto the print next to Don was a picture of Robert Duvall pointing his finger and yelling as "the Great Santini" in the movie version. Don was far too much of a testosterone-driven warrior to show any signs of weakness. He may have been hurt by the way Dad depicted him, but he was trained well. He dusted himself off and soldiered on. Before long he had made himself into a minor celebrity. Although he would never admit it, I think it was clear that Don knew Dad was speaking his truth in *The Great Santini*. I believe he admired Dad's courage.

Within the pages of that book Dad exposed his own damaged, gentle heart. The humanity and poetry in Dad's words and the love Dad sought from Don could not have escaped even a man as hardened as Don was. Perhaps it was Dad's call for help within the pages of his book or Don's own need for help when the love of his life left him that prompted Don to move to the Darlington on Peachtree Road.

It is an understatement to say that Don was not the greatest role model as a father. He was deployed as much as he was at home when Dad was a child, and his abuse when he was around is legendary. Like Don, Dad was absent most of the time when I was a child. He divorced my mom when I was six and left for months at a time to write. He was often battling his own demons. When he was around we were always thrilled to see him. He could be combative and difficult to contend with at times. But he was just as larger-than-life to his family as he was to his fans. I was always excited for the teasing, the stories, and the dark humor. Because of Dad's dark humor I have found myself often having to suppress the desire to laugh at unfortunate circumstances as an adult.

There were times as a kid when I understood Dad's humor better than some of the older people around me. Whenever we had a babysitter, Dad would say, "Make sure to beat the kids before they go to bed." Those babysitters who didn't get the joke made the decision to ignore his request. But there was one babysitter who seemed to think he was dead serious—the only male babysitter I recall having. I'm not sure why Dad decided to hire him. He might have been out of options. Or maybe this babysitter came off differently to adults than he did to kids. To be honest, I doubt Dad put much thought into the decision. When Dad gave his go-to babysitter speech before leaving, which included nothing of practical interest to any babysitter, I watched this babysitter's reaction closely. "I'll give you extra money for each beating you give my children," Dad said. Unlike the previous babysitter, who simply rolled her eyes at this comment, I saw a glint in this guy's eyes. As soon as Dad left, the babysitter lifted up his pants cuff to show us the bayonet strapped to his shin. The night progressed slowly, with the three of us—Megan, Jessica, and me—warily staying in line to avoid the wrath of his bayonet. When it came time for bed, he tucked us in and read us a story. Then things came back around to what Dad said.

"Time for your beatings!" he said.

"Dad was only joking," Megan replied.

"He didn't seem like he was joking to me."

"No, he really was joking, I promise."

"You better be right, or next time you'll get double!"

To this day I do not know whether he was beating Dad at his own game of dark humor, disappointed that he didn't get to beat three girls, or relieved that we gave him an out on the beatings. That was the closest we ever came to getting a beating through Dad.

After Dad died, I went to his gravesite with several people, including his best friend, Bernie Schein. Bernie proclaimed, "One of the biggest shocks of my life was watching Pat die with dignity. I mean the guy was a marshmallow!" I think Bernie was right. There were certainly ways in which Dad was similar to Don. He had faults he was unable to own. Like Don, there were too many layers of hurt (both self-inflicted and created by others) to explore. But, there was also a sweetness to him. An untouchable, almost unbearable sweetness. He had a huge heart that sought out recognition and love from others but struggled to express love for those closest to him.

When Dad was dying, he told me and my sisters that as a boy he struggled to receive the love he needed, and because of that he didn't know how to love his own children. He didn't know how, but he tried. It's funny how now that he is gone, so many people are pointing out the way he would sign every correspondence "Great Love." That suspicious baby in me wants to point out that he always went slightly overboard in his effusive praise to make up for his inabilities in other areas. But now I find his effusiveness incredibly touching. I felt his great love, too. He had a beautifully big heart. He gave to the world with that heart. As an author, he doesn't belong to our family, he belongs to the world. We are all lucky that he left so much behind for all of us who love him back.

The Endurance of Love

~ MAGGIE SCHEIN

> For a long time, I thought I was born into a mythology instead of a family.
> —Pat Conroy, *The Death of Santini*

For a long time, I thought I was born into a family instead of a living mythology.

Pat Conroy was my father's best friend. He was always a teacher at heart and an imp by nature. He was with me, influencing me, holding me up, challenging me, pissing me off, inspiring me, helping me, disappointing me, making me laugh, and quick to tell me how it's done (at least *his* way), and instructing me how it's *not* done, "kid," at pretty much each formative transition of my life: birth (mine), childhood, adolescence, career changes, marriage, and, of course, death (his). Pat is as natural a part of my life as my fingernails—and sometimes as ratty. He is woven into the very fabric of my family tapestry. That remains true after his death.

For a long time, until I started publishing my own fiction, until I dipped a few aspirational digits into the world that he had lived in so long, I took the tightness of that weave for granted. I was, at the time, unable to answer prompts like, "How did Pat influence you most?" or "What is your strongest memory of Pat?" I am not sorry for that. I am happy for it. I didn't reflect on Pat as being "Pat Conroy." Or on his family. He and they were as fucked up and as exquisitely a part of my life as my blood relations. I don't think that is enough to make my experience of him unique. Rather, that is the aspect of the experience of Pat we all share: that majestic and precious intimacy he welcomed, though sometimes that was for worse rather than for better. At all times he is a great teacher of our accountability to love and of being responsible to and for one's own art. I could not be more grateful to him for that.

On Shoes

The Pat who occupies my earlier recollections is the Pat who came over nearly every day to our house in Atlanta, in the same gray sweatpants with a hole in the left rear, and drank bourbon and Coca-Cola with my father in the living room, paid me a nickel to either put on a dance show or get the hell out—depending on whether or not he and Bernie were bored with each other that day—and who punctuated my after-school hours with the sounds of his trademark "Shee-*it*! Are you fucking kidding me?" followed by, "Well, Gaahaadayamn!"

In addition to acclimating me to the subtleties of rhythmic, harmonic, and distinctively southern cursing (of which, the sticklers be damned. If Pat Conroy thought "you're fucking shittin' me!"* was the most effective and poetic arrow to a communicative target, then I dare them to argue. I'm pretty sure I learned at least one-third of my language sensibilities from the cursing exchanges between my father and Pat), he also taught me to tie my shoes.

Shoe-tying is, as we know, quite the rite of passage and the call of freedom—not just for the child but for the crouching, cursing adults who can't get on with their day until they supplicate themselves to the toddler's feet. I, however, was an obstinate, disrespectful screwball of a learner. Whether I chose not to learn from my family to keep them in servitude to my shoes or I just couldn't learn to tie them I don't remember.

In response to my family's well-earned exasperation, Pat announced one day, "Gaahaadayamit, Schein, I'll teach her to tie her goddamn shoes!" He dragged me into my father's writing studio and shut the glass doors behind him. He took one shoelace, laid it out to one side, took the other, laid it out

---

* In gleeful rebellion against one of his few explicit writing instructions to me: "I hate exclamation points! Never use them!" I have included exclamation points where I deemed necessary. Ironically, they are almost exclusively in relation to his direct quotes.

opposite. He gave each of the shoelaces names and said that they wanted to be friends. He put the left over the right so they touched. He explained that they just met and asked me if that were enough to be good friends. I shook my head. "Why not?" he asked. He threw them apart and said, "'Cause there's nothing holding them together, right?" And so he looped the one under the other and pulled. He asked again, "And now?" I wasn't sure. He said, "Okay, so maybe they need to *do* things together?" And he talked me through the adventure that took each one around the other until they were bound together as best friends forever—that seemed about right, since he had tied a double knot (always in need of an editor, he was), just to annoy my big sister, whom he knew would then have to teach me how to *untie* a double knot. I wish I remembered the adventures of left-string and right-string, but I was too proud at that moment to pay attention to silly stories about whatever-their-names-were. I could tie my shoes!

He was never my formal writing instructor. I took no lessons or critiques from him, but he helped construct the grammar of my learning and inspiration, of my understanding of love and friendship, and my inability to escape story. And, he taught me about the responsibility to that—to love and to story—by failures as well as successes.

On Authoring, Not Writing

As an adult trying to get published, I was as stubborn as a child learning to tie my shoes. I was frustrated with the industry, with editors, with, quite frankly, doing anything I didn't want to do. I complained with hidden-fist angst to Pat about what one "had" to do—Press kits? Interviews? Signings in the August heat that no one comes to? Presentations one pays for oneself? I just wanted to write!

I will say that rant lasted as long as it took Pat's metaphorical hand to spank the living daylights out of me. He said, "You love to write? You want anyone to read it? Then you just asked your best friend to jump off a cliff with you, your baby, and his baby. If you don't understand that as an author you are responsible for the relationships you've just created, then you should abort your own book and jump off a cliff by yourself." And it was with his relentless philosophy of responsibility to love (not necessarily of individual people but of the fact of them) that he taught me to grow the hell up as an author. And so I learned of the gloriously gracious, selfless, secret, and extraordinarily draining commitment he gave back to his readers, to bookstores, to publishers, and to editors.

For one example, he never left a signing line (no matter how many hours long), no matter if he had to pee, and he never left an open hand unshaken. I know this. I was severely scolded by him for doing so myself on my first engagement when I went for a pee break. He would, without complaint, with only a Diet Coke for company, routinely sit in the backs of warehouses signing thousands and thousands of books. Why did he do these things? He didn't respond with, "To sell more books." He didn't say, "Because I am supposed to" or "Because it is strategic." He said, "Because I *love* them, kid." And so he taught me how unselfish being a loving author is. It is not the same as just being a good writer. It is a commitment on and off the pages; it is a commitment to where the words go.

On Living and Dying in Great Love

During the hushed-but-well-known hiatus of friendship between Pat and my father, my gut felt concave. Mind you, both of them are serious pains in the ass, and both can be downright silverback chest-thumping knuckleheads (Bernie and Pat would make a joke here about compensating, but I'll leave that to your imagination), but I was eighteen, living in New York, mostly alone. And I wondered, *Who do I have who knows me now other than my parents and my sister?* At that time, because my own trajectory had been vastly different from friends I'd grown up with, I had only my new roommate and my two cats. I could not help but recall those afternoons in Atlanta when, as a child, I had hidden behind the sofa listening to Pat and Bernie talk about their youth over and over with itching repetition. And I thought, *What in the name of God is wrong with these two idiots! After thirty-odd years of friendship, years that can never, ever be re-created, years that were melded from broken moments made whole, from years anticipated that fractured into even more years, from brilliant moments never expected, and from accomplishments only shared in whispers of secret anticipation, they refuse to speak to each other for reasons neither one can remember?* And I did ask them both at that time, and neither one remembered. *What the fuck is wrong with these two?*

They had taught me friendship. I'd grown up seeing their legendary friendship in live action. And damn them to hell if they were going to betray that. Damn if they were going to tell me that wasn't really possible. That story had only one possible ending if the grammar of the world they gave me were to create coherency.

And hell if they didn't end up proving my fear a completely unfounded adolescent panic—a lack of faith in the solidity of proper narrative harmonies, discords, and resolutions.

Shame on me.

At Pat's death, as his face and body finally were able to relieve themselves into their innocence, and while the rest of us were in whole-body contortions of pain, Bernie, who hadn't wanted to leave Pat's side, held it together for a few seconds. And then he, too, crumpled over Pat's newly pain-free face; he brushed his infamous and half-century-old comb-over, palmed his cheeks, kissed his forehead, and looked at him as if no one else was there and whispered, "I love you, Bubba. I love you, Pat. I will always love you. Your heart is my heart. It will always be my heart." It was not great literature. I'm sure Pat would want it rewritten, and I'm sure Bernie will rewrite it. But, unadorned and abandoned by the Guard of Decorative Words, in that raw split second, against the ripples of the creek lapping up the last of the crimson sun, appeared the two fifteen-year-old boys right at the beginning of their adventures together. Great love, indeed. They kept true to their lesson of friendship and the endurance of love.

Pat was there at my birth; I was there at his death. That man involved me in part of one miraculous, beautiful, reverent and irreverent, sloppy-ass knot that I can never undo.

Old Men and Young Bucks

~ STEVE ONEY

"Remember the night I couldn't stop you at the Paideia School? You kept pounding your body into the lane and the ball into the hoop. You're a fighter, bred to it and excellent at it."

Three weeks before Pat Conroy's death, I e-mailed that note to him. The author of *The Prince of Tides* was suffering from pancreatic cancer. Although he had vowed to beat the disease, I couldn't find any realistic grounds for hope. Still, I wanted to give Pat all the encouragement possible and do so in a way that recalled a moment of triumph for him. That I had participated in this moment and that it had been chastening for me were more than incidental details. Accompanied by much banter, what had passed between us and the others involved was at heart a matter of life and death. Which was why, with Pat in extremis, it seemed urgent to remind him. Not that I thought he'd forgotten. It was the kind of thing you never forget.

An Affair of Honor

The air that November evening was metallic and brisk. Autumn had come to Atlanta, and with it the leaves had gone brown and the cicadas silent. Set back from Ponce de Leon Avenue on the southern fringes of the Druid Hills neighborhood, the Paideia School (in 1980 just nine years old) was already becoming one of the city's elite private academies, taking a place alongside Lovett and Westminster. Not quite as snooty—but snooty enough—Paideia

This essay originally appeared in the *Bitter Southerner*, 2016.

provided a fit venue for an affair of honor between the princes of the literary establishment and a group of young bucks who had thrown down the gauntlet. Besides, a gym with glass backboards anchored the campus, and it was ours for as long as the business required.

The Lineups

Pat's team was exactly that—his. This was not merely because at thirty-four, thanks to his 1976 novel *The Great Santini* and the 1979 film based on it, he was the rising star in Atlanta's small but impressive constellation of writers. Pat had been an all-state high school basketball player in South Carolina and a starting point guard at The Citadel. Now that the Hollywood money was rolling in, he was thickening around the middle, but he remained a threat. Equally impressive was Lee Walburn, editor of *Atlanta Weekly*, the magazine of the *Atlanta Journal-Constitution*. At six-four and in his early forties, Lee, a LaGrange, Georgia, native, had played basketball at West Georgia College. Then there was Bernie Schein. The model for Sammy Wertzberger, the flamboyant son of Israel whose family owns the "Jew store" in *The Great Santini*, Bernie had been Pat's pal in their hometown of Beaufort, South Carolina. He was thirty-five, five-eight, and, in appearance, a shambling clown. His idea of proper attire for our confrontation was Bermuda shorts, untucked polo shirt, baggy socks, and off-the-rack tennis shoes. My initial impression of Bernie was that he'd been invited to participate simply because he knew Pat and because, as a Paideia faculty member, he'd secured the court.

As for their opponents, we were in our mid-twenties—old enough to have experienced disappointment and hurt but not old enough to know that sometimes there's no remedy for them. Long-legged and well-muscled, we were impelled by the youthful delusion that we were answerable to no one but ourselves. Michael Haggerty, at twenty-eight the eldest, had recently moved to Atlanta from Austin. He was so fast off the dribble that we called him Speedball. Jim Dodson was a droll North Carolinian whose preferred sport was golf but who knew his way around the hoop. I was twenty-six and had done much of my growing up in Atlanta, where I'd been a mediocre reserve center for the Peachtree High School Patriots. But thanks to graduate-level courses on asphalt I'd become a dangerous outside shooter. What we had in common was not only our youth: We were all staff writers at *Atlanta Weekly*, which made us potential usurpers to the throne. While the *Weekly* had been founded in 1912 as the *Atlanta Journal* magazine (Margaret Mitchell worked there in the 1920s), it had drifted along in sleepy irrelevance until 1979 when Nancy Smith, Lee's predecessor and a *Texas Monthly* alumna, gave it a makeover and a mission, which we interpreted as carte blanche to question authority.

Tout le Monde

During warm-ups, as I drained mid-range jumpers and Pat and his teammates stretched and practiced layups, the Paideia gym filled with Atlanta's literati. Anne Siddons, author of the novel *Heartbreak Hotel*, was there along with Heyward, her dapper advertising executive husband. So, too, was short-story-writer Paul Darcy Boles, in an ascot and blazer a refugee from an already extinct world where one could earn a living peddling five-thousand-word morality tales to the *Saturday Evening Post*. Michele Ross, the lovely book editor of the *Atlanta Journal-Constitution*, was on the sidelines, as was Cliff Graubart, proprietor of the Old New York Book Shop on Juniper Street. Cliff's store, which sprawled through a craftsman house, anchored the city's writing community. He sold first editions as well as paperbacks, and whenever authors within a hundred-mile radius published new works, he gave parties that lasted long into the night. This was tout le monde, and it was Pat's crowd. Not that this was surprising, for the person in attendance who drew the most attention—the person everyone had come for—was a sainted figure to the old order: Jim Townsend. The best editor in town, Jim was the paterfamilias to a generation of southern writers and a mentor to Pat. He was also, at forty-seven, dying of cancer. Chemotherapy had left his skin ashen and taken his hair. Age, youth, and bragging rights were on the line, but as Pat had for weeks been telling anyone who'd listen: "We're gonna win this for Jim."

The Hands of Dear Heart

It had all started a month earlier during a gala yet sobering affair at the Atlanta Public Library. The occasion, which Pat had organized and would emcee, was intended to give Jim Townsend a resounding sendoff while he was still healthy enough to enjoy it. The attendees included most of those who would later congregate at Paideia, journalists Marshall Frady, Paul Hemphill, and William Hedgepeth, novelist Terry Kay, and a cross-section of business and political leaders.

That the turnout was big and cut across many layers of Atlanta society was a testament to the guest of honor. A native of Lanett, Alabama, James Lavelle Townsend had founded *Atlanta* magazine in 1961. During Townsend's editorship the city had sailed largely unscathed through the racial travails that bedeviled the rest of the South, and he deserved some of the credit—not because he was a great thinker or tactician but because he was a great believer, and the object of his belief was Atlanta. His organ for expressing that belief was *Atlanta* magazine, and he filled its pages with the work of the people in whom he believed most—the city's writers, artists, and photographers.

Sadly, however, Townsend's future was now behind him. In need of comprehensive medical benefits, he was spending his final months in the *Atlanta Weekly* offices on the seventh floor of 72 Marietta Street, headquarters of the *Journal-Constitution*. There, at a desk next to mine, he wrote a column called *Dear Heart*. The pieces, most of them homages to the simple pleasures of his Alabama childhood, were by turns humorous and warm and always winning—and I was part of them. On the day the art director scheduled the photo shoot for the logo—an image of fingers flying over a typewriter keyboard—Jim went home sick. I posed for the picture. For the 575,000 subscribers who received *Atlanta Weekly* on Sundays, I was the hands of *Dear Heart*.

The Umbrage Taker

During the cocktail hour that preceded the Townsend fête, Jim Dodson and I got into a conversation with Lee Walburn and Pat about basketball. We young *Weekly* staffers had been playing almost nightly at a YMCA around the corner from 72 Marietta, and we weren't shy about our prowess. For some time, in fact, the idea had been in the air that we might get up a game with these long-ago college stalwarts to see if they could still put on a jockstrap—just for fun, it was understood. We'd always left it there, and that's where we again left it before the event began. But that's not where it remained. All that was needed to transform this notion into reality was provocation, and as anyone who has attended a wake for the living can confirm, they are fraught with opportunities for provocation—especially when the speeches start.

After the assembled took seats in a conference room around a scattering of tables with Townsend at the head, Pat began soliciting testimonials. As is typical of such things, the speakers to a one sang Jim's praises—as well they should have. But after the sixth or seventh encomium, the atmosphere grew heavy. Overuse of the words "brilliant" and "nurturing" has a way of casting a pall. For his part, Townsend was thanking people when they finished, and he seemed touched. Still, it felt as if the crowd was burying him alive, so when Pat nodded at me, I made the ill-advised decision to say something original. It was a privilege to sit beside this revered editor at *Atlanta Weekly*, I began. I was receiving a priceless education in writing. But—and here I stepped through the ice—what I found most remarkable about Jim was how he got so much work done while spending most of his time on the telephone sweet-talking literary ladies from across the South who knew him from his years at *Atlanta* magazine. This struck me as an innocent deviation from accepted doctrine. Not only that, but it was true and flattering to Jim—he remained devilishly among the living. The lone place such a comment might not fly, I thought, would be church. The coughs that greeted my stab at irreverence told me that church was exactly where we were. Worse, Pat took umbrage.

Pat, of course, was one of the all-time umbrage takers in American literature. His heroes frequently use grievance to uphold virtue (see Meechum,

Ben, in *The Great Santini*). By the same token they abhor piety, especially as embodied by institutions (see McLean, Will, in *The Lords of Discipline*). Pat's ability to negotiate the contradictions between these poles was one of his literary strengths and one of the elements that makes his fiction southern. (Is there any other part of the country whose people are so simultaneously devout and incorrigible?) Unfortunately, Pat saw me on this night as a defamer, not a sprite, and he would call me to task. Once the program concluded, he, I, and various seconds negotiated terms in an unintentional parody of the *code duello*. Our teams would meet in a best-out-of-three, half-court basketball tournament, all games to eleven, one-point buckets, win by two. As for the stakes, they would be ten dollars per participant, payable by each member of the losing team to his winning counterpart. Not serious money but sufficient to add a sporting element.

Defense, Defense, Defense

The opening game was all about defense, both by those who could play it and those who could not, and Pat, who would guard me the entire evening, could play it. While I had been taking those flashy jumpers prior to the onset of hostilities, he had been studying my tendencies. What he saw was that at six-three with a high release point on my shot, I could, if unchecked, soar over the top of his six-foot frame at will. Which was why, on the initial occasion that our team got the ball, Pat not only bodied up on me but began slapping my wrists and grabbing my elbows. It was like the worst first date ever. From my preferred high-post position, I would fake to the inside, pivot back out, then sprint to a corner, where I was typically deadly. But there was Pat, staying with me stride for stride and keeping my arms pinned to my torso. I couldn't have caught a pass, no matter how well thrown. As if this weren't enough, Pat also worked me in the midsection. All shooters are vulnerable there, but on this night I was more so than most. A few weeks earlier, a girlfriend had dumped me by figuratively sticking a shiv into my heart and raking it down to my testicles. Pat didn't know this, but having grown up the son of Marine Corps colonel Donald Conroy—aka the Great Santini—he was a student of pain and sensed where it resided in others. So he continued to hammer. Had this been a friendly game I would have called a foul, but from the start it was clear that unless someone slammed you to the floor, there would be no fouls this evening.

Luckily for us, what Pat tooketh away Bernie Schein gaveth back. Bernie, who guarded Michael Haggerty, was a slacker on defense. On top of that, he couldn't comprehend a fundamental truth about Michael as an athlete—he was left-handed. Bernie overplayed him to his right, which meant that Michael was able to blow past him for uncontested layups. Thanks to that and several jumpers by Jim Dodson, we won this one, but only by a couple of points. As soon as it was over, Pat, gasping for breath, burst through the heavy doors that gave onto the Paideia parking lot. He was on the verge of collapse, but as the breeze from outside rushed in, I wasn't focusing on him. While we'd drawn first blood, we were in trouble. Our opponents were playing with greater resolve.

Thanatos and Eros

Only a few seconds into the second game it hit us that Bernie Schein, far from being a schlub, was a sniper in camouflage. Bang, bang, bang, bang, bang—he sank three, four, five consecutive jumpers. Pat set up each shot by laying shuddering screens on Michael that freed Bernie twenty feet from the hole and forced me to chase him out there. Every time, I arrived a second too late, and a second was all he needed. Bernie may have looked like a clown, but it was in the same way that the great Harlem Globetrotter Meadowlark Lemon did. He was for real. More crucial, he and Pat had been playing together since they were teenagers, and Pat—ever the point guard—knew how to get the ball to his buddy. With Bernie on fire and Lee Walburn sticking in put-backs on the few occasions when Bernie missed, Pat's guys won going away. Yet here again, they were the ones who afterward seemed out on their feet. Bernie's wife, fearful that he might have a heart attack, waded into their midst to suggest that we should just end things as a draw. That wasn't going to happen. What had been implicit in the buildup now was explicit. This was war. As I waited for the finale to begin, I let my eyes wander the sidelines, where they landed on the figure of Jim Townsend. He was having a terrific time, but he appeared so gray and frail that I averted my gaze. I then stared at Michele Ross. She was among the most beautiful women I knew—and she adored books. There it was. Thanatos and Eros were in the house, just as they are in every house, and always have been and will be. These games may have been for Townsend, but they were about coming to terms with mortality.

A Pat Conroy Novel

The end was brutal, but it couldn't have been otherwise. We were now playing for keeps. In an effort to shut down their main scorer, I guarded Bernie, the theory being that with my height advantage I'd smother him. The strategy failed because Pat kept setting solid screens for his old friend. The strategy also nearly led to fisticuffs. In order for me to match up on Bernie, Jim took Pat, and Michael took Lee. There was animosity between Michael and Lee stemming from Michael's resentment that Lee had replaced Nancy Smith, who'd recruited Michael from *Texas Monthly*. The two promptly tangled. Lee maintained that Michael kneed him in the groin. I missed that, but I did see him elbow Lee in the head. Once again, no fouls. This was how it would go as we exchanged leads, fighting down to the finish. With our opponents up 10–9, Lee grabbed a rebound and whipped the ball to Pat. We knew what to look for, so we collapsed on Bernie. But Pat, rather than pass to him, faked, turned, and drove to the basket. The fake gave him a half step on Jim, and a half step is enough for an ex–college athlete. Pat was gone, exploding to the rim and laying in the shot. The old men had prevailed over the young bucks. It was like something out of a Pat Conroy novel.

Our Winning Season

If there was celebration, I do not remember it. If there was commiseration, I did not partake. I threw on a sweatshirt and drove downtown to the *Atlanta Weekly* office. I always felt at home there, especially after hours when it was empty and I could write in peace. Although I had work this night on a story due later in the week, I ended up just sitting. As much as the loss stung, I appreciated that the victory by Pat's team was dramatically satisfying and morally right. How could you not root for them? They were the underdogs, and we were cocky. They played for something bigger than themselves. We had it coming, and they gave it to us. They taught us a lesson: you can't win them all. I wrote Pat a check and stuck it in an envelope.

As it turned out, Pat later had his own thoughts about defeat, and he expressed them in *My Losing Season*, his 2002 nonfiction book about his basketball career at The Citadel, which saw his team whipped too many times. He wrote: "Loss is a fierce . . . uncompromising teacher, coldhearted but clear-eyed in its understanding that life is more dilemma than game, and more trial than free pass. My acquaintance with loss has sustained me when . . . despair caught up."

Yet I don't believe Pat, who over the decades did me literary favors and with whom I stayed in friendly contact, viewed life as a tragedy—and as my last e-mail to him suggested, I no longer think the moral of what occurred at Paideia involves loss. After Pat's funeral I phoned Bernie Schein, who now resides in Beaufort, where Pat lived at the end. "Those games were as important as hell to Pat," Bernie said of our tournament. "There wasn't a year that went by that we didn't talk about them." Bernie's remarks confirmed my evolving view. Pat's team didn't show us how to lose. They showed us how to win. Jim Townsend's generation is mostly gone. (The hands of dear hearts could not hold them.) Pat's generation is going. Mine is getting ready. It doesn't stop. But there are moments—the Atlanta shootout was one; and, by God, Townsend's dying flirtations another—when grit and gumption buy us another round of what hoopsters call hang time. We rise above the floor and for an instant float. Soon, gravity pulls us to the earth and then puts us under it. But for a second we are up there. Such moments are what matter, never more so than when time and fate begin to circle.

In Walked Conrack

⌁ NIKKY FINNEY

I was a part-time graduate student at Atlanta University and a part-time copy clerk at a Kinko's copy shop in Atlanta. Circa 1984. I worked at Kinko's because I could copy my poems cheaply and use the computers without cost. I had just started to send my work out into the world. One day the door flies open and in walks this tall, rumpled man. "Conrack," I whisper. Nobody knows who he is but me.

These were the days of dreaming of being a writer. I was only twenty-six. I had no map. I read everything I could, especially South Carolina writers. I knew who he was and had read everything he had written to date. His writing moved me. There was so much poetry in his prose. His empathy struck a chord deep within me. His striving to tell the truth. His willingness to stand up for the children of Daufuskie moved me.

I know who he is because Daufuskie Island held my history, too. When I realize who just walked in, I gasp and turn away from the counter momentarily. Then, as if endowed with something else, I turn back to the counter and shoo the other clerks away. I walk up and face him eye to eye. He is jittery and looks a little out of place holding a sheaf of papers in his hand and waiting for help.

"May I help you?" squeaks out. He half smiles and says, "I need two good copies of this," and sets the sheaf on the counter. I pretend that I don't know who he is and I take over the extra-large Xerox machine—known for its

Portions of this essay originally appeared in the Columbia, South Carolina, *State* newspaper, January 2013.

Olympic collation capabilities. I am already whispering a prayer to the service tech gods that the machine is not having a bad day. Most Kinko's customers leave the counter and walk away and have a seat or even come back
later. Not Conrack. He stands there with his hands on the counter watching
me as if I might be putting his child into the document feeder. I totally realize that this is a fresh manuscript just out of the word processor and only I
can take care of it.

The title page reads "The Prince of Tides." This means nothing to me—
then. Instead of the usual forty or so pages that I normally put into the
feeder, I carefully put in ten or so. I am sweating. I want no machine jams on
this order. None. This is very important. It takes much longer to get through
the two hundred–plus pages.

I never look at him. I keep my eyes on the pages. I don't care if I am holding
him up. I have to get this right. I have moved his order up to the front of the
line, and none of my coworkers understand why. They get out of my way. The
machine performs brilliantly. I stack the two copies, dividing them with a
piece of generic gray card stock, and then lay them in a cardboard manuscript
box. I tally his copies at three cents per page and take his money.

He pays me in Conroy cash. He says, Thank you.

I say, You are welcome.

Only after watching him walk out of the door and turn the corner completely does my head fall in absolute amazement and wonder.

⌒

Fast-forward thirty years, four books, and one National Book Award. I had
been teaching at the University of Kentucky for twenty-three years when
I received the news that my father was in the throes of a major illness. I
have spent my entire life talking and writing about being a Black girl and
woman from South Carolina. I know my family needs me closer. I accept the
University of South Carolina's offer of a teaching job in African American
studies and English. I have not lived in South Carolina for thirty-five years.
I return to Columbia in the fall of 2013. I am walking home one day after
instructing an exuberant class of impatient undergraduates. I feel both
exhausted and grateful as I walk across campus. A car on the street near

me slows down, pulls over, and stops. The USC dean of libraries, Thomas F. McNally, is driving. On the passenger side, through the open window, is once again the face of Conrack. I smile a big smile. I had heard Pat Conroy was coming to town to attend the dinner being held in his honor by the Thomas Cooper Society. My teaching and travel schedule had not allowed me to commit to attending.

"Nikky!" Pat calls out as he comes out of the car like a flash.

"Pat!" I call back as I walk toward him my arms already open.

We embrace just for a minute—like long-lost kin. He says something quickly and shyly, something like, "I'm glad you've come home." I think that's what Conrack says to me. That's what it feels like he said. In two minutes he is back in the car and gone with a wave out the still half-open window. It is only the second time in both our lives that we have met. It is the first time ever we will meet as two South Carolina writers standing on South Carolina soil. I don't know if he ever got to hear the story about the young unknown poet working in the copy shop who had recognized him that day many years before and tenderly copied his brand-new manuscript with all the care and precision—and excitement—her South Carolina self could muster.

In the Dom Rep with Conrack

~ CLIFF GRAUBART

Pat walked into my bookshop in Atlanta in April 1973, less than one year after the publication of *The Water Is Wide* and before *Conrack* was in the theaters. He often said publicly, to much laughter, that I wasn't friendly. That I didn't have a welcome mat out for customers. In fact he compared me to Don Rickles, only without the jokes. I told him, "I'm from New York. You're lucky I didn't shoot your ass!" To me, Atlanta then was a small town and appeared cliquish. But Pat, too, was an outsider, and he would disarm me of any feelings of not belonging. Two weeks after we met, he invited me to his home for dinner with friends. Three years later, he would invite me to travel with him on his return trip to the Dominican Republic.

When *The Water Is Wide* was made into a movie in 1974, Pat Conroy received some attention from it, resulting in a few speaking engagements. A memorable one for him was when he spoke before an audience of students and teachers in the Dominican Republic, and he looked forward to visiting again there someday.

It was the winter of 1976 in the Dominican Republic; our summer, their winter. He returned this time to stay with one of the student teachers, a beautiful twenty-five-year-old named Maria Marguerita Jiménes Grullón, and her parents. Maria, black-haired and fair-skinned with dark, intelligent eyes and a quick laugh, lived in a small but grand home once owned by a family member of Rafael Trujillo. It was ironic because her father, Juan Isidro, had plotted to kill Trujillo in 1934 and was exiled until Trujillo was assassinated in 1961, and he was able to return and even run for office. But her father's politics had changed; once a conservative he now was the ideological leader of the left, writing books criticizing the West, especially John Barlow Martin and the United States' involvement in the Dominican Republic.

When Pat invited me to come along with him, nothing was planned except to stay with Maria Marguerita and her parents. I didn't think about what we would do, I just remember wanting to go because there was something about being with Pat that I experienced with no other. He would be more than the highlight of the trip, he would *be* the trip. It would be interesting to stay in the home of the ideological communist leader of a country, even if my politics did not lean that way.

For some, communism is evil, plain and simple; for others, it can be almost romantic as when we read of John Reed and Louise Bryant. Pat was introduced to the "blacklist" when he met the author and screenwriter George Sklar while he was in California working on the screenplay of *The Water Is Wide*. While staying with Sklar, Pat witnessed an episode in which Sklar was offered some work by a former "rat," and George suffered recriminations from some of his friends who were blacklisted years before by merely considering taking on the work. Sklar decided to decline the offer, giving Pat a true insight into the world of the blacklist. So it was logical for him to be intrigued by this youthful, electric beauty and her leftist background. I was happy just to be at the party.

Maria Marguerita's mother was a pretty, middle-aged matron from Cuba. Her name was "Cuca." Unfortunately for her, we learned that "Cuca" in Venezuela meant vagina. This was information that should never have reached the ears of Pat Conroy and myself, as we felt compelled to greet Cuca every morning as our paths crossed in the house with, "Hola, Cuca de Venezuela!" Her English was poor, but she understood the greeting and laughed so hard she couldn't hold her water and dripped on the tile floor, causing even more laughter. This ritual prevailed through the almost three weeks of our stay.

Maria Marguerita's father hardly noticed any of our comings and goings for he was a serious man who continually sat at his desk writing. He was almost thirty years older than Cuca, and his life was now devoted to exposing "American imperialism." He also spoke very little English. When I would walk by I tried to speak with him in my college Spanish. Sometimes he would pick up a book and say, "Muy importante." It was invariably a critical work on the United States. That's about all he said to us. Pat couldn't speak with him either. Next to Pat I was practically Berlitz.

Pat was reading *One Hundred Years of Solitude*, beginning a love affair with Latin American literature in concert with what I would soon learn was his new love for Maria Marguerita. I was reading proofs of *The Great Santini*. Years later he wanted to include a chapter on Latin American literature when he was writing *My Reading Life*, but his publisher was pushing hard for him to finish the manuscript and cut him off before he could get it on paper. He always wanted to write about Maria Marguerita, and he hoped that book would be the vehicle to accomplish it. He regretted that he didn't do what he usually did in those situations—ignore his publisher's demands.

We motored around the island in an old white Corolla not knowing exactly where we would eat or sleep, but it always seemed to be by the water under palm trees with soothing salty air blowing over our skin.

"Maria, what is this?" we would ask as we stared at the menus written in Spanish.

"Goat. You'll like it." There was banter between the three of us as we talked history and politics, though admittedly I think Pat and I were on the learning curve, open to Maria's ideas more than she to ours. "I could never make love with a fascist," she once said. "I think I could work around it," I said.

One thing I recall vividly was Pat stating that when the "revolution" came, it would be people like him—the writers, the intellects—who would be lined up against the wall for execution first. She thought Pol Pot was pure—we thought he was pure hell.

Then there was La Victoria. Maria Marguerita asked Pat if he would talk with a friend who was accused of murdering his mistress over an affair he was involved in. "But it's all political," she said. He was in prison because he was a Communist, she added. With the success of *The Water Is Wide* and the film *Conrack*, Pat was thought of as a crusader and was ambushed by the request but willing to oblige. So on a bright Saturday morning the three of us and the prisoner's wife found ourselves on a long line at the entrance of a yellow concrete fortress, Penitenciaria National–La Victoria, along with scores of women and children. As we entered I saw a handsome, light-skinned colonel with piercing blue eyes looking at every entrant, saying nothing. Just looking. I realized that he was probably familiar with everyone he saw, knowing whom each was visiting, unless it was for a new prisoner. He looked straight at me, Pat, and Maria Marguerita and stopped us. A short interrogation ensued. But when he saw the prisoner's wife with us he understood the situation. Again he stared at me and Pat, probably for affect. I wondered what I had in my pockets. Would I get in trouble? But he let us pass.

"Did you see that guy? Gives me the creeps," I said.

"Welcome to the Dom Rep, big boy. Nervous?" Pat asked.

"How do you say, 'I need toilet paper' in Spanish?"

"I told him you were gay."

"I told him you were my husband, Patty."

Pat's levity masked an uneasiness he always felt around authority, and this was new territory for us. We inched through the building in a long line until we found ourselves in a circular field among the prisoners and their families. From the inside it looked like a one-story Coliseum with cellblocks on the perimeter and this huge field in the middle. All the cell doors were open, and all the prisoners were mingling with the visitors. Under a hot morning sun we looked for our prisoner. Many eyes followed us. One thing you realize when you travel abroad is that your clothes are like flags of your country. Surprisingly our meeting was passionate, even fun, and of course useless for the prisoner. He is probably still there, and as Pat and I assumed privately, probably guilty as charged, an idea we never conveyed to our hostess.

Traveling together all over the island and sharing three meals a day taxed our conversation. I would say something, and Pat would look up, appear astonished, and proceed to make believe he was writing down my every word, an act performed so often that a truce was finally called over a dinner one night.

Our trip to the Dominican Republic was my first taste of travel with Pat, and it whetted my appetite for more. But it was only one of my Pat Conroy stories. It seemed every author in the South had a Pat Conroy story.

He also stirred in me an urge to write.

One day Pat came in to the bookstore and I handed him an article I had written and wanted to submit to the *Atlanta Gazette* for publication. He went to the coffee pot and grabbed his cup off the wall. (All the regulars had cups with their names glazed on them.) He sat down on the couch and read the 1,500-word piece, and the *obras completas* of Cliff Graubart, while I sat anxiously at my desk. He walked back, turned around with my manuscript in hand, and mimicked the act of wiping his behind with it. I froze. Then he said, "It works. Here's what I would do." And he edited it. I couldn't think of a title, so he titled it and the next few articles I wrote. Looking back, I was never so pleased to see someone wipe his butt. Pat, I miss you.

Conroy Redux

⌒ ANNE RIVERS SIDDONS

If Pat Conroy hadn't existed, it would have been necessary to invent him.

I never met anyone else whom that old saw applied so aptly. Whether you knew him personally or through the words of his novels, he filled thousands of hearts. When he died, there were Pat-shaped holes in those hearts. Most will never be filled.

I first met him at a dinner at the Governor's Mansion that the then–Georgia governor, Jimmy Carter, gave for the Atlanta press. Most of us were eager to attend; the idea of drinks and dinner with our compatriots all together was a delightful one. Writers tend to drink a good bit. Writers also tell outrageous and enthralling stories. No one cares if they're true or not.

I was walking down a marble-floored corridor that led to the formal dining room, my heels clicking on the floor. Pat was coming around a corner, facing us. We smiled. He smiled back.

"I like your shoes," he said. I looked down at them. No one had ever complimented my shoes before, at least no man ever had.

"I'm glad," I said. "They're not very fancy."

"At least you didn't say 'these old things,'" my husband said.

"I like them anyway," Pat said, his face flushing bright red.

"I'm Pat Conroy."

"Anne Siddons," I said.

I was Anne to him only a short time. After that it was Annie, and later still, Annie Lou. No one seemed to know where the Lou came from. No one else called me that.

We went in for drinks together. Drinks were sodas, fruit juices, and sparkling water. We eyed each other, eyebrows lifted. Surely, though, wine with dinner. Dinner came with coffee or sweet tea, southern style. Eyebrows went further up. After dinner a young blind man played the piano brilliantly. When the evening ended there was a mad rush for the door and up Paces Ferry Road to the first bar in Buckhead. The proprietor later told me he'd never had a better night.

It took me only that evening to realize that this Pat Conroy person was, though seldom consciously, as electric as a bolt of lightning. Even when he was angry, a state I seldom saw, that easy charm winked through the thunderclouds.

Besides being a man from whom words and charm flowed endlessly, he was the son of a Marine fighter pilot who was a severe disciplinarian and a beautiful mother who read *Gone with the Wind* aloud to him. He lived all over the South on Marine bases. He went to The Citadel in Charleston, largely because his father would only pay tuition to a military school. Three of his closest friends were Cliff and Cynthia Graubart, who had a wonderful shop called the Old New York Book Shop, and the outrageously ebullient Bernie Schein, who taught English to reeling high-schoolers at a private school. Together they were incredibly and bawdily funny.

Sometimes darkness rode him like a harpy, but still. Funny. My Lord, he was funny. Even when his life was ricocheting from city to wife to book to tragedy—of which there were more than a few—he remained one of the funniest men I ever knew.

Like the time he lived in Trastevere and had a party on his flat rooftop for Cliff and Cynthia, who were being married the next day in the Piazza Michaelangelo. Up the hill behind his house, inmates of the Queen of Heaven Prison wailed ceaselessly, "I want a lawyer! I want a woman!"

Across the street, retired nuns struggled up the stairs of the house next to them with trays laden with food, wine, cigars, and only God knows what else for the retired priests lounging there. In the street below, tourists and residents mingled. Gazing fondly down at them all, Pat spread his arms and intoned, "These are my people."

On the Night of the Forbidden Fingers, at the train station in Rome, we were boarding a train to Venice. I have a habit of making a circle with my thumb and forefinger to denote "Okay, good." Beside us sat a young woman and her small daughter. The child was trying unsuccessfully to open a little train case. I smiled and said, "Here," and produced a nail file with which I successfully opened the case. Mother and child smiled up at me and I smiled back at them and made my "okay" finger circle. The mother gasped and rushed away with daughter. Pat, Cliff, and my husband laughed uproariously. Apparently the finger circle means something other than "okay" in Rome.

On that same trip I stood with Pat at the Trevi fountain and tossed in a coin, which was supposed to mean that I would come back to Rome someday. The floor of the fountain was inches thick with coins. "Do you think they'll all come back?" I asked him.

"No," he said. "They've got it all wrong." He took out a handkerchief and withdrew something from its folds and tossed it in. It sank and rested atop the coins.

"That's not a coin," I said.

"Nope," he said. "Dried pigeon shit. You should only offer a fountain something organic and local."

Oh, Conroy. As your universally loved wife said, "The water is wide, and now he's crossed it." I know that. But, still, when my phone rings, I expect for a moment to hear, "Hey, Annie Lou, it's D.P."

And I always will.

A Recipe for Tall Tales

~ NATHALIE DUPREE

Pat Conroy never let the truth get in the way of a good story, particularly about me. For instance, in *The Pat Conroy Cookbook*, he wrote about a dinner I cooked once at the request of a beau. Pat neglected to say the dinner of mountain oysters (also known as lamb or other animal testicles) was a surprise meal for the man's Oklahoma mother, who loved them and missed them in New York.

Instead, Pat said I devised the meal for a tall, dark, handsome stranger on a first date, ignoring the fact that no sane woman would try to woo a man by serving him a plate of testicles that had been held on a long fork next to the burner until the skin was popped off, then peeled. The unfortunate fact that I had also purchased live snails rather than dead ones, which then escaped and lined the walls of my beau's elegant kitchen, was added to the story—and that was true. My husband calls the story an affectionate caricature. There are many other stories I wish Pat had told. I would say at least he spelled my name right, but he didn't. I caught it and alerted Pat's editor, Nan Talese.

I met Pat in the mid-'70s in Atlanta when I was director of Rich's Cooking School, and Rich's was hosting the Gourmet Gala fundraiser for the March of Dimes. Celebrities were asked to cook, and my cooking school assistants and I organized the food, pots, and pans for them.

Pat already had a reputation as someone who loved to cook or he wouldn't have been invited, and he was fearless in his cooking at the benefit and jovial with everyone who came by his stove and chatted with him. I didn't know who Pat Conroy was, what he had written, or how his prose had begun to etch itself indelibly on the hearts of his readers. I had been living in England, then was chef of a restaurant in rural Majorca, and was now owner and chef of a restaurant in rural Georgia as well as a cooking school. My spare time was spent reading *Gourmet* and *Food and Wine*. I only knew Pat had written books that had been made into movies I hadn't seen.

He projected such charisma. Pat was a big man with a boyish face, whose personality was so strong it swallowed up a large portion of the air around him, and he had a smile to match. People attached themselves to him like fringe on a suede jacket, going a few feet away and then coming back to hear his next story. Meanwhile, gowns dazzled, couture was at its height, and the food passed muster.

Sometime later I managed to cultivate a friendship with Cliff Graubart, the owner of Atlanta's Old New York Book Shop, not too far from my new home in Ansley Park. Cliff was a close friend of Pat's and of many authors, including Terry Kay and Anne Rivers Siddons. It was a literary coup to be on his mailing list for book parties. I would go and drink cheap champagne, meet authors and newspaper writers, and schmooze.

One of those crowded, smoky evenings I talked with Pat again. By now I had read *The Great Santini*, *The Boo*, *The Water Is Wide*, and anything else of his I could put my hands on. Talking to Pat was like reading his books. Four-letter words tumbled out of his mouth followed by phrases that created so much music I wanted everyone in the room to be quiet while I absorbed them. His voice was so sensual that a man once asked me what happened to my voice, because he'd considered Pat's impersonation of me on the audiobook of *The Pat Conroy Cookbook* to be my real voice and accent.

Pat's father, Don, the Great Santini himself, was often with Pat at these book parties. They said terrible things to one other with an amazing underlying affection. Pat was a military brat and so was I, something we have always had in common. We both were very nervous, for instance, when not on time (or early, even). We both operated best when chaos was around us, of our own making or fate's.

Whenever Pat and I met we talked nonstop about food. We talked about Paris and eating and the lowcountry, and tried to beat each other at discovering and purchasing Cliff's collection of old cookbooks, with Junior

League cookbooks and Escoffier tucked under our arms mingled with auto-graphed books by Anne Rivers Siddons, Robert Coram, Stuart Woods, and others. I stayed on the invitation list because I was such a good customer.

Pat decided to form a group to take cooking lessons from me at Rich's. He showed up with his fiancée Lenore, his attorney Jim Landon (in whose apartment he married Lenore), and a couple of other people. They were all good cooks, and I had them make a list of what they didn't know so we could work on those areas. They laughed robustly, invented both disgusting and marvelous recipes, and ate with gusto. Pat had a touch of seasoning in his hands, a necessary if indefinable ingredient for a good cook.

When *The Prince of Tides* came out, Pat told me I was "responsible for all the food in the book," a bit of verbal embroidery. Lila Wingo, the mother in the story, wanted to be part of the cookbook committee, and she cooked and cooked. When her husband criticized the ongoing parade of food, she served him dog food dressed up as hash. (This part did not come from me, I hasten to say.)

Before Pat and Lenore moved to Italy and settled in their grand apart-ment in Rome, I introduced Cliff to Cynthia Stevens, my comely television producer, and hosted a slam-bang poolside engagement party for them for which I cooked tenderloin of beef and other good dishes. They discussed getting married in Rome when Pat and Lenore were settled, and Pat insisted he would take care of the paperwork and details. I knew Pat well enough to recognize this as a grandiose promise with no possibilities of being fulfilled. He was to be best man and I, the matron of honor.

I offered to cook the wedding supper, anticipating just Cliff, Cynthia, Pat, Lenore, and Anne and Heyward Siddons, who also were coming. After all, Cliff and Cynthia knew no one else in Rome, and seven for dinner would be easy no matter what the circumstances. Suddenly Lenore had invited about fifty people for a rooftop party. Cliff and Cynthia frantically ran around Rome trying to do the undone paperwork, encountering numerous snags, and finally having to hire a marriage "arranger" who led them through the byways of Italian bureaucracy. Lenore and I shopped in the local market and picked up the poultry, olives, red peppers, and other things, some of which I had ordered by fax from home. We were talked into buying ripe cherries by an Italian man selling them in the market who said, "These cherries are better than a night of love." Who could resist?

When I returned, Pat was boiling water for the pasta and had started on the mound of olives, and one of his children was juicing lemons. My menu was ripe Italian melons with prosciutto; lemon-grilled Cornish hens, chickens, and quails piled up grandly with grilled zucchini; roasted red pepper salad; Pat's spinach tortellini salad with Parmiagiano Reggiano; and olives, fresh cherries, cream puffs, and cream. The grill was part of a European wall oven, which blew fuses whenever it had been on for a period of time, to our constant frustration. Occasionally I would have to hang up my apron to do something important like go with Pat, Cliff, and Cynthia to sign our names in the huge registry Rome uses to record marriages and witnesses.

Pat made the tortellini salad (appropriating the Parmiagiano Reggiano that Stuart Woods had left for Cliff and Cynthia's wedding present) and helped me peel the red peppers and pit the olives. Our hands and arms were saturated with olive oil, but we finished the meal in time. The bride was beautiful, the party with Rome at our feet successful, the food all cooked, and I wasn't sorry. We toasted Cynthia and Cliff, and Pat orated a history of their life and love. I cried then and when they were married the next day at the Campadello.

Pat was a wonderful speechmaker. I have heard him at funerals, weddings, and other events. Listening to him talk, combining his storytelling ability with his love of language, was a sacred experience, like listening to fine church music. It was my ardent hope that he would outlive me so he could speak at my funeral. Instead he included me in his cookbook and wrote the foreword to a book I wrote with Cynthia Graubart, *Nathalie Dupree's Mastering the Art of Southern Cooking*.

In Atlanta, Pat and Lenore would come to my parties. Seating was sometimes awkward because I invited too many people and had to add an extra table. One night I was forced by space confines to have two tables in abutting rooms with Pat at one and Calvin Trillin at another. By evening's end, Pat was in the room with Calvin, and they were vying for floor space with tales that were wonderful, some of them perhaps even true.

Later, Pat was in Oxford, Mississippi, where my husband, Jack Bass, and I had a home. Pat's entourage included his father, his father's lady friend, his editor Nan Talese, his publicist, his high school English teacher Gene Norris, and John Berendt (author of *Midnight in the Garden of Good and Evil*), who was doing an article on Pat for *Vanity Fair*. I had told him the night before that he would have a hard time booking a meal for that many people, so not to put it off. He didn't pay me any attention, didn't book, and called late Sunday afternoon desperate for a meal for all of them.

We were redoing our kitchen, so we had no stove or oven, but my dear husband lit the charcoal grill, I threw on a tenderloin straight from the freezer, cooked grits with Parmiagiano Reggiano on a plug-in hotplate, made a panna cotta with strawberries, and we had a wonderful meal ready in no time. I assigned Pat to watch the red peppers on the grill as they charred so we could peel them for a salad. Fortunately charring wouldn't hurt them and was even desirable, because he wandered off to do something more interesting without telling me. We all ate on a couple of tables put end-to-end in the living room and laughed. I was glad they couldn't find a restaurant to feed them all.

There is more, of course, including the time here in Charleston I had a bad cold and asked him to turn the lamb under the grill (it was already marinated and cooked on one side) and a few other things so I wouldn't pass my cold along to him and his wonderful wife Sandra by handling and plating already cooked food. As Pat told it, he cooked the whole meal. As far as I'm concerned, that's the mark of a fiction writer. As long as he spelled my name right whatever he said was fine.

The last time I ate with Pat was at a meal arranged by Mary Alice Monroe for me and Jack, Pat and Sandra, Mary Alice's husband, Markus, and the manager of the private club where it was held. During the meal, the manager bemoaned the fact that the club members hated tattoos and she had a hard time hiring front-of-the-house staff who didn't have them. At the end of the meal a slip of a young woman in chef's whites sidled into the private dining room. I asked if I could help her. She said she had a tattoo she wanted to show Pat. I asked to see it first, and she lifted up the side of her chef's coat and showed me, going down the side of her body from armpit to waist, the opening lines of the prologue to *The Prince of Tides*. I called Pat over, and it was the first and last time I saw him openmouthed in awe. He had long since given up drinking, and he was sobered even more by this young woman's adoration in the form of permanent ink.

My relationship with Pat began and ended with food, so I'll leave with this: *The Pat Conroy Cookbook* is worth the price. Pat made his famous crab cakes for me once, and they are truly a pièce de resistance, requiring timing and fearlessness. I was, and remain, impressed, and consider them his best dish. But better yet, the book even has some of my worst recipes in it, including one for a Jell-O mold.

An Angel to Watch over Me

~ CYNTHIA GRAUBART

Although I didn't know it at the time, the man with the baby blue eyes holding court among friends in my living room was studying me. Sizing me up.
When I joined the conversation, he stopped talking and sat back to watch
the pot he had stirred start to bubble up. Opinions and insights were vol-
leyed back and forth. I would discover later he had been reading us like
a book, noting our strengths and vulnerabilities. And he had a particular
knack for noting the wounded. And he became my friend.

"I brought you something, kid," he bellowed as he entered my kitchen
several years later. In his outstretched arm was a flat object wrapped in tissue paper. As he handed it to me I saw the business card of Red Piano Too
taped to the paper. Red Piano was a favorite folk art gallery on St. Helena
Island, South Carolina. The card was signed "To Cynthia, much love, Pat"
in his unmistakable hand. I was certain the object was metal, but clueless
beyond that. Beneath the tissue was indeed metal, as flat as a board, cut into
the shape of an angel, like a one-dimensional Christmas tree topper. And it
was painted white and gold in a folk art style. "It's an angel," I exclaimed with
a hint of incredulity. After all, an angel was not something one expected to
receive from Pat Conroy.

"It's to watch over you," he said.

"Here in the kitchen?"

"Yes, it's your kitchen angel. For the room where you make your magic."

I was speechless. I was so touched by his thoughtfulness. I hadn't known
I needed to be looked over.

"It's to remind you that you always have someone who's watching out for you, kid," he said. "Like me."

Pat had sized me up that night long ago. We shared a common bond as military brats with an emotionally unavailable parent. We'd always been the new kids at school, moving so many times during childhood. And we were always waiting for the other shoe to drop. Our good fortunes in life surely weren't permanent. The wound we shared was permanent, not something that ever healed completely. We knew we would never be good enough. We didn't know what bad thing was lurking just ahead of us.

Like so many writers who crossed paths with Pat, I too received care and encouragement from him on my writing. For his blurb of my very first book, a cookbook written for new mothers, he wrote that it was a cross between Betty Crocker and Dr. Spock. Oh, Pat.

We also shared a love of good food. He pronounced nearly every dish I put in front of him as among the best he'd ever eaten. When I was a young bride, this meant everything to me.

My kitchen angel found a home above the sink where she indeed watched over me. I would find myself on occasion turning my head to look at her hanging from the side of the adjacent cabinet. She always made me smile.

On occasion, my angel would fall into the sink for no apparent reason. Just a random act, or so it seemed. She made quite a clanging sound, but she never seemed the worse for wear.

After a few years I began to notice a pattern with her descensions. I could swear she fell ahead of bad news—about two to four days ahead. It was a sultry day in July when she went clanging into the sink one summer. My mother-in-law passed four days later. One February she fell. That was three days before my grandfather died. I was packing a suitcase to visit my sister one spring when the angel clanged again. My sister received her cancer diagnosis while I was on that trip.

My adoration for this kitchen decoration deflated, and I tried to cast off the pattern as coincidence. But it wasn't to be.

As the pattern continued, I recalled what Pat had said my angel was supposed to do. Watch over me. And I recalled what Pat and I had in common: When was the bad thing going to happen? How fitting that the angel did her job. Her clanging announced that a bad thing was coming and that she was looking out for me.

My husband and I flew to New York for a few days to celebrate our son's engagement. We flew back to Atlanta when we got the news about our dear Pat and rushed to switch out our suitcases for the drive to Beaufort. Before we left, I walked by the kitchen. My angel was in the sink. How did she know?

Pointing at Pat Conroy's House

⌒ WILLIAM WALSH

In May 1988 I was completing my first book, *Speak So I Shall Know Thee: Interviews with Southern Writers*, having traveled throughout the South in a yellow Volkswagen convertible, down dirt roads, blue highways, and the rolling countryside to meet the writers who would become a part of my literary DNA. Once, the exhaust pipe on the VW loosened and filled the car with blue smoke so I had to drive back to Atlanta in January with the top down and the heat blazing. As I began to see the book reach its completion, my mother suggested I interview Pat Conroy. I had thought about interviewing Conroy many times but was intimidated by his literary stature. Years ago, that same trepidation had filled my heart when I spoke to Harper Lee's literary agent requesting an interview. She said, "You'll have a better chance getting the Lord God Himself." She was, of course, right. Without reason, I felt the same about Pat Conroy. Not only was he a literary giant, he was an iconic figure in my house.

It was my mother who read Conroy and suggested I read *The Great Santini*. I believe there's a little bit of Santini in every father, and every mother knows and fears this. Our mothers, deep down, hope their sons will circumvent this character flaw and grow to be men like Pat, who was aware of his behavior, understood the sensibilities of women, and respected all people. Mothers pray that no hand will ever be lifted to strike their sons, nor their sons raise a hand to strike their wife or children. Because Conroy was from the South and living in Atlanta, which was clear from the many articles in the *Atlanta Journal-Constitution*, my mother kept up with him. She clipped articles from the paper and saved them for me, and now, looking back, I see she was wishing that I might turn out to be like Pat Conroy. Thirty years later, it has dawned on me as I reflect in this article that not only did my mother wish for me to be like Conroy, but that she also saw in herself a little bit of Conroy's mother, Peggy. Pat's mother was from Alabama while my mother was from Lakewood, New York. They lived contrasting lives in the geographical sense, but there was a connection between them. They were women of manners. They were both beautiful women with difficult financial lives and husbands who, at times, probably did not live up to their dreams, women who, in the end, placed their stock in their children. Like Peggy Conroy, my mother instilled in me a Victorian awareness of gentlemanliness.

When the Conroy interview came about, my mother, who loved reading biographies of famous people and the celebrity that accompanies fame—her mother grew up with Lucille Ball in Celeron, New York—was more excited than I was. She may have told every friend and relative that I was interviewing the famous writer.

"Do you know where he lives?" my mother asked one day over the phone.

"Sort of."

"Let me show you. I'll take you over there."

Pat Conroy lived on Palisades Road in the upscale Brookwood Hills neighborhood of Atlanta, a few blocks from my mother's office at Southern Engineering on Peachtree Road. A few days before the interview, I visited my mother's office, took her to lunch at Huey's (best beignets outside of Café du Mode in New Orleans), and afterward, in my Volkswagen, we drove down Palisades.

"Drive slow now. His house is just down the street," she said.

I was looking on the wrong side of the street when she said, "There it is."

It was the second house on the right, but I was looking at the red-brick house across the street.

"No, not that house. This one."

As I turned to look right, I raised my hand off the stick shift and pointed my index finger, "That one?"

"Don't point. He'll see you." My mother grabbed my hand and pulled it down below the windshield.

"He's not going to see me pointing at his house."

"Yes, he will. It's not polite."

Down the road I turned around and drove back up the hill as my mother instructed me how to drive—not so slowly that I was conspicuous, and I certainly shouldn't stop in front of his house. That would be rude and I might tie up traffic (mine was the only car on the street).

"What are you wearing to the interview? Not blue jeans, I hope."

"No, a pair of khaki pants and a polo shirt.

With my mother satisfied about my wardrobe, I waited for her to remind me to wear clean underwear, as if Pat would ever know, as if I was destined to be in a car accident and rushed over to Piedmont Hospital a quarter mile away, where the doctors would refuse to treat me.

"I'm sorry, Mrs. Walsh, we cannot treat your son's head injury. He isn't wearing clean underwear."

My mother simply wanted the best for me, wanted me to be polite and well mannered, and wanted Pat Conroy to like me because then he was apt to like her. Deep down, she wanted any novel I was writing to be successful so, much like Peggy Conroy, she could say, "That's my son." In fact, when my first book was published, my mother was at Waldenbooks at the mall and saw my book on the checkout counter and said to the cashier, "That's my son's book."

Pat Conroy was and still is an iconic figure in our house. Just today, I called my mom to ask if she still had the books Pat signed for her.

"Oh, yes. I'd never get rid of those."

She grabbed one from the shelf and read me the inscription.

To Elaine Walsh, who has fabulous taste in sons. Pat Conroy

At Pat's seventieth birthday celebration, I was in Beaufort for three days of lectures, readings, celebrations, parties, visiting with old friends, and making new ones. I hadn't seen Pat in twenty-seven years. Toward the end of the week's program Pat was on a Q&A panel. As expected, afterward he stood around for an hour talking, hugging friends, laughing, having photos taken, and signing books. I had a copy of *Beach Music* and *The Death of Santini* I wanted him to sign for my mother. As the crowd dwindled, I waited patiently to ask for his signature.

I've always remembered his politeness, his kind words, and the time he spent with me that afternoon in Atlanta and how he needed to pick up his daughter from school so we drove over in his car. Now, here we were twenty-seven years later in Beaufort and Pat remembered the interview.

Then he signed my book.

To Elaine, Whose son pointed at my house and I saw him. Pat Conroy

What I Miss Most

~ JONATHAN CARROLL

What I miss most, Pat, are the conversations. Because I live in Europe, we rarely had a chance to meet face-to-face, but our phone conversations pretty well filled the gap. The telephone would ring and your oh-so-familiar voice would always say the same thing in a kind of southern twang basso pro-fundo–mock scold: "Of course it is up to me as usual to keep this thirty-year-long friendship going . . ." I would break out my biggest smile and settle into that cozy chair by the phone because it was you and time for one of our never-ending chats. You didn't like people calling you—the Conroy phone almost always went immediately to the answering machine. So I rarely did, knowing sooner or later you'd get in touch. Our conversations were almost always long because we talked about everything, but most of all we laughed. God, no one could make me laugh like you did. The stories, the insights into people, the writer gossip—whether true or not—the talk, and the laughter just went on and on for three decades. Everyone who knew you spoke of the same things—your warmth, your kindness, your generosity to all, your intense curiosity about people and the way the world worked. Your wonderful books were a testament to all that. It's said that we really shouldn't meet our heroes because they rarely live up to our expectations. But there are exceptions, and you were one of them. Times ten.

When Pat Conroy Came to Stay

~ RYDER CARROLL

When I was in early high school, my parents told me we were going to have a guest stay with us in Vienna. We're a private family and didn't often have visitors, so I knew they must love him and that he'd probably be a character.

The last guest we had stay with us, "Uncle" Bob, lit up the sky over the old city with a flare he launched—from our apartment window—with a teargas bullet. I liked having guests.

All I knew about our guest-to-be was that he was one of my dad's author buddies from way back. Honestly, all I really cared about at the time was a girl, Rosamunde. She'd started attending my school that year and was way out of my league. She was a nerd, a jock, a Nordic beauty, and worst of all, genuinely kind. I was (am) none of those things. I was that weird teenage art kid with pre-trend ADD and shoulder-length hair who listened to bands like Cannibal Corpse and smoked. A real catch.

Undeterred, I'd been trying to figure out an excuse to ask her out on a date. I scored tickets to a fancy private press screening of the biggest movie in the United States at the time, *Toy Story*. It wasn't set to arrive in Vienna for another six months. I thought it was pretty cool, and apparently so did she because she agreed to come, even though it was at 7:45 a.m. . . . on a Sunday.

I'd been all nerves asking Rosamunde, but it was way worse after she'd agreed. I'd asked her that Monday, and each passing day felt like taking yet another irreversible stride toward some spectacular disaster. I've always

This essay was originally published on Medium.com, 2016.

had terrible stage fright, but back then it paled when compared to "date fright."

When Pat Conroy arrived for his visit, we had no guest room to offer, but that didn't seem to bother him at all. He got a kick out of staying in my father's study, where he slept on the massive leather couch with our sixty-pound bull terrier, Beehive.

Early one cold morning my father and I couldn't find Beehive anywhere. Exasperated, we quietly entered the study and found Beehive happily stretched over Pat's big belly, rising and falling with his sleeping breaths. We laughed so hard that we woke him up. Momentarily confused by the rude awakening, Pat looked at us, then at the ridiculous dog inches from his face, and started to giggle. "Well, hello there!" he said petting her long head. His giggling belly jostled the dog, which made Pat break out laughing.

Though it ebbed and flowed throughout the day, that laughter never really went away. Since he'd arrived, Pat's company charged the air like the first warm days of spring.

With him around, the week passed quickly. The night before the big date, my mother had gone all out fixing us supper. In the short time Pat had been there dinner had become something we all looked forward to, especially to his wild and wonderful stories. As we sat there at the table we started to hear an unmistakably aggressive swell of sound rising from the street outside. We looked out the window and saw a massive protest rally passing by our building. To the great chagrin of my mother, Pat, my father, and I raced down to get first-row tickets to the unfolding spectacle.

The three of us stood there rubbernecking in yellow lamplight as the shouting mob made its way past us and collided with the police barricade down the block. The angry mass pooled and oozed into the night toward the old center of the city, leaving tattered banners and bottles in their wake.

The evening left us all wired. Not that I was going to get much sleep anyway. I was wide awake at 5:00 a.m. and watched the rising sun fill the thin skin of window frost with light. All gussied up, I headed out. I sported one of my father's snazzy gray Italian trench coats for God knows what reason and had tied my damp hair neatly back into a ponytail.

Although the cinema was right up the street from our place, I left an hour early—you know, just in case. Rosamunde and I had agreed to meet at 7:45

a.m. inside the movie theater . . . or was it outside? Better wait outside. It's cold, but, you know, I'll seem "cooler" if I shrug off the cold. Around 7:30, when my hair began to freeze, I was feeling *really* cool. By 7:45 I was getting a little concerned for my life. My teeth were chattering, but I couldn't honestly tell if it was the cold or anticipation. Around 8:00, the cold was the last thing on my mind.

I was sitting on a bench outside the cinema, scanning the far ends of the street, when I noticed people looking at me strangely. I shrugged it off assuming they thought of me as some burnout still partying from the night before. Finally, a concerned woman approached and asked me if I was all right. Confused, I looked down and noticed that my lap was covered in blood, a lot of blood.

It was so cold I hadn't felt the blood streaming from my nose. I got up, and it looked like I had been stabbed. I was covered. Despite all this I looked at my watch, and it said 8:30. Reality set in. She was not coming, and for good measure, the universe had punched me in the face. Totally defeated, I bled my way home.

I walked into the living room and fell into the first chair I could find, blood and all. I heard shuffling as Pat sleepily emerged from the study. "Well, how did it . . . boy, what the fuck happened to you!?" he shouted.

He stood in the doorway in his pjs and patiently listened as I told him what had happened. He came closer and pulled up a chair but didn't say anything for a while. Then he smiled, and involuntarily so did I. He began to tell me about the romantic misadventures he'd had at my age. In no time I was laughing so hard that the caked blood was crumbling off my face.

We sat and talked for a long while until my parents returned from their early breakfast. We quickly folded them into the conversation. A lot of terrible stories about heartbreak were shared that freezing morning, but not a tear was shed.

It was long ago, and I can't for the life of me remember what he told me that morning. What I can remember is how he made me feel: like I wasn't alone and that it would all be okay. This was just an epically ridiculous moment—the first of many—that would make for a great story to share with others one day when they were feeling low. Thank you, Pat. I think it's time.

Doing What It Takes to Keep This Dying Friendship Alive

~ MARK CHILDRESS

I first met Pat Conroy in 1980 at the uproarious publication party for *The Lords of Discipline* at Cliff Graubart's Old New York Book Shop in Atlanta. Conroy was the radiant star of the evening. His father was in attendance, overplaying the role of the Great Santini and cursing his son every time he passed through the room.

I asked the senior Conroy what he thought of the book his son had written about him. "My son does not have the balls to portray the actual genius, the greatness of the Great Santini," he said.

Pat just laughed.

The party carried on well after 3:00 a.m. The next morning, at his insistence, I met Pat back at the bookstore at 9:00 a.m. sharp. He shrugged off his hangover and started helping to clean up the epic mess his admirers and fans had created. He drank coffee and wielded a broom while entertaining everyone with his renditions of comic highlights of the party. He lugged sacks of trash and poured red cups of leftover beer out the window.

That has always been my ideal for how a famous person should behave. Every good novelist has a massive ego—it's an essential tool for the job—but Conroy's ego was contained in a package of sweetness, comedy, and full-Irish savagery that made him irresistible.

At that time I was a twenty-three-year-old editor for *Southern Living* magazine sent to interview him. Conroy called my editor to complain that I was too young for the job and advised him: "Next time, send a sperm."

But he liked the piece I wrote about him. He stayed in touch. He encouraged me to finish my novel, and when I did, he gave it the most wonderful blurb any first novelist ever got. (I wasn't the only one so blessed; Pat holds the modern American record for generous blurbing from a big-name author.) After that, we became friends.

For a while in the early 1990s we both wound up living in San Francisco. Conroy bought a big house and threw fancy parties with famous people in attendance, but that life didn't really seem to suit him. He preferred a long, boisterous lunch, preferably Italian, with one or two friends in North Beach.

Our adventures at that time mostly consisted of watching several close friends die of AIDS. Somehow we had managed to arrive in San Francisco just as the epidemic reached its peak.

Conroy and I would meet every week or two at Rose Pistola or Trattoria Contadina to eat too much pasta and garlic, get hopped up on iced tea, and talk about death or anything other than death. We agreed that we were truly awful human beings, enjoying that beautiful city when everyone around us was dying. "Death is overrated," he said.

We both thought that one day we might write fiction about the plague, but it was too soon, while it was happening. There was no way to gain perspective. He wrote about it twenty years later in *South of Broad*. I'm still waiting for that perspective.

Whenever one of us would get in touch after some time apart, Conroy would bark, "Hey, Childress! I guess it's up to me to keep this *dying friendship* alive!" This was a line he used often, on many of his friends. I knew it was a joke, but it always felt nice to know that Pat considered ours "a friendship" and that he was working hard on his end of it.

When *The Prince of Tides* was number one on the *New York Times* best-seller list, I was driving Conroy home from lunch one day in my '65 Thunderbird down Market Street. On the steep hill that leads down toward the Civic Center the brakes failed.

My two-ton car went faster and faster. I stomped the brake pedal to the floor again and again. Finally Conroy said in a casual tone, "Hey, does this car have an emergency brake?"

When he said that, I remembered that yes, it did. I stepped on it and managed to stop the car by running it into a curb.

Afterward, Conroy had a great time writing imaginary headlines for that incident. His favorite was "Number One Best-Selling Author Dies in Car Crash with Minor Writer." I may have shaved a couple days off his life that day. If so, I apologize.

Through a turn of circumstance, we both happened to be at the Writer's Guild of America awards the year Pat was nominated for his screenplay of *The Prince of Tides* and Fannie Flagg for *Fried Green Tomatoes* (both of them lost to *The Silence of the Lambs*). Conroy spotted me and announced that in order to make one more try at keeping this dying friendship alive, he was, by God, going to introduce me to Barbra.

I demurred. I was too much a fanboy and far too intimidated to meet her.

He dragged me over to her table anyway. Tiny little thing, she is. He introduced us. Barbra said, "Oh another southerner! You're everywhere tonight."

To which I replied, cleverly, "Yes, we're like worms coming out of the woodwork."

Conroy got a terrible gleam in his eye. "So, Childress! Big fan of Barbra, loved her all your life! Always wanted to meet her, now you've met her and you've just compared yourself to a worm!"

Until that moment I didn't know Barbra Streisand could howl with laughter, but she did. She may have even slapped her thigh. I don't know, because everything went a little hazy for me right then.

In subsequent years Conroy enjoyed introducing me to others as "Barbra Streisand's favorite worm." The story of my humiliation got better each time he told it. As his family knows, to be teased by Conroy was to be loved, and I always felt plenty of love when he was around.

We both moved away from San Francisco not long after that, but whenever our paths crossed, it was old times again. The last time was at a book festival in Texas. Conroy was given a chair in a room where his job was to sign about three thousand books. He appointed me to keep him company. The eager readers who waited in line to meet him got his best performance—charming, roguish, occasionally sarcastic, but always warm and interested. In between, he shot observations and one-liners in my direction.

"This is my friend, Mark," he told one lady. "I blurbed two or three of his books. I don't really have friends, you know. Just people I've blurbed."

"Hey!" I turned on him. "Did you just tell her we're not friends?"

He grinned. "Look," he said, "I'm just doing what it takes to keep this dying friendship alive."

Okay, Conroy. You did your part. I guess it's up to me now.

The Relationship We Never Had

~ JANIS IAN

It was 1988 when a singer named Marti Jones said she wanted to record a song of mine called "Ruby." Would I come to Charlotte, North Carolina, and play piano on the session?

Amtrak was running a big special; for sixty-nine dollars you could buy a round-trip ticket and make three stopovers anywhere in the country. I was pretty broke at the time, and taking a long train ride sounded romantic, so I booked myself via "the southern route" and made my plans. I'd stop in Charlotte, continue on to New York to see my mother, then swing through San Francisco and visit my dad before returning to my home base in Los Angeles.

The very idea of journeying without a book in hand made me break out in a cold sweat, so a few days before departure I indulged myself at our local bookstore. I hunted down three of the fattest new releases, then took a seat and began to choose.

I'd always been a fast reader, preferring large tomes I could skim through quickly rather than small, serious books that insisted I pause and philosophize with them. *The Prince of Tides* looked like a keeper—a stunning 704 pages with lots of dialogue. I checked the table of contents; no list of characters or family tree, something I'd watched for ever since picking up a copy of *Anna Karenina* and discovering I couldn't follow the plot without a flow chart.

Idly flipping through the pages, I read, "It is an art form to hate New York City properly."

I stopped, looked twice, read it again. And again.

No matter the form, a writer is a writer. We respect and admire one another's worlds, but although the rules of each form are similar, there are subtle differences known only to the practitioners. For songwriters like me, brevity has an urgency unknown to most novelists. Right placement of single words is as important to us as Right Speech, Right Action, and Right Livelihood are to Buddhists travelling the Eightfold Path.

Pat's sentence could easily have been "It's an art form to hate New York," losing the gentility of "It is" and the completeness of "New York City." Or perhaps he might have written "It's an art form to hate New York properly," which any New Yorker would know was poorly written because "New York" is a state, not a city.

But no. *It is an art form to hate New York City properly.*

A perfect sentence. Read it aloud. Listen to the cadence. That author might have been a songwriter himself, and a damned fine one at that.

I promptly bought the book, and a few days later I was seated in the club car of the *Silver Eagle* meeting Pat Conroy for the first time.

In memory, the trip has become a series of snapshots overlaid by the book. I was completely enthralled, occasionally lifting my eyes to stare out the window at an unknown land. I can see the images to this day: an old man on a ramshackle front porch, face covered in shaving lather, while the woman behind him slowly strops a straight razor. Barefooted children running beside the train, waving as they disappeared into dust. Heat waves rising from the pavement. Louisiana swampland, alien and forbidding.

The South.

Conroy's book stunned me. It elevated me. It reminded me of all the reasons I'd become a writer. His fecundity of language gave me something to strive for as I began thinking about my own next album. I had no money and no prospects, but Conroy's prose reminded me that I, too, had a talent with words. A reminder I sorely needed. Peering through the smoke-stained picture window, I found myself reading aloud, something I'd never done before. The language was too beautiful to keep inside. It needed the air, to breathe.

"It was my sister who forced me to confront my century." That sentence, along with a couple of films (*The Maids*, *At Play in the Fields of the Lord*), dictated the kind of writer I resolved to become.

Years later, having finished *Breaking Silence*, an album seven years in the making, I wrote to some of the artists who had influenced the songs. It was an eclectic group, one that included Whoopi Goldberg, Mike Resnick, Kathy Bates, Orson Scott Card—and Pat Conroy. I sent him a copy of the album along with a heartfelt cover letter. I didn't linger over the writing of it; if I took too much time I'd lose my nerve.

I kept no copy, but if memory serves, I thanked him for many things. Chief among them was giving me a framework for the South, where I'd moved five years earlier. It was a very different place than I'd imagined growing up in the Northeast, and in large part I have Conroy's work to thank for my earliest introduction to the rhythm of the land and her people.

Much to my astonishment, Pat wrote back, on a sheet of yellow legal paper with a hand-stamped family crest in the upper right. His response began, "What a lovely & generous letter."

He called my album "superb & haunting & beautiful."

He confessed that try as he might to look me up on his next trip to Nashville, he became shy at the thought of contacting me, but "you don't have to let shyness be a two-way street." He asked me to call if I got to San Francisco and promised, "My family's nice & we cook well."

I didn't get to San Francisco for a while, and by the time I did, Pat had moved. I was embarrassed that I'd never used the telephone number he'd so generously provided. By this time *The Prince of Tides* was a film, *Beach Music* was soon due, and I was afraid to look the sycophant.

So I let the opportunity slip away, as I let it slip away decades later when, narrating an audiobook by his beloved gatekeeper and goddaughter Maggie Schein, I took for granted his offer to "show me around Beaufort" and cook me a meal.

I took for granted that he would be there when I was ready, when I'd managed to grow up enough to get over my own shyness at the thought of meeting him. Somehow, the intensity of his work had already made him eternal in my eyes. Ever changing, ever growing, much like his beloved South. But also immutable. Always there.

In the last line of his letter to me Pat wrote, "You sing like a fallen angel."

I like to think we had that in common, at the core of the relationship we never had. That Beaufort, South Carolina, and Farmingdale, New Jersey, could come together in mutual rebellion against the gods of our childhoods, be they parents, teachers, or a world that refused to believe what we instinctively knew from the start—that words have lives of their own stretching far beyond anything we could have dreamed in our youth. And that we spend our entire lives trying to catch up to them.

My Hero

~ KATHY L. MURPHY

Every once in a great moon, through a series of fateful meetings and divine intervention, you meet someone who forever changes the way you experience your life. That man for me was Pat Conroy. I have since read all of his books, had the pleasure and the privilege of his company, and in turn have found one of my personal heroes.

I related to his upbringing. My family stayed in one place, and I only had two sisters, not a whole passel of siblings, but something resonated in me when I read his words—I had found someone just like me. Someone too afraid to speak out and then someone who was ashamed for not standing up for my siblings and myself.

My father was a Korean War veteran who was pushed to the limits trying to support his family of girls. He worked all his life on the oil rigs, and if home, never let us sleep in. "Get up, you mattress backs," he'd say as he ripped off our covers. We were commanded to mow and clean up the yard. "Wash the cars, help your mother." We were not allowed to lounge around, and we all got jobs at a fairly young age.

My father had a temper. He struck hard and fast; you never saw it coming. I could relate to *The Great Santini*—he reminded me of my father, who also mellowed with age, and we actually became great friends. I was crushed when he died.

My parents had a weird love/hate relationship. From the outside we looked like the American dream family—beautiful parents dressed just right, driving a big Cadillac, belonging to the Eureka Country Club—but behind closed doors it was just that, a story to be kept hidden.

When I discovered Pat Conroy's words, it was the first time in my life I felt I was not alone. The first Conroy book I read was *The Lords of Discipline*. I could not put it down. Next, *The Water Is Wide*. I cried for days over the ending, and on to *The Great Santini*. I found my own family in that book, my tribe.

In 2008 when my book, *The Pulpwood Queens' Tiara-Wearing, Book-Sharing Guide to Life*, was about to be released, my mother called my publisher and tried to stop the presses. I called Pat Conroy and cried. He listened until he could stand no more. He told me his mother got angry, too, about his books and would not speak to him for years, but she got over it. I told Pat I did not think that was going to happen to me. "Fuck her," he said. "You have the right to tell your story, so tell it." Those were his words, not mine, but this was one time I let that word slip on by.

My cherished friendship with Pat had begun years earlier.

In the 1980s I was a children's manager/book buyer for a local independent bookstore. I attended Book Expo, the largest publishing convention in the country, where Pat Conroy was going to be signing copies of *Beach Music*. I stood in line forever waiting to meet my American hero. As the line inched closer I could see him, his rosy, cherubic cheeks, his smile, but I could not believe my ears. People were angry. His book was not ready. He was handing out copies of *The Prince of Tides* that he was signing along with a *Beach Music* tote bag as its replacement. As I got closer, the couple in front of me went ballistic. As Pat reached out to shake the couple's hands, they began to berate him: Why in the world wasn't his book ready? They had stood in line for hours. Pat graciously began to take each book they were carrying and sign them. I watched in horror. Pat apologized, smiling, and told them he just did not get it done, but his book was coming. After getting armfuls of books personally signed, they stormed off in a huff. I was next, and I could not face him. As I turned to run, the publicist shoved a book bag at me with the signed copy. Her look pleaded with me to stay, but I could not. I was mortified by the bad manners of these two booksellers.

Soon after, Pat's publisher held a *Beach Music* contest to win a visit from him. I came up with this grand scheme to bring in a kiddie pool and who-knows-what-else, and lo and behold, I won. But for some reason Pat Conroy could not come to the bookstore. Perhaps I could come to Dallas to meet him. Could I ever!

I was supposed to meet him at a Texas Rangers ballgame, but after I spent an afternoon waiting anxiously in the hot summer sun, his plane was late. Could we meet at the bookstore? You bet.

Finally, my moment arrived. When I walked up with my complete stack of Pat Conroy books, he looked me right in the eye and said, "Now Kathy Patrick [my former married name], what are you doing here?" I was so shocked that he was speaking directly to me I was momentarily speechless. I finally found my voice, and he signed all my books. Everyone else disappeared as I became the most important person in the room. What a gift. I was in love.

I gave him an Auntie Skinners ball cap, and he told me that no one had ever given him such a magnificent cap. I beamed. I'd done good. I had accomplished my dream: I got to meet the author of my dreams.

I left for a while then came back to take the book rep, Ken Graham, out to dinner. I was waiting patiently for him when an arm went around my shoulder. I looked up, and it was Pat Conroy wearing my Auntie Skinners ball cap. He said, "So, what are you doing, Kathy Patrick?" I was so flustered he again remembered my name that I blurted out, "We are going to dinner, Pat. Would you like to join us?" He said when he was on book tour he practically starved and died of thirst because most people forgot to offer him even a glass of water. We walked arm in arm out of the bookstore, and never in my life have I felt more loved.

A Cajun eatery called Pappadeaux's was packed to the rafters with Saturday night diners, but a round table in the center of the room suddenly opened for us. Pat pulled out my chair for me and announced as he sat, "This looks like a fried food place, let's order some fried food." We closed that place down, and I never laughed so hard in my life. I never wanted the night to end.

Years later my bookselling friend and mentor, Mary Gay Shipley, of That Bookstore in Blytheville, Arkansas, called. Pat Conroy was coming, and she asked if would I like to come up to the book signing. I drove for hours and was seated on a stage in a theater, chatting away, eating dinner when Pat

Conroy came. Everyone kept asking me where I was from and why I came. I told them I had had the pleasure of meeting Pat Conroy, and we had had dinner together, and he was an absolute delight. I could see all the eyes at the table registering serious disbelief. "Oh, it's true, you all. You are just going to love him."

Then Pat strode onto the stage. He immediately came over to my table, walked up to my chair, and hugged me, "Why, look who is here, my dear East Texas friend Kathy Patrick, all the way from Jefferson." To see the looks on the faces of all those women at my table was priceless. How did Pat Conroy know?

I was now writing for *East Texas* magazine. I had never interviewed any-one before. Reporters and television stations were there to cover the event, and he made them all wait. I began scared to death. I had my paper and pencil but nothing would come out. Pat goes, "So Pat," he encouraged me, "Pat, tell me about your new book. What is the story?" I repeated his cue and on and on until we were finished—the kindest and most generous thing anyone could have ever done.

In the years since I met Pat, I'd gone on to open my own beauty/book-shop, Beauty and the Book. I began the Pulpwood Queens, the largest book club in America. I'd been featured on Oprah Winfrey's Oxygen Network and kicked off *Good Morning America*'s READ THIS Book Club with Diane Sawyer. I still thank my lucky stars that Pat Conroy, Cassandra King, and Doug Marlette were among the sixty-plus authors who blurbed my book. Pat's former publicist, Marly Rusoff, who put on the *Beach Music* contest I won, became his literary agent, and later became mine. The Pat Conroy connection expanded my circles and my world.

It seemed like twenty years that I tried to get Pat to come to East Texas when one day the stars aligned. He agreed to be a keynote speaker at my annual Pulpwood Queens book club convention, Girlfriend Weekend. We flat sold out. Pat Conroy brought people to my festival I had never seen before. To say the event was a huge success is a supreme understatement. Nearly four hundred copies of *South of Broad* went out to the luncheon guests.

Pat's speech ran way over, and nobody cared. His line for signing books lasted all afternoon, and nobody minded. In the midst of my running around crazy, Pat, his daughter Melissa Conroy, and Pat's friend author Janis Owens all wanted to see my shop. I gave over the keys, wishing I was showing them my Beauty and the Book. But I bit my tongue. I had a book festival to run. Later, I had saved a seat so at least I could sit at times with Pat at the festival, but alas, another Pulpwood Queen had nabbed the spot and was not budging. I was on the brink of tears. Would I ever get to talk to Pat Conroy? Not much. Time was not on my side that year.

A month after the event I received a phone call from Pat. I was beside myself. He told me, "Kathy"—I can still hear his voice—"I thought the book-publishing world was over, I thought no one really reads anymore. Then I came to your event, and I was wrong. I have never seen anything like your Girlfriend Weekend. Do you realize what you have created?" Pat went on and on and then he asked me, "Has an author ever invited himself back to your Girlfriend Weekend?"

Pat Conroy did come back, this time with his new book, *My Reading Life*. I finally caught him in a brief moment when he was not covered with reading fans. I quickly blurted out what I had been trying to tell him all these years—that his books made me realize I was not alone. I tried to convey to him that someday I wanted to sit down with him and have a heart to heart. He looked up at me with very solemn blue, blue eyes, apple blossom cheeks, and said quite seriously, "It's never going to happen, Kathy." I knew then without saying another word I would probably not see Pat again.

I was devastated when Pat died. No one could ever make me want to read as much or make me feel as important as he did. He was the most generous author I've ever known. I will never forget him standing in line for all the authors who came to Girlfriend Weekend to buy their books, including mine. He never complained but was a champion for mentoring others still finding their way to best-sellerdom. His words are important, but his actions went beyond the call.

The members of the Beaufort High School *Breakers* literary magazine editorial staff, 1963: Pat Conroy, Julie Zachowski, Stephanie Edwards, Daralee Dragon, and Becky Vernon. Conroy, Zachowski, and Edwards all went on to have careers in literature. Courtesy of Beaufort County School District.

Pat Conroy, #13 on the Beaufort High School Tidal Wave basketball team. In his senior year, 1963, Conroy was team captain and voted MVP. He was also voted senior class president, Mr. Congeniality, and Best All Around. In 2017 Conroy was inducted in the Beaufort High School Hall of Fame. Courtesy of Beaufort County School District.

Pat Conroy as a Citadel cadet, circa 1966. Courtesy of the Pat Conroy Estate and the Pat Conroy Archive, Irvin Department of Rare Books and Special Collections, University of South Carolina Libraries.

The Conroys in Pensacola, Florida, 1968: (seated) Peggy, Tim, Tom, and Don; (standing) Jim, Carol, Pat, Kathy, and Mike. Courtesy of the Pat Conroy Estate and the Pat Conroy Archive, Irvin Department of Rare Books and Special Collections, University of South Carolina Libraries.

The Conroys during the filming of *The Great Santini* in Beaufort, South Carolina,
1978: (back) Pat and Don; (front) Pat's daughters Megan, Melissa, and Jessica.
Courtesy of the Pat Conroy Archive, Irvin Department of Rare Books and
Special Collections, University of South Carolina Libraries.

Pat Conroy and Cliff Graubart, circa 1979. Courtesy of the Pat Conroy Estate and the Pat Conroy Archive, Irvin Department of Rare Books and Special Collections, University of South Carolina Libraries.

Pat Conroy, circa 1980. Courtesy of the Pat Conroy Estate and the Pat Conroy Archive, Irvin Department of Rare Books and Special Collections, University of South Carolina Libraries.

Pat Conroy, circa 1980. Courtesy of the Pat Conroy Estate and the Pat Conroy Archive, Irvin Department of Rare Books and Special Collections, University of South Carolina Libraries.

Pat Conroy on book tour for *The Prince of Tides*, circa 1986. Courtesy of the Pat Conroy Archive, Irvin Department of Rare Books and Special Collections, University of South Carolina Libraries.

Pat Conroy with Barbra Streisand following the New York premiere of the film *The Prince of Tides*, December 1991. Courtesy of William E. Dufford.

Cassandra King Conroy and Pat Conroy with dogs Tom and Virginia Woof on Fripp Island, South Carolina, 1998. Courtesy of the Pat Conroy Estate and the Pat Conroy Archive, Irvin Department of Rare Books and Special Collections, University of South Carolina Libraries.

Citadel '67 classmates John Warley and Pat Conroy at a signing for Warley's novel *Bethesda's Child*, 2010. Courtesy of the Pat Conroy Estate and the Pat Conroy Archive, Irvin Department of Rare Books and Special Collections, University of South Carolina Libraries.

Pat Conroy speaking at a fundraiser at the University of South Carolina Beaufort Center for the Arts for the Open Land Trust, February 2010. The remarks he delivered appear as the title essay in his posthumously published collection *A Lowcountry Heart*. Courtesy of the Open Land Trust.

Pat Conroy signs a copy of his novel *The Great Santini*, 2010. Courtesy of the Open Land Trust.

Pat Conroy with his former assistant Margaret Evans, publisher of *Lowcountry Weekly*, in Beaufort, South Carolina, 2010. This event, held at the USCB Center for the Arts, was an Open Land Trust fundraiser to preserve the Green in Beaufort's historic district, the Point. The Green appears prominently in *The Great Santini*. Courtesy of the Open Land Trust.

Pat Conroy, 2010. Photo by Steve Leimberg/
UnSeenImages.com.

Five of the Conroy siblings at the South Carolina Book Festival in Columbia, May 2014: Mike, Kathy, Pat, Jim, and Tim. Photo by Lauren Lyles.

Pat Conroy biographer Catherine Seltzer on stage with Conroy at the historic Newberry Opera House, Newberry, South Carolina, May 2015. Photo by Ted Williams, courtesy of the Newberry Opera House.

Pat Conroy with actors David Keith and Michael O'Keefe at the Pat Conroy at 70 festival, University of South Carolina Beaufort Center for the Arts, October 2015. Photo by Susan DeLoach.

Ron Rash, Patti Callahan Henry, and Pat Conroy at the Pat Conroy at 70 festival, University of South Carolina Beaufort Center for the Arts, October 2015. Photo by Susan DeLoach.

Ellen Malphrus and Pat Conroy at the Pat Conroy at 70 festival, University of South Carolina Beaufort Center for the Arts, October 2015. Photo by Susan DeLoach.

Jonathan Haupt and Pat Conroy in Columbia, South Carolina, February 2014. Photo by Anne McQuary.

Cassandra King Conroy and Pat Conroy in Pat's writing room at their home on Battery Creek in Beaufort, South Carolina, 2014. Photo by Rob McDonald.

Pat Conroy's desk as he left it, at his home on Battery Creek, Beaufort, South Carolina, photographed after his death on March 4, 2016. Photo by Ellen Malphrus.

The Pat Conroy Literary Center at 308 Charles Street, Beaufort, South Carolina. The Conroy Center opened to the public in October 2016 and by October 2017 had been named South Carolina's first affiliate of the American Writers Museum and South Carolina's second American Library Association United for Libraries Literary Landmark. Photo by Maura Connelly.

Andy Marlette's memorial cartoon for Pat Conroy, appearing originally in the *Pensacola News Journal* on March 7, 2016. The cartoon is inspired by a similar piece in memoriam for Don Conroy, the Great Santini, created in 1998 by Marlette's uncle and mentor, Pulitzer Prize–winning cartoonist Doug Marlette. Courtesy of Andy Marlette.

Goodnight, Sweet Prince

~ ALEX SANDERS

Donald Patrick Conroy, born on October 26, 1945, was the best storyteller of our time—very possibly any time. The Spanish philosopher George Santayana said that those who cannot remember history are condemned to repeat it. Pat Conroy said that anybody who ever heard that quote was condemned to repeat it. Kipling said the same thing better. "If history were written as stories," he said, "nobody would forget it." We will never forget Donald Patrick Conroy.

Pat came to live in South Carolina on orders of the United States Marine Corps. In 1961, his father, Col. Donald Conroy, a Marine aviator who went by the nickname the Great Santini, had received orders to report to the air station in Beaufort, South Carolina. Pat was sixteen years old. He received the news of his impending South Carolina residency with dread. He had attended ten schools in eleven years, and Beaufort High School would become his third high school.

When Pat's mother, Peg, drove her seven children into Beaufort County, none of them knew that they were driving toward his literary destiny. As they crossed the Whale Branch Bridge Pat caught his first glimpse of the tidal marshes of the lowcountry. That vision remained with him all of his life. He was a marsh-haunted boy from that moment on. Remember that first sighting of the marsh in the opening frame of the movie *The Prince of*

Portions of this essay were first delivered as Pat Conroy's eulogy on March 8, 2016, at St. Peter's Catholic Church, Beaufort, South Carolina, and later appeared in *A Lowcountry Heart: Reflections on a Writing Life.*

Tides and recall how Barbra Streisand praises the inexpressible beauty of the landscape. Of course, those were Pat Conroy's words. Both the book and the movie are his love songs to South Carolina.

Peg died of cancer and is buried in the National Cemetery in Beaufort, beside Colonel Conroy. Pat supported nothing more strongly than the Hollings Oncology Center at MUSC. He and The Citadel, the other Charleston school in his life, eventually kissed and made up and became great friends. They had a rocky relationship following publication of *The Lords of Discipline*. That ended in compromise: Pat promised not to write any more books about a fictitious military college in South Carolina, and The Citadel promised to stop using his books as kindling to heat the barracks.

He told me that The Citadel was one of the big reasons he became a writer. While other students of his generation were going to fraternity or sorority parties, he spent his four college years reading during evening study period. He became a member of the Dock Street Theater, the Charleston Ballet and Symphony. He learned about the beauty and charm of cities by studying Charleston and Beaufort.

Thirty years ago he wrote these words: "My wound is geography. It is also my anchorage, my port of call," the opening words of *The Prince of Tides*. He told me he didn't know where these words came from or why a fictional character named Tom Wingo was saying them. But he knew at that moment *The Prince of Tides*, his most widely acclaimed novel, had begun.

These words would soon follow:

> I would like to take you to the marsh on a spring day, flush the great blue heron from its silent occupation. Scatter marsh hens as we sink to our knees in mud, open an oyster with a pocketknife, and feed it to you from the shell and say, "There. That taste. That's the taste of my childhood." I would say "Breathe deeply," and you would breathe and remember that smell for the rest of your life. The bold aroma of the tidal marsh, exquisite and sensual, the smell of the South in heat, a smell like new milk and spilled wine, all perfumed with sea water.

Through his eloquent words he took us to that unique place on earth.

Pat had a turbulent personality, a complex mixture of joy and despair, but through it all, great love. He loved books and independent bookstores, especially the Old New York Book Shop in Atlanta. He loved his friends, his brothers and sisters, his children and stepchildren, his grandchildren, his legion of readers, who hung on his every word and were enchanted by his characters, the descriptions of the South Carolina lowcountry, and his stories—always his stories.

But he loved no one more than Sandra, his steadfast wife, Cassandra King Conroy. She smoothed out the rough places for him and calmed the turbulence in his life. She loved him unconditionally, as he loved her. She brought him peace at the last.

More than anything, he had an acute sense of social justice and his own place in the scheme of things. His own ideas of right and wrong lurked within his writing, sometimes not readily apparent but always right below the surface. He could cause you to do the right thing without embarrassment. He was the most unselfish human being I ever knew. Other than my family, he was my favorite person on earth.

In the acknowledgments to *The Prince of Tides*, Pat Conroy magnanimously thanks me for telling him many of the stories in the book. Of course, I was grateful—to a point. When he wrote the stories down, he got them all mixed up. I'm glad for this opportunity to set the record straight.

The tiger at the Esso station in *The Prince of Tides* was Happy the Tiger, who lived at the Exxon Car Wash on Gervais Street in Columbia. But Happy never ate a rapist like the tiger in the book. When Columbia finally got a zoo, Happy went to live there. She had to be kept all by herself at first, having forgotten she was a tiger. And according to some reports, she could not go to sleep at night without a tape recorder playing, over and over again, the sounds of the car wash. The car wash had become her own personal Bengal, and its sounds were for her the sounds of the jungle.

The baby in the freezer, in Pat Conroy's words, "born dead, baptized in a sink and deep frozen with a hundred pounds of shrimp," was not really a baby but a cat. A lawyer in Columbia named "Tuck" Rion kept dead cats in his freezer. Why is another story.

The character in the book who waterskied from Beaufort to Charleston was in real life state senator Ryan Shealy. He really did waterski from Columbia to Charleston in a misguided effort to prove that the Congaree

River could be made navigable for commercial shipping. All he succeeded in proving was that it was possible to waterski from Columbia to Charleston, something no one had ever doubted.

The white porpoise in the book, Carolina Snow, was "Carolina Snowball," the white dolphin who lived in Port Royal Sound, near Hilton Head. She really was captured by a group from the Miami Seaquariam in Florida and became a major tourist attraction. I'm sad to say, unlike the porpoise in the book, she was never returned to the wild. Pat was able to give his Carolina Snow a happier ending. While the real white dolphin never returned home, life-size models of Snowball and her offspring Sonny Boy are now part of an educational display at the Port Royal Sound Foundation Maritime Center, near the waters where the real Snowball once swam.

The story in the book of Amos Wingo and his cross was based on the old man who carried his cross down Two Notch Road in Columbia every Good Friday. He eventually got so old he had to put wheels on the cross.

Pat named another character in the book Papa John, for Papa John Valahos, the chef at the Elite Epicurean Restaurant on Main Street in Columbia and my wife's uncle by marriage.

The town described in the novel that was wiped off the map to build the nuclear plant was really New Ellenton, South Carolina. The town was moved in the early 1950s, lock, stock, and barrel, including even its grave-yards, to make room for the hydrogen bomb plant in Aiken County. New Ellenton thus became the third town destroyed by a nuclear bomb, the first two being Hiroshima and Nagasaki.

The first story in the novel is about the boy who killed the bald eagle and was made to eat it by his father. That was me and my daddy. But it wasn't a bald eagle. It was a robin. A robin probably tastes a lot like a bald eagle but makes for a less dramatic scene in a Pat Conroy novel.

Pat may have mixed up my stories, but the truth of the matter is that the mixing of them was part of Pat's art and what has earned him worldwide recognition and adoration. In telling and retelling our stories and his own, Pat honored all of us and his adopted home. He may have come to live among us involuntarily, but he stayed among us by choice and enriched us for more than fifty years. Many of us saw ourselves reflected in his published words.

Some of us he entertained grandly. Others of us he outraged greatly. To all of us, however, he gave a rare gift. He came to us from afar, like Faulkner and like Wolfe. But I respectfully suggest that, in ways more real and more loving than either of them, he gave to us the opportunity, in the phrase of Burns, "to see ourselves as others see us." For this alone we should be forever grateful to Pat Conroy, our very own prince of tides.

> Good-night, sweet prince.
> May flights of angels sing thee to thy rest.
> (*Hamlet* V.ii)

Sea Island Magic

⌒ LAWRENCE S. ROWLAND

Pat Conroy is now part of Beaufort's history. For forty years his novels and their movies have brought more people to Beaufort than anything other than the U.S. Marine Corps. Many have been so captivated by Conroy's Sea Island aesthetic that they bought property and moved here to work or retire. Pat Conroy was responsible for his own microeconomy, and his adopted hometown has prospered because of it. It was one of his many gifts to his readers and to his neighbors.

The Sea Islands, which stretch along the southeastern coast from Charleston, South Carolina, to Jacksonville, Florida, are a uniquely beautiful part of America. They are an amalgam of land and sea buffered by vast salt marshes and dotted with green, magical isles. The Carolina lowcountry is a flat land where surging tides mix daily with lazy, swamp-fed freshwater rivers. This mix produces the vast spartina grass marshes. The Sea Island salt marshes are the most productive ecosystem in the world and have provided easy sustenance for millennia of human inhabitants.

The horizon is always visible in the Sea Islands, orienting sailors by day and night. Land and sea often merge in the summer haze. The humid salt air has a particular effect. It softens the borders between land and sea, creating a world that is sonically muted and visually impressionistic. This world between two worlds surrounded and permeated Pat Conroy, the man and the writer. He began *The Prince of Tides* with these short sentences: "My wound is geography. It is also my anchorage, my port of call."

The journals left by the earliest Western visitors to the Sea Islands record the beauty and bounty of the lands they explored. In 1514 the first Spanish explorer, Pedro de Salazar, noted in his journal of the voyage the health and stature of the Native American inhabitants, a result of the Sea Islands' abundant shellfish and marine life, and called his new discovery "the land of the giants." René de Laudonnière, in his chronicle of Jean Ribaut's 1562 voyage to found the first Protestant colony in the New World, noted the bounty of the Sea Island estuaries: "so many sorts of fishes that ye may take them without net or angle, as many as you will." Ribaut named the harbor and surroundings Port Royal and concluded famously that there was "no fayrer or fytter place then Porte Royall."

The Spaniards who settled Florida built the city of Santa Elena (1566–87) on Parris Island. One of the settlers, Bartolomé Martínez, in a letter to King Philip II of Spain, described his Port Royal home as "the healthiest country, with the most abundant shooting and fishing and very good for cultivation, which is all that can be desired." The Spaniards abandoned Santa Elena and retreated to St. Augustine as their empire diminished.

Into this vacuum strode aggressive English adventurers. In 1663 Captain William Hilton reconnoitered the Sea Islands on behalf of the eight English aristocrats who had been granted the Carolina Charter from King Charles II. Hilton concluded his report to the Lords Proprietors by commenting on the beauty and bounty of the Sea Islands: "The ayr is clear and sweet, the country very pleasant and delightful. And we could wish that all they that want a happy settlement of our English nation, were well transported thither."

Despite years of destructive wars with Native Americans and decades of colonial conflict with Spanish Florida, the English made permanent their claims to the Sea Islands, chartering the town of Beaufort in 1711. They introduced cattle, rice, indigo, Sea Island cotton, and African slavery to the lowcountry, creating one of the wealthiest plantation societies in North America. The children of that wealth had time for leisure and literary pursuits. William J. Grayson (1788–1863) became the poet laureate of the Sea Islands, which he described in his poem "Chicora."

> . . . those isles of the summer seas,
> Where stories say, no winters come . . .

In the blessed land, the spirits home
A richer verdure spreads the ground,
The sky is of a softer blue,
And scattered in profusion round
Are flowers of every shape and hue;
Their fragrance on the unsated breeze
Floats exquisite and evermore
On purple vines and bending trees
Are various fruits, an endless store;
Innumerable birds prolong,
With chattering joy, their dainty cheer,
Of brighter plume and sweeter song
Than meet with mortal eye or ear. (Abridged)

Grayson's friend and contemporary William Elliott III (1788–1863) made an international reputation by describing the Sea Island world and the leisure pursuits of the planter class. Elliott's *Carolina Sports by Land and Water* is a classic of southern literature, kept in print by sporting enthusiasts on both sides of the Atlantic for 160 years. Elliott's most famous essay, "Devil Fishing," inspired the defining misadventure in Conroy's *Beach Music* when four boys in a small outboard motor boat harpoon a giant manta ray off Port Royal Sound. The great fish, one of the most powerful in the ocean, encircles the boat, disables the engine, and tows the boys and the boat far out to sea before they are rescued. Elliott's story took place in 1817 when he and his friends harpooned the manta ray, wrapped a heavy line around the anchor post, and let the giant tow their longboat around Port Royal Sound until it exhausted itself.

The American Civil War ended the world of the planter class and created a new world of freed slaves, small farms, and Yankee industry. But Union Army occupiers and their cadre of northern missionaries to the newly freed slaves were also entranced by this rare place. Charles Nordhoff, correspondent for *Harper's New Monthly* magazine, arrived in spring 1863 and penned his first impression: "Coming from the blustering and bleak March winds of New York, the climate here was enchanting. The breezes are soft, the skies have a tropical radiance; the yellow jassamine was in full bloom . . . and filled the air with its strong perfume."

When the war was over and the slaves were freed, Supreme Court Chief Justice and President Abraham Lincoln's wartime Secretary of the Treasury Salmon P. Chase (1808–73) toured the defeated former Confederacy. His guide was Reverend Richard Fuller (1804–1876), Beaufort native, Harvard graduate, and one of the most famous Baptist ministers in America. Accompanying this distinguished party was Whitelaw Reid (1837–1912), a young journalist with the *Cincinnati Enquirer* who would become a candidate for vice president with President Benjamin Harrison in 1892. They toured Beaufort and Port Royal, where the Reconstruction of the South began. They left Beaufort at night to travel by steamboat down to Hilton Head Island and continue their journey. Their conveyance was the packet steamer *Planter*, and their captain was Robert Smalls, hero to freedmen and Unionists alike and a future Beaufort statesman. It was an auspicious moment in Beaufort's history not lost on Whitelaw Reid, who recorded the magic of a Sea Island summer night in his published journal of his southern tour: "The breeze over the island was delicious; not a film of mist flecked the sky; and down to the very meeting of the sky and water, we caught the sparkle of the stars, brilliant with all the effulgence of a tropic night."

The Civil War's end brought an era of prosperity to the Sea Islands. In 1873 a new railroad connected Port Royal Sound to Augusta, Georgia, and the Sea Islands to the mainland for the first time. Lumber and coal were delivered to the port, and Atlantic maritime steamships made Port Royal both a coaling station and a port bustling with imports and exports. A U.S. naval station was established in Port Royal Sound, and the Navy bought Parris Island as a shipyard and coaling station. U.S. Marines followed. Phosphate rock, a source of mineral fertilizer, was mined from local river bottoms, providing thousands of industrial jobs for Sea Island freedmen.

Prosperity disappeared with the deadly Sea Island Hurricane of 1893. In the early twentieth century, Beaufort County declined in wealth and population. Between 1890 and 1940, 52 percent of the African American population of Beaufort County moved away. But the magical beauty of the

Sea Islands remained. Ruth Batchelder, whose family had migrated south from Peru, Vermont, visited Beaufort by steamboat from Savannah and left this comment in a 1917 article in *Travel* magazine: "Perhaps the longest to retain the romantic atmosphere of antebellum days are the picturesque Sea Islands of the lower Carolina coast. . . . There has always hung over these charming islands of the sea a veil of delicate mystery which the commercialist of the present age has not been able to penetrate." Batchelder called Beaufort, where her brother had a hardware store on Bay Street, "the queen city of the Sea Islands."

During the 1930s, in the depths of Beaufort's poverty, the town became a bit of a mecca for artists and writers, all drawn by the compelling beauty that had attracted people for centuries. The center for this literary group was the Gold Eagle Hotel that Kate Gleason built at the corner of Bay Street and New Street on land once owned by Henry W. DeSaussaure, the first director of the U.S. Mint. The hotel opened in 1930 and counted among its prominent guests Edison Marshall (1894–1967), author of fifty-seven books and two Hollywood movies and winner of the O. Henry Award in 1921; and Francis Griswold (1902–2001), the author of *A Sea Island Lady*, the most famous novel about Beaufort published before Pat Conroy embarked on his literary career.

More famous novelists sought refuge in Beaufort during World War II, including W. Somerset Maugham and Erskine Caldwell. The most permanent literary luminary in Beaufort was Samuel Hopkins Adams (1871–1958), a winter resident for twenty-three years, who wrote fifty books between 1905 and 1955. Seventeen were made into Hollywood movies. He was a member with Dorothy Parker and Alexander Wollcott of the famed "Round Table" group at New York's Algonquin Hotel and the literary critic for *New Yorker* magazine. Sam Adams never forgot his first arrival in Beaufort in 1935 and the effect it had on him. He described it in an article in *Lincoln-Mercury Times* 1950:

> The spell was cast as we turned off the main route, pursuing the vague report of an old and quiet city out among the sea islands. . . . The approach to Beaufort threads through broad marshlands and across shining rivers. . . . We entered the town proper between a long, double row of royal palmettos and rounded a

curve to blink amazedly at a floral riot in a private yard. There were camellias enough to choke the largest display window on 5th Avenue. Overhead a pair of chinaberry trees were festooned with the soft gray of the Spanish moss and spangled with the golden traceries of the wild jasmine. For background there spread the broad expanse of reed and river with a lordly white yacht on its way to Florida.

Pat Conroy was not the first writer to describe the special world of the Sea Islands, but he may have been the best. One of the places that influenced Pat's work was Dataw Island, where my family farmed for half a century. Pat had the run of the place and took imaginative possession of it when he made Dataw the model for Melrose Island in *The Prince of Tides*. He put the Wingo homestead on Jenkins Creek, where my father had built a cinder-block cottage with his own hands in 1936. When we were young, Pat and I and several friends spent many happy days there fishing and crabbing and watching the moon rise in summer skies. Through Tom Wingo's eyes Pat described Dataw in his prologue to *The Prince of Tides*: "It is growing dark on this long summer evening, at the exact point her finger had indicated, the moon lifted a forehead above the horizon, lifted right out of filigreed, light-intoxicated clouds that lay on the skyline in attendant veils. Behind us, the sun was setting in simultaneous, congruent withdrawal and the river turned to flame in a quiet duel of gold." For five centuries, explorers, settlers, travelers, and commentators have written about the beauty of the southern coast. In all that time, no one has captured the magic of the Sea Islands better than our Pat Conroy.

A Rare Kind of Generosity

~ ASHLEY WARLICK

The first time I ever heard about Pat Conroy I was probably ten years old. My parents were getting dressed up, heading out, leaving us with a sitter. They were having drinks with friends and then going to see a movie called *The Lords of Discipline* that was about my dad.

It was really a movie about the college my dad graduated from, a place I knew ran by its own set of strange and ritualized standards, and it was the source of many of my dad's best stories. There was the one where he got caught selling ladies' underwear. There was the one where he threw the test geology rock out the classroom window. There was the one where he orchestrated a tunnel to be dug through the dirt floor under his footlocker all the way to the car he had parked off-campus. Knobs ferried the dirt away in their laundry bags. He got caught one Thanksgiving break, a picture of the commandant standing in the tunnel broadcast to all the local papers. He was demoted from company commander to cadet private and barely allowed to graduate.

I loved these stories. They flexed and shifted with each telling, sometimes more detail, sometimes new details. But they were always funny, with a scoundrel's sense of a hero, and nobody got hurt. My parents returned from the movie, and I remember my mother was fairly horrified at the glimpse it offered into this time in my dad's life before she knew him. "They made the freshmen walk in the gutter," she said. "No son of mine will be going to that school."

My first real experience with Pat Conroy was reading *The Prince of Tides*. I was a college freshman, believed I wanted to be a writer but had yet to write a word, and I picked up a fat paperback copy on Christmas break. The movie was about to come out, and I wanted to read the book before I saw it.

I was both conflicted and absorbed. Pat's sentences were big and beautiful and graphic in ways that impressed me, and the story was dark, tangled, and laced with family. Family I understood to be based on his own family. Events I understood to be based on events that had happened to him.

This made me profoundly uncomfortable.

The ease with which he drew from the private places in his life—abuse, suicide, shame—seemed to me to be somehow cheating. I was eighteen years old, and I knew my own dark things, protected my own family secrets. Those were not for telling, and novels were supposed to be imagined. Before I went back to college I talked my brother into cutting class, and we went to see *The Prince of Tides* in the middle of the day. I cried in all the sad parts, even though I knew what was coming next.

The first time I met Pat in person we were attending a literary festival put on by the Hoover Library in Birmingham, Alabama. Pat was on hand to introduce his good friend Anne Rivers Siddons, who was being honored, and I had just published my first novel. My parents had driven down from Charlotte to meet me for the weekend, and we were gathered backstage when Pat walked up behind me and my mother and put an arm around each of our shoulders. He said, "I heard tell there was a novelist here by the name of Ashley Warlick. Now, I knew a Frank Warlick at The Citadel, but he couldn't even read, let alone raise a daughter who could write a book."

My father was just walking up with glasses of champagne.

They laughed and shook hands, and I was aware, given what I knew about the culture of The Citadel, that my father had undoubtedly made Pat's life hell once upon a time. That night, Pat told stories about my father I'd never heard, stories that made my father go quiet with something like contrition or maybe loss, something I'd never seen happen before. Watching his face, I thought about why we protect what we protect, and what kind of protection silence really is.

Later in my writing life, Pat offered kind comments on my novels, single-sentence five-hundred-word e-mails, booming messages on my answering machine, and invitations to meet for breakfast when he would come to town. He gave encouragement and advice and bear hugs freely, and went out of his way to do so. I believe it gave him joy to see other writers succeed, which is a rare kind of generosity.

In 2015, I and three other women opened M. Judson Booksellers and Storytellers in Greenville, South Carolina. We invited Pat to be our guest for a special ticketed dinner as part of our community campaign. He agreed immediately, and that evening he signed book after book for friends and family and for our shelves. We had worked on the menu with a fantastic local chef, and before each dish was served we read a passage from one of Pat's books that had inspired it, quite literally feasting on his words. Pat would laugh and clap and say something self-deprecating. When it was time for dessert, the chef came out from the kitchen to read the passage from Pat's cookbook about his mother-in-law's pound cake, a pound cake that spoke volumes to him of the woman he'd never known but who was responsible for his beloved wife, Cassandra. The chef cried. I cried. We all cried.

And then Pat stood, and he told us how proud he was to have been a part of opening our bookstore. He said, "A bookstore to me is more important than all the churches. It does more for the spirit." And it was communion there for a moment. It was one of the great evenings of my life.

After everyone had gone home, I walked Pat to where Sandra had pulled the car around. He was physically spent, and I wonder now if he knew he was sick. But they were headed to Winston-Salem that night for a literary festival where Pat was to lend support to a group of writers he'd championed in his Story River Books imprint, and the Conroys wouldn't be arriving until after midnight. The last thing Pat said to me was this: "Tell your father I forgive him for all the horrible things he's done."

He said it with that twinkle in his eye that was both teasing and reflective of his giant spirit. He really did forgive and love and champion, and all of those things are bound up in complicated ways with my father, and with telling stories, and with what really happened. Which I am learning, by example, to be generous with.

The Great Yes

~ TIM CONROY

In 1993, eight months before our youngest brother, Tom, committed suicide, I visited Pat at his house on Fripp Island. It was in late November, one of those rare opportunities when I would get to spend time alone with Pat surrounded by a thousand books in the geography he loved best. This was going to be an epic brothers' weekend. And that meant drinking Pat's liquor and wine, enjoying his wizardry with fresh seafood, discovering what he was reading, prying out information about what he was writing, and talking about everything and everyone. I was excited to tell him about a poem I was struggling to write about Einstein and how our lives are a womb-to-tomb blur or some such bullshit.

He was working on *Beach Music* at the time. Neither of us had an inclination that he would be forced by events to add this line in the dedication of his novel: "And to Thomas Patrick, our hurt brother and lost boy, who took his own life on August 31, 1994." Our youngest brother, Tom, who struggled with paranoid schizophrenia, was thirty-three years old when he died.

I was living in McClellanville and working as a special education teacher at Browns Ferry Elementary near the Black River in rural Georgetown County. Honestly, both Pat and I were messes. Pat's second marriage had failed in epic proportions, and my marriage was flirting with disaster. Terrye and I would reconcile in part because of the grief and pain we shared over Tom's suicide. I would pour what was left of myself back into her generous arms.

But during the fall of '93, Pat called me weekly late at night. "Bro, Bro, Bro, Bro," he would tease. We began our favorite game of dissecting the bloodline. No one was spared and no truth left out. "Heard from Carol?" He would laugh when I answered as the Great Santini, "Negative, pal." When Mike's turn came, we would praise him like he was Saint Jude for all he was doing to help Tom. Next was Kathy gossip, then Jim time, but we struggled when we got to Tom. We spoke in brief, anguished exchanges and could only salvage the moment with a tragic but hilarious Tom story to help us get through it. The family decoder ring: *tragedy becomes the fodder for Conroy humor.* That's how we survived it all.

I knew little about the storyline of *Beach Music* except that Pat referred to it as a "brother book." I suspected later that his invitation was somewhat motivated by a chance for him to observe me like a lab rat so I might reveal the finer oddities of Tee McCall, the pitiful and vocabulary-challenged character he created in mockery of me in *Beach Music.* In other words, the writer brother was mining family material again. But that didn't matter a bit then or ever to me.

The weekend was magical. Pat told story after story, and I did my usual gut spilling. He loved to hear about my teaching, but he was especially interested in hearing about my struggle with writing poetry. I told him about my poem idea and that I didn't know where to begin or how to pull it off.

Pat flew into action. He piled up book after book in my arms, explaining that I had to read the poems of Robert Penn Warren, James Dickey, C. P. Cavafy, and countless others. I followed him around like a puppy as he scoured bookshelves for prose and poetry to give me. If they showed any interest in an author or a genre, no guest or visitor ever left Pat's house without a stack of books.

That's when he launched into a story I'd heard many times before and would hear many times again. He opened the Cavafy book of poems and read to me "Che Fece . . . Il Gran Refiuto." The message of the poem is stark and foreboding. There comes a day when we each must choose a path with conviction. Some will recognize that moment and say the "Great Yes," but others will say the "Great No," and that No becomes the repetitious No of their lives. Those who choose the Great No defend their mistake and forever deny the path of the Great Yes. As teenagers, Pat and Carol would tease one another relentlessly about who would have the courage to choose the Great

Yes and who would ruin their lives with the Great No. Theirs was a literate and tenacious sibling rivalry.

I'm sure we finished the weekend watching football and falling into the companionable silences that happen when you know someone well. As I was packing on Sunday, Pat brought in a red legal-sized journal to add to all the books he had given me. I tossed it in my bag, we said our good-byes, bear-hugged, and he told me to visit again soon. The weekend had been emotional for me, and on the drive home I was contemplating if I had said the Great No by mistake long ago.

That evening, back in McClellanville, I opened the journal. In the miniscule scrawl of Pat's hand, I read the following:

To my beloved brother Tim,
Know you are greatly and deeply loved by a large number of carefully and not so carefully selected people. That you are going through a rough year, and the rough ones seem to provide grace and insight and wisdom that leads to serenity and understanding. Write in this journal. Find your own voice. Most people never find theirs. But you have a deep, rich, and exciting one that you are still trying to find. You've got to write down what you think or you never hear what you are trying to say.

The advice in the inscription, though written for me (especially the phrase "not so carefully selected people"), was what he told everyone who ever dreamt about becoming a writer. He could spot the person who needed to tell a story within a split second of entering a room even if they didn't know it yet. Whether it was Bernie Schein or John Warley or Valerie Sayers or Terry Kay or Doug Marlette or a stranger in line at a marathon book signing, his was a resounding message of encouragement to any aspiring writer.

We have stories we must tell. He believed this down to the worn-out Crocs on his pudgy Irish feet. If you are willing to read great books and work your ass off to write down what you are thinking and find your voice, it's possible to emerge as a writer. To Pat there was no more sacred and worthwhile calling. You only need look at the example of wonderful books and courageous voices he championed in his Story River Books writers.

Pat was my oldest brother and I am left stunned by his absence. I miss how he would call bullshit on me and how he would insist I dig deeper as a writer. His phone calls were an art form—a comedy routine, a passionate rant, instructive advice—and while these conversations came intermittently, I never wanted them to end. I will miss the random call late at night for the rest of my life. Like the one a few years after Tom's death when he called to read me Mary Oliver's poem "Wild Geese" and we both wept for ten minutes as I asked him to read it again and again. Somehow the release of guilt and slow healing over Tom started then for both of us. The tragedy of Tom's death wreaked havoc, changed our trajectories in mysterious ways, and brought our family closer together than it had ever been before.

Pat finished writing *Beach Music* and it was published in 1995, the same year he met Cassandra King. He fell in love with a gifted writer, an idiosyncratic truth teller, a farmer's daughter, a weed puller, a barefoot mystic and seeker who brought him a serenity he had never known before. He loved her family and her sons like crazy. Those last few months, I watched her care for him like he was a tender perennial for as long as she could. Sandra was the master gardener of his life, and whenever you are near her, know that you are as close to Pat's heart as you can ever be.

Pat will never write another word of his own, but he is still inspiring the words of others. On behalf of his great love for aspiring writers of any age, let the advice in Pat's inscription be for you too. Make your voice be part of his legacy. Read great books. Bring truth and pain and joy to the page. Write at high and stormy tides with interesting verbs and adjectives, throw surprise punches, use tragedy, use hope, drive your family crazy, pepper us with insults and humor and friendship, put nothing off limits, then go deeper to tell it all while connecting our souls to the vibrancy of your surroundings. Love and live and write as long and as big as you can. Say the Great Yes and discover the stories only you can to tell. But do my family one favor: when you finish your first book, list Pat Conroy next to a beloved sibling or a supportive friend in the acknowledgments.

I never finished that poem about Einstein and the blur of time. But somewhere along the path I found conviction. After Pat's death, my poem "Theology of Terrain" was used as part of Kathleen Robbins's installation

"Descent: Mississippi Delta photographs 1999–2014" at the Columbia Museum of Art. The exhibit curators converted my work into a six-foot poem, about the height of Pat, and displayed it next to Kathleen's remarkable photographs.

What happened next Pat would describe as one of the curious circles of life that you notice if you're lucky to live long enough. In the main exhibit hall, photographs of Daufuskie Island taken by Jeanne Moutoussamy-Ashe were on display. Included with her "Daufuskie Memories" exhibit in a glass case in the middle of the room was Pat's original handwritten manuscript of *The Water Is Wide*. My poem was a hundred feet away from Pat's masterpiece. Such is the magic, power, and honor of the Great Yes. Pat whispered it years ago in Beaufort, the two words that change a life forever.

The Great Conroy

An Homage to a Southern Literary Giant
and a Prince of a Guy

~ RICK BRAGG

He left the message every few months, the same message, word for word.

"Bragg? This is Conroy. It is now obvious that it is up to me to keep this dying friendship alive. You do not write. You do not call. But I am willing to carry this burden all by myself. It is a tragedy. Ours could have been a father-son relationship, but you rejected that. And now it is all up to me to keep this dying [bleep, bleep, bleepity, bleeping] friendship from fading away . . ."

And then there would be a second or so of silence before:

"I love you, son."

That part always sounded real.

I would always call back, immediately, but the voicemail just told me it was full, always full. I would learn, over decades, that it was full because I was not the only writer or friend he had adopted, or even the only one he left that same message of mock disappointment and feigned regret. But now and then I would actually be there when he called, and we would talk an hour or two about writers and language and why I should love my mother, and he would always, always tell me he had read my latest book and how proud he was of me.

Then he would tell me how he did not mind that I had neglected our friendship and that his broad shoulders could carry the weight of my indifference, and the phone would go dead.

This essay was originally published in *Southern Living*, May 2016.

My God, I will miss that.

Pat Conroy died on the edge of spring. I won't try to add anything to the gilded language said over him; those who have read him know of the elegance there. I just know he was different from others at the top of his craft, different in his generosity. He was a champion, even for those who pretended not to need one.

Some two decades ago, when my first book was just months from publication, he wound up with a bound galley and actually read it all, and he sent a message to my publisher with his thoughts. We call such endorsements, inelegantly, "blurbs." This was the best blurb ever written, lustrous and— now that I have had twenty years to consider it—undeserved.

But a thousand people since have told me they read it because he told them to and quote the last line of that blurb to me: "I wept when the book ended . . . and I sent flowers to his mother."

But it was what happened months later that mattered most. He and his soon-to-be wife, the fine writer Cassandra King, came to visit my mother in Alabama and brought her half a German chocolate cake. (My mother was too kind to ask what happened to the other half.) As he left, he offered to take my mother and elderly aunts home with him. "I'll cook for you," he said. He told me later he was impressed by my big brother and my sister-in-law. He looked in their faces and saw the utter absence of Old South pretension and fell in love with that, too, a little.

As he left, I knew I was now only the second most popular writer in our home; *The Water Is Wide* is my mother's favorite book. Because of Pat we see the good in Santini and know that any man, no matter how wounded or damaged, can be a prince of tides. We will miss the words he had still to write.

We will miss a damn sight more than that.

Pat's Choice

∼ CONNIE MAY FOWLER

Amid the toil of day-to-day travails, sometimes the universe is abundantly kind, delivering to us at just the right moment the exact person we need to meet.

It was 1995 and my second novel, *River of Hidden Dreams*, had been published a few months earlier. Much to my dismay, the novel and I—conjoined for life—found ourselves in turbulent waters.

The previous spring a close friend and mentor had introduced me at a prepublication reading, telling the audience I was experiencing "the second book curse." This was news to me but would turn out to be prescient.

My publisher, who largely behaved as if I did not exist, chose not to promote the book in any appreciable way. And when they did promote it, I felt as though their plans were forged with one purpose: humiliation.

Case in point: At the American Library Association convention during a ritual I had come to dread—the author signings—my publisher gave away the books of all the authors present except for *River of Hidden Dreams*, for which they charged full price. I sat there like the Maytag Repair Lady. Librarians aren't known for their deep pockets, but I think they felt sorry for me, sorry enough to avert their eyes, a coping mechanism I do not hold against them.

Reviews for the book were largely positive, but the negative comments were the ones that stuck, a Gregorian chant of glib barbs playing ceaselessly through my brain.

After two months of what I can only describe as constant misery and belittlement, I ended up at a book soirée in some southern city—Nashville or Memphis, I think—and I was whipped. What once felt like my greatest accomplishment—getting published—now felt like the latest cruelty in a long line of mean moments—my parents' violent relationship, my father's death when I was six, my mother's madness that manifested in both physical and psychological abuse.

This writer needed kindness.

Amid the throngs I stood alone in a hall during the soirée's opening-night author reception. I knew no one. Shy by nature in the best of circumstances, I wanted to disappear, to erase my corporeal and spiritual selves from this public aspect of a writer's life. To very possibly never, never pick up the pen again.

Gripping my chardonnay, I scanned the room for the quickest route out. Everyone seemed to know each other. Everyone seemed happy. Everyone seemed beautiful, talented, smart, self-assured. If I left, no one would even notice. I ordered my feet to do the one thing required of them in this life: ferry me to where I wanted to go, which in this case was the isolated safety of my hotel room. Nope, not going to happen. Immobilized by fear, dread, self-consciousness, I had, without any effort, become a potted plant.

If I stood still long enough, perhaps no one would even glance in my direction. Or if they did, they would mistake me for a waiter. They would hand me their empty glasses and glide on by.

Yes, I should give up writing and wait tables again. You truly are a fraud. Just a big fat mistake. Leave now before you embarrass everyone here.

I willed myself not to disintegrate into tears. Crying had become my number one hobby, something I was really, really good at. Once I started, boy oh boy, the waterworks were nearly impossible to shut off. I felt the threat rise, a tsunami behind my pupils. *Please, dear God, no.* I downed my chardonnay in one great gulp and was just about to crawl out if my feet continued to play lame when a portly, cherub-cheeked man walked up and said, "Hey, aren't you Connie May Fowler? I love your books. You're the real deal, girl."

I looked at that face. Sweet openness. No guile. Not a stitch of meanness.

"Y-y-y-yes," I stammered.

"Don't you just hate these things?" he asked, and by the tilt of his head and the bemused light in those blue eyes I knew he really wanted an answer.

The pressure evaporated. The tsunami receded. My frazzled nerves rebraided themselves, and I felt my universe tilt toward something that resembled alignment.

That's how Pat Conroy saved me, by walking over to a young woman whom he probably sensed was in way over her head and saying something kind.

We found a table away from the madding crowd, and he asked me how things were going. I told him. Pat, who was there to promote his latest novel, *Beach Music*, was not a man with whom you equivocated. It was all the truth or nothing. When I finished my tale of woe, he said, "Let me tell you something. The publishing world is full of a lot of good people. But it also has more than its fair share of shit asses."

Shit asses. Yes. Those were the words one of the finest writers of our time used to describe the folks who held our futures in their hands. Shit asses. How delightful! How true!

Over the years I would come to learn his words were pure Pat: no pretense; just unvarnished honesty delivered in as deadpan a manner as a southerner can possibly muster.

He then went on to tell me in detail exactly why they were shit asses. His reasoning was not petty, cute, or mean-spirited. It was just the facts, the world as Pat perceived it, one in which cruelty or ignorance surely sometimes owned the day but never totally won out.

In his dissection, his keen intellect and penchant for self-deprecation shined bright, as did his belief in the basic goodness of people. Over one glass of wine it became clear that Pat was a man who called them like he saw them, but in the calling never compromised his humanity or considered himself superior. He was engaged with the human condition like no other person I've met before or since.

Pat and I stayed in touch through the years—not as much as we should have, but that was my fault as much as his. Life happens, as we say. And he seemed to have a preternatural sense about when people were in crisis and needed a listening ear, a hearty laugh. When we did talk or e-mail or meet at some literary function, it was as if no amount of time had passed. We took up where we left off, brother and sister, comrades in arms against hubris, comrades in arms in support of the miracle task that chose us: the curious act of writing.

I have seen Pat sit for hours at a table in a large convention hall and sign books, remember names, remember babies' names, engage with fans as if they were truly important to him. And they were. I don't think Pat perceived them as fans. He saw them as fellow travelers. That's how big his heart was. The human race was his family.

I've often wondered why Pat and I were simpatico and why his honest assessments of people and situations—even when they carried the funny stench of shit asses—thrilled me so. And then one day, when I was research-ing his work because I was mentoring a student whose critical thesis was a comparative study of *The Great Santini* and *The Prince of Tides*, I ran across this quote of Pat's: "My father's violence is the central fact of my art and my life." I must have read that sentence aloud a dozen times. "My father's vio-lence is the central fact of my art and my life."

And then I knew. I could just as truthfully assert that my *mother's* vio-lence is the central fact of my art and my life.

Pat could have allowed the cruelty to harden him, make him mean, make him repeat the sins of his father. But Pat made a conscious decision, I believe, to live a life that stood in total opposition to the violence. He found for-giveness through writing and grace in a life well lived, a life we will always remember not only through his books but also in his innumerable small and great acts of kindness to both strangers and beloveds.

Pat gave me the example of how to be a writer in this hard world. His kindness to me at a moment when I was imploding is a seminal reason I get up every day determined to be understanding—to try to love without blinders, to approach my fellow humans with bountiful measures of intel-lect and insight—sinners, saints, and shit asses all.

To Catch a Thief

∿ WILLIAM A. BALK JR.

Very soon after I had moved back to Beaufort, South Carolina, and begun working in a venerable downtown bookstore, on one of those quiet days booksellers learn to cherish, I looked up from shelving newly arrived titles to see a rather shambolic character coming through the front door in well-worn clothes and with a noticeably distracted manner. Something about him set off my shoplifter-detection radar, so I shifted into my big-city observant detective mode.

Odd characters were nothing new to me, not in Washington bookstores or in Beaufort. The bookstore regulars were often odd, or characters, or both; they fit in easily among the grandes dames, power brokers, students, hipsters, housewives, and the occasional street person who made up our clientele. Oddballs and characters were always welcomed and were always offered assistance.

The ones you had to look out for were those you couldn't "read," the ones whose intentions were obscure. Sometimes this meant that some misguided soul had wandered into the bookstore intent on slipping out with a few hot volumes to fence down the street—a sad prospect with little likelihood of reward.

I couldn't "read" this guy who had just come in making a beeline for the back of the store. Disheveled, a ruddy, round face inadequately topped by a breeze-tousled comb-over, and an expression that hinted at something mischievous—well, I knew at least that this guy needed to be watched.

A version of this essay was first published on WeeklyHubris.com.

Thanks to all that training in Washington bookstores, I rarely had reason to be fearful of someone planning on shoplifting a book, and I wasn't uncomfortable approaching such a person in the store. Summoning determination, I headed to the back where our special section of books on the lowcountry was shelved—books hard to find, books especially sought after by our clientele, books often bought and shipped all over the country. My suspicious customer was there going over the more unusual titles on the shelves.

I offered my assistance with as much geniality as I could muster. I had found in the past that persistent offers of assistance often resulted in a hasty retreat.

Instead, my suspect's countenance lit up when I offered my assistance; he assured me he didn't really need assistance, but would I suggest something for him to read? *Dammit!* I thought. This was either a skilled riposte by a mastermind bent on thwarting my antitheft techniques . . . or the engaging response of a joyful reader.

I am a practiced—even skilled—hand seller of books. I need a bit of history, some interesting tidbits about a reader's responses to books already read, to formulate a rough idea of where a reader's interests lie. This guy was revealing nothing to me. Then he proceeded to inquire about my own reading discoveries recently—most of which he had either read or had acquired but not yet opened.

If he was planning on shoplifting, this suspicious character was a past master at disarming store security. He was charming, witty, engaging, and unassuming. We spoke for a little while, I found several titles I was fond of and that he had not read, he thanked me, bought them, and left. His credit card read "Donald P. Conroy." Pat Conroy.

It would be the first of many encounters.

Not too long after that first meeting, I looked up to see Pat coming into the store and headed straight for me. He looked at me very directly and said, "So! You're *that* Will Balk!"

When we had met that first time, when I had been so suspicious of him, we had not introduced ourselves. I was more than a little surprised that he had learned my name somewhere.

At the time, Pat's new novel-in-progress was infamously delayed. Rumors abounded throughout the book business about its subject, about its length, about whether it would ever be finished. The book would be titled, it was said, *Beach Music*, a title that resonates with particular meaning for Carolinians of a certain age; and it would reputedly center on the lives of a group of 1960s radical students who encounter each other years after a defining action in which they had all participated. It would as well draw on characters and events Pat knew intimately—as does everything Pat wrote.

"So! You're *that* Will Balk!"

Pat had been at a dinner party the night before with mutual friends, he said, and much of the discussion was about *Beach Music*. The guests remembered well the real events and real characters from the '60s that Pat's long-delayed novel centered on. It was only in that raucous dinner discussion, Pat told me, that he learned that I—the overly suspicious bookseller he had just met downtown—had been one of the central figures in the actual events on which the book turned; that I was one of the core group of real-life friends whose fictional intersecting lives provided the crux of the story he was writing.

So, indeed, I became "*that* Will Balk."

A customer of our store since high school, Pat had his first book signing for his first book, *The Boo*, there. He had signings there—often several—for every one of his books that followed. By the time I met him so awkwardly, Pat had been all over the world and had become "Pat Conroy, celebrity," a fact that left him both grateful and dismayed. He was now settled back in Beaufort, where he would spend the rest of his life.

In those halcyon days of bookselling, publishers would often send galley copies before publication to influential booksellers. I had been sent an early copy of Michael Cunningham's *The Hours*, and I was so taken with the novel that I began telling everyone I could find to read it when it was released. It became an astounding success for us, selling hundreds of copies in both hard- and soft-cover.

Pat was a frequent visitor to the store, and he always asked for recommendations. Every visit, I would try to get him to read *The Hours*, but Pat would always decline. Finally, just a day before he was to leave for a trip to Ireland, he came in to get something to read. I handed him a copy of *The Hours* and told him, "I'm buying this for you. Now take it." Somewhat reluctantly, he did.

A week later, I got a call from Pat at JFK Airport in New York. "Listen, damn it! How the hell you did that, I will never know! Here I am flying back from Ireland, I finished that damn *The Hours* over the Atlantic, I open my *New York Times* . . . and plastered everywhere is the news that *The Hours* not only won the PEN/Faulkner Award, but it won the Pulitzer as well. How the hell did you know?"

I laughed and said of course I couldn't have known so long ago.

"Shut up and listen," Pat interjected. "I got off the plane and called Jonathan Galassi . . . " (NB: the editor of Farrar, Straus and Giroux, who published *The Hours*) " . . . and told him there was this crazy bookseller in tiny little Beaufort, South Carolina, who had singlehandedly sold thousands [sic] of copies of this book, and who had personally forced me to read it against my better judgment. I told him," continued Pat, "you owe this guy. I mean it!"

Within a week I had received a gracious handwritten note from Mr. Galassi along with a copy of *The Hours* inscribed with a note from Michael Cunningham.

I ran into Pat at the Pat Conroy at 70 festival in Beaufort in October 2015. He called me over, disregarding for a moment the crowd of fans yearning to speak with him. He wanted to introduce me to his companion, Jonathan Galassi, who had flown down from New York for the celebration. It had been fifteen years since that phone call from JFK Airport, yet Pat related the entire story, in every detail, to Mr. Galassi.

In the twenty-odd years I knew Pat Conroy, whenever I would encounter him, in places distant from Beaufort or near, he never failed to offer a huge embrace or a warm kiss on the cheek. I have been surprised in train stations and concert halls in major cities to hear Pat's booming voice call out, "Hey! *that* Will Balk."

That was no thief I pursued ages ago in the bookstore. Thousands of us willingly, happily, offered up our hearts to him, and he treasured those gifts. There was nothing for him to steal—it was all his.

An Invitation into His World

～ JUDY GOLDMAN

"Judy! Your book is about Jews!"

That's Pat Conroy sounding like God delivering a proclamation. I'd never met him, never received a phone call from him before this Sunday morning in 1998.

My husband, Henry, and I were having a late breakfast on the screened porch. I lowered the speaker part of the phone, pointed to it, silently mouthed to Henry, *Oh my God it's Pat Conroy the Pat Conroy right now calling me!*

And then I spoke into the phone with all innocence: "Does this mean you don't want to read it?"

"Actually, I *do* want to read your book," Pat said. "Jews are my subject!"

I had called him weeks before to ask if he'd consider reading my soon-to-be-published first novel and maybe write a blurb, at which point he'd told me he was a "blurb slut," but that Dannye Powell, our mutual friend who'd shared with me his contact information, should stop plastering the walls of public bathroom stalls with his phone number. He told me to have my publisher send him an advance reader's copy and he'd get back to me. In that same conversation, which lasted more than an hour, we also talked about Monica Lewinsky's stained blue Gap dress and how much we both still liked Bill Clinton.

Every few hours over the next two days, he called to discuss what he'd just read. "Did this really happen?" he'd ask. I'd fill him in on the background. Because my novel was so autobiographical, there was plenty of background to fill him in on. He asked a million questions about my family, my world. And, because my book was about sisters, he had his own stories to tell.

If you knew Pat, you know how this is going to end. Of course he wrote the blurb. Not just any blurb. A marvel of a blurb. Crafted in such a way that anybody reading it would feel like a complete idiot if they didn't buy my book.

But a blurb was not all he gave me.

He also gave an invitation: "Judy, I want you and Reid to come to my daughter's wedding next weekend on Fripp Island."

For a minute I didn't know who Reid was. Was he fixing me up with a date? Then I got it. Reid was the husband of the narrator in my novel. Pat knew that the character was loosely based on my real-life husband. So, instead of using his real name, Pat called him Reid. He continued to call him Reid all the years of our friendship. Much later, Sandra, Pat's wife, told me, "I never knew your husband was named Henry!"

"No, no, we can't come to your daughter's wedding," I said. "A wedding is for family and close friends. We should *not* be there."

"You have to come," he insisted with that pure doggedness I came to know as one of his main traits. "You invited me into your world with your book. Now I'm inviting you into mine."

So we spent the next weekend on Fripp Island. There was the rehearsal dinner Friday night in Pat and Sandra's backyard, which is where we first met the two of them. Then the wedding and reception on Saturday followed by the small, bustling family brunch in their kitchen Sunday morning.

Reid (Henry) and I were right there with all the relatives and close friends, and we felt Pat's protective arm around us the whole time. "I'd like you to meet Judy and Reid," he'd say to a brother or sister-in-law. I'm sure they wanted to ask, *Who are you?* Instead, they smiled and nodded and brought us into their conversations, into their world. I kept telling Pat, "We're fine, you don't need to look out for us, we're having a great time."

As time went on, I realized I'd been invited into a much bigger world than just a wedding weekend.

He loved to offer publishing advice. When he gave me his blurb he said, "This is the last good thing that will happen to you as a result of publication." He was right. He understood that having a book published is never all it's cracked up to be—like everything in life that's supposed to be utterly transformative, but isn't.

Eventually, he told me the reason he gives so many blurbs is that he could not get a single established writer to say yes to him for his own first novel.

Everyone who knew Pat knows you did not call him. If you tried, you got his mailbox, which was usually full and not accepting messages. It had been a fluke I got through that first time.

Every few months he called. Each conversation began with: "I'm working hard to keep this dying friendship alive."

He always asked to speak to Reid. They argued over which was worse— Jewish guilt or Catholic guilt. And which was rougher—growing up with a military father or with a Jewish mother.

Pat invited me into a world shaped by his ability to make the people he connected with feel as though we'd been made new, as though we had become a better thing. Publication had, in fact, been transformative, just not in the way I'd expected. Instead, it gave me Pat. And his immeasurable attention. His immeasurable affection. Like the man himself, his world was unconfined excess—an excess of wonderfully wrought tales, good food, bursts of exclamations, and laughter. It was a world that did not know its own ending and was shocked by it.

Santini's Son Was More Heroic Than Tragic

~ ANDY MARLETTE

We are gathered here today to thank God for Pat Conroy.

America's greatest living author died a little more than a week ago. But like the tides that seep and swell within his beloved South Carolina marshes, his words return eternal.

News reports memorialized the tragic figure of Conroy—the famous author raised and abused by the equally famous fighter pilot; the eldest child of the Great Santini, the beaten boy, the broken son; the brilliant artist forged by a tortured childhood. All of it was true. So much of the man's life was scarred by sadness.

But he was also one of the funniest, toughest, and most heroic humans I ever met. A brief story of that heroism:

Conroy and my late, great, cartoon-drawing uncle, Doug Marlette, were best friends. Not like Facebook best friends. They were talk-on-the-phone-every-day-for-hours best friends. I do not know what they talked about other than everything. National headlines and college basketball. Thomas Wolfe's brilliance and the Clintons' narcissism. The virtues of creative assertiveness and the social treachery of passive aggression. Had they not been such admirers of the English language I would have suspected they'd invented their own vernacular the way some twins do. They were brothers.

Having been convinced by Conroy to try out the highfalutin art of novel writin', Uncle Doug's first book, *The Bridge*, came out in 2001. It was based on the town of Hillsborough, North Carolina, where our family roots ran back

This essay originally appeared in the *Pensacola News Journal*, March 12, 2016.

to the good ol' days of textile mills, labor abuses, and government-enforced violence against poor folks who dared speak up for better rights. Decades later, modern Hillsborough became hip. Duke University professors, vegans, and liberals of all stripes bought cottages and lattes on the same streets where my grandfather once ran barefoot during his childhood. "These days the town features an advanced white-wine-and-brie-in-bulk community of writers and other bourgeois bohemians," my uncle wrote.

Well, upon reading *The Bridge*, some of those bourgeois writers abruptly choked on their organic granola. They saw themselves caricatured in the book's description of modern Hillsborough—and they were not amused.

One writer resorted to weeping. Another tried to convince my uncle to edit down his novel. A third threatened a young publicist away from a job promoting the book. Anonymous reviews trashing it began to appear on Amazon. A bookstore at nearby University of North Carolina was pressured into canceling a signing. Weird, hand-written threats arrived in the mail, and the book was baselessly labeled "homophobic" within tolerance-preaching academic circles. Such is the treachery of passive aggression.

But then there was Conroy. He adored *The Bridge* so he stood up for it. Spoke up for it. Praised it and promoted it. Fought for it. And the clamoring clansmen of Hillsborough's offended, brie-breathed literati couldn't have collectively matched his wit, heart, and talent if there had been ten thousand of them. I have no idea what it's like to do battle in the realms of literature, intellectuals, and New York publishing houses. But it surely helps to have a literary giant fighting on your side.

The underhanded efforts to torpedo *The Bridge* ultimately failed. It won awards. It sold movie rights. And everyone in town read that book about poor folks that a few feckless elitists wanted banned.

After my uncle was killed in a car crash in 2007, Conroy delivered one of his eulogies. It read like a beautiful chapter from one of his books. And there was fight to it. In front of all the mourners, Conroy proposed titling his next book with a commandment to bring him the head of the weepy author who tried to have my uncle's book banned. He also pledged to annually dump one hundred of his own novels in the front yard of the other Hillsborough writer and set them ablaze lest those authors forget the "fine art of censoring books and being the enemies of free speech."

It was a moment of utter heroism: to defend art in the midst of the artist's death. But through The Citadel and Santini, Conroy was highly trained for such warfare.

Later in 2007, several parents in Charleston, West Virginia, sought to have a school board ban two of Conroy's books from its classrooms. The parents cited violence, profanity, and sexual content. A freedom-fighter student from the district wrote to notify Conroy. That young West Virginian was named Makenzie Hatfield. The gods of symbolic irony smile upon the world's great writers. So Conroy responded with the greatest letter to the editor I've ever read. Here's an excerpt:

These controversies are so commonplace in my life that I no longer get involved. But my knowledge of mountain lore is strong enough to know the dangers of refusing to help a Hatfield of West Virginia. I also do not mess with McCoys.

My English teachers pushed me to be smart and inquisitive, and they taught me the great books of the world with passion and cunning and love.... Few in the world have ever loved English teachers as I have, and I loathe it when they are bullied by know-nothing parents or cowardly school boards.

About the novels your county just censored: *The Prince of Tides* and *Beach Music* are two of my darlings which I would place before the altar of God and say, "Lord, this is how I found the world you made." They contain scenes of violence, but I was the son of a Marine Corps fighter pilot who killed hundreds of men in Korea, beat my mother and his seven kids whenever he felt like it, and fought in three wars. My youngest brother, Tom, committed suicide by jumping off a fourteen-story building; my French teacher ended her life with a pistol; my aunt was brutally raped in Atlanta; eight of my classmates at The Citadel were killed in Vietnam; and my best friend was killed in a car wreck in Mississippi last summer. Violence has always been a part of my world....

People cuss in my books. People cuss in my real life. I cuss, especially at Citadel basketball games.... The world of literature has everything in it, and it refuses to leave anything out....

The school board of Charleston, West Virginia, has sullied that gift and shamed themselves and their community. You've now entered the ranks of censors, book-banners, and teacher-haters, and the word will spread. Good teachers will avoid you as though you had cholera. But here is my favorite thing: Because you banned my books, every kid in that county will read them, every single one of them. Because book-banners are invariably idiots, they don't know how the world works—but writers and English teachers do. . . .

I salute the English teachers of Charleston, West Virginia, and send my affection to their students. West Virginians, you've just done what history warned you against—you've riled a Hatfield.

And all the English teachers say, "Ooh Rah!"

Such was the bravery and heroism of one of America's greatest authors. Books. Truth. Speech. With all the ferocity of a fighter pilot, the son of the Great Santini went to war for life's most sacred things. Thank God for Pat Conroy.

Pat Conroy and Telephone Noir

~ TERESA MILLER

Whenever I used to get late-night calls, I pretty much knew what to expect: a scam artist, a prankster, or one of the great writers of our time. And for nearly a decade I was unbelievably lucky—we're talking about the kind of luck that wins lotteries—for more often than not my caller would be Pat Conroy, author of *The Prince of Tides* and, yes, a telephone genius.

Naturally, this begs the question: Why would a master storyteller be calling me when he could ring up the likes of Barbra Streisand or John Grisham? So it wasn't easy explaining my role to a Delta flight attendant who phoned saying she'd discovered Pat's journal in the lost-and-found locker. Apparently, it included dozens of phone numbers, but my name and contact info had stood out, most likely because I wasn't famous, and she felt freer to reach out to me.

So this is the backstory: I knew Pat before I *knew* him. Naturally, I'd met him first through his novels and such classic lines as "My wound is geography," which gave place to the hurts so many of us carry. When you come from Oklahoma, the earthquake and tornado capital of the United States, those words even carry added meaning for you.

But it was our mutual friend, novelist and Pulitzer-winning cartoonist Doug Marlette, who eased Pat into my life in such a way that their history became part of what was to be our history. I'd known Doug for years, but after he moved to Tulsa we started having coffee every week—with Pat. Not in person, obviously, but Pat and Doug had daily phone chats, and before long we all became part of each other's conversations. So much so that Doug startled me one morning by announcing that Pat, haunted by my writer's block, had ordered my out-of-print books and was reading them.

A quick disclaimer here. I was only one of several writers that Pat did his best to mentor. And it's worth noting that, though many of these coffee chats included some pretty harsh critiques of politicians and other public figures, he never relayed criticism of another writer, be it a novice or a seasoned professional.

Needless to say, he already knew most of the country's major writers and regularly called them, too. But I did get to introduce him to one of his idols, Earl Hamner, creator of *The Waltons*, a particular favorite TV show for those of us from dysfunctional families. In fact, my grandmother had banned the show in our home, convinced that focusing on such a happy family would give me false expectations. It was a story that seemed to delight Pat, and he would regale me with his own tales about listening to the Waltons' good-night endearments even as the Conroys worked through their own repertoire of end-of-the day expletives.

It's only now, as I look back to that time, remembering how happy Pat was in Earl's company, that our essential history becomes clearer to me. We both had trouble finding grace in the night. We were, as he was to say later, of the same tribe.

That seemed especially true the morning Doug was killed in a freak car accident on the way home from his father's funeral. For it was later that same day that Pat called me for the first time, sobbing but leaving the line open even after silence overcame him. That was his message to me—there was still a connection between us.

He began to call me intermittently after that, usually late in the evening, that tricky juncture for both of us when we could navigate the darkest hours together. Suffice it to say, when I'd see *Donald Conroy* listed on the caller ID readout I'd breathe a sigh of relief, knowing that I'd have a restful night after all.

We always picked up where we'd left off because we had a regular canon that informed our visits: memories of Doug, best wishes for Earl, worries about family. Then we were free to cover the gamut, talking about his karaoke outings with his daughters, his nephew-in-law who was competing to be a "Bubba of the South," or such Oklahoma anomalies as thunder snow.

I mean, no one could work a phone like Pat. Even over a bad connection he could make you feel interesting. But he never learned much about the device itself. He once called from a hotel line, when he was on tour, to say that the cell phone his publishers had given him was basically inoperable. Translation: he was old school, way too chivalrous to resort to speed dial—or fool around with voicemail.

That's why I learned early on in our friendship not to leave a message. Instead, I'd just send an e-mail and he'd get right back to me. A word about Pat's e-mails—they were always in lower case. No name, whether it referred to his beloved *charleston* or the great *harper lee*, ever got that capital distinction.

I should also add that an e-mail to or from Pat was always risky, for he was likely to inadvertently forward to it to any number of his regular correspondents. One time I was in his e-mail loop for a YouTube video, "Nana Dancing," featuring an elderly woman getting down and jiving. This came without explanation or any sort of follow-up. You just had to accept Nana and jive with her yourself if it came to that.

Pat's calls, on the other hand, couldn't have been more exclusive and were definitely in all caps. Shortly before his final illness he invited me to come to Fripp Island to work on my book. When he sensed some reluctance on my part—related to my pets—he encouraged me to bring all three with me, declaring with total Conroy bravado: "MY FATHER-IN-LAW USED TO HAVE FORTY DOGS."

And then there were those wonderful closing moments, after an hour or so visit, when he'd sign off by reassuring you: "WITH CONROY IT'S THE REAL DEAL—GREAT LOVE."

Sometimes, though, our conversations took a darker turn, like the night he told me he didn't have many friends. I was stunned; he routinely alluded to dozens of people he kept in touch with on a regular basis. Of course, there'd once been Doug—like a brother to him. Then there was his former student Sallie Ann Robinson—like another daughter. So he was right to this extent: he didn't have many friends, because after someone was a friend for a week or two, he automatically granted them family status. In other words, he had a huge family.

It was usually as a last resort that we focused on writing. For despite Pat's great success as an author, he found the process of putting together a book, fiction or nonfiction, to be incredibly painful, in part because he dug deep and then forced himself to dig deeper. Think *The Death of Santini*, a memoir about what it meant to be a son, a brother.

He was struggling with the book even as he toured with *My Reading Life* and stopped in Memphis. *MRL*, his homage to such classics as *Gone with the Wind* and *To Kill a Mockingbird*, was a particular fan favorite, so he enjoyed a full day of book signings and parties. But he returned to his hotel room only to confront the defining loneliness of his *writing life*. Not that he questioned the constancy of family—or extended family. Like Tom Wingo in *The Prince of Tides*, he understood he was "a well-loved man." He just didn't know why.

He was especially puzzled when it came to his fans and their unabashed affection for him. Still, if being Pat Conroy and autographing a book or posing for a photo could brighten someone's day, he was all in. One year during a visit to Tulsa he was so seriously compromised, due to his diabetes, that he had trouble standing. His wife, Cassandra, was my ally and helped me relieve his burden without letting him know, simply by suggesting he sit on stage—cozier, we told him. It only worked until we got to the luncheon, when he skipped eating altogether, fighting his own pain, so he could move from table to table and shake hands with everyone who'd come to see him.

There was a last phone conversation that ironically focused on time, but we weren't maudlin about getting older. He even told me he was feeling better, that he was looking forward to resuming work on his new novel, that . . .

Sometimes the phone still rings after the rest of the world is already asleep, and I can't let it go. I mean, once Pat Conroy's rung through the night, you know what it means to really be called. So I remember my friend, pick up the receiver, and listen.

Farewell to Pat Conroy, Whose Words Made Him the Sexiest Man Alive

~ KATHLEEN PARKER

Soon after *The Prince of Tides* became a blockbuster movie in 1991, *People* magazine put the film's leading man, Nick Nolte, on its cover as the "Sexiest Man Alive."

This couldn't possibly be true, I thought (and wrote) at the time. Nolte, who played protagonist Tom Wingo, was a good-looking actor who did well by his role. But what made him sexy was the character created by beloved author Pat Conroy.

Conroy, I wrote, was the sexiest man alive.

It was Conroy, after all, who had crafted sentences so sensuously lush and true that they begged to be read aloud. He wrote that " . . . salmon dreamed of mountain passes and the brown faces of grizzlies hovering over clear rapids. Copperheads . . . dreamed of placing their fangs in the shinbones of hunters. Ospreys slept with their feathered, plummeting dreamselves screaming through deep, slow-motion dives toward herring."

It was Conroy who described South Carolina's seductive lowcountry as something you breathe: "the bold, fecund aroma of the tidal marsh, exquisite and sensual, the smell of the South in heat, a smell like new milk, semen, and spilled wine, all perfumed with seawater."

Ever after, there would be no point in anyone else trying to describe animal dreams or the marsh. Forevermore, the world would experience the lowcountry through Conroy's eyes.

Several years after that column, I met Conroy at a Naples, Florida, hotel where, serendipitously, we happened to have adjoining rooms. We discovered

This essay originally appeared in the *Washington Post*, March 8, 2016.

this while speaking to each other on the phone, a conversation that I was simultaneously hearing through the hotel wall.

Wondering whether we might be next-door neighbors, we poked our heads out our respective doors, receivers to ears, and were delighted to find ourselves face-to-face.

Over drinks later that evening, Conroy regaled me with stories, including that cartoonist Doug Marlette had teased him mercilessly about my sexiest-man-alive column. We talked about friends, family, children, and writing.

Why, he asked, hadn't I written my own father-daughter novel? I began to answer, "I was waiting . . . " when he interrupted to complete the sentence: "for your father to die."

Yes.

"I wish I had," he said. At the time, his father—the Great Santini—was up in their hotel room waiting for his son to escort him to the family wedding that had brought them to Naples.

Before we parted, I asked him, "What's it like to be Pat Conroy?"

He threw back his head and roared with laughter: "It's a dream!" he said, though I was never sure he really meant it. Sometimes, as his readers know, it was a nightmare, too.

One painful irony was his recognition that his books had liberated throngs of fellow sufferers—the depressed, the abused, the father haters—not to seek therapy or write books but to share their miseries with Conroy at book signings. This was unwelcome duty for a writer who wasn't inclined to guide others through their self-realization. Writing is not group therapy.

But such was the price Conroy paid for exposing so much of himself and his family, book after book, as he sought to explain his tortured childhood to himself.

When he wasn't writing Conroy was reading—four hours a day—or talking to Marlette on the phone, nearly every day for decades. Marlette, who wrote two novels of his own before his death in a 2007 car accident, also drew cartoons and comic strips. While he doodled he liked to talk to his friends.

One can only wish to have had a party line with those two, both raconteurs with razor-sharp vision, a wicked sense of humor, and a flair for expressing what most others hide or never notice.

The last time I saw Conroy was, alas, nine years ago at Marlette's funeral, where we were two among ten eulogists and became forever bonded as members of what Conroy dubbed "Team Marlette." Bereft beyond measure, we were nearly staggering with grief and choking on tears as we rendered our words of farewell. Conroy loved how, as we returned to our seats, the others would pat us on the back and offer commendations as though we'd scored a touchdown.

He found this both funny and heartbreakingly lovely. Now we are heartbroken again, our losing season upon us, another of our most brilliant players down. At least there is consolation in knowing that Conroy and Marlette can roar together now, laughing and weeping at the glory of it all—as ever the envy of the living.

.

III

Tributaries and Delta

◠ Sustained and Sustaining Friendships, Lasting Legacies

(Back to the lowcountry, Beaufort, the South, and Beyond)

Pat Conroy's Not-So-Secret Love Affair

⌒ WALTER EDGAR

On August 11, 2009, Pat signed a copy of *South of Broad*: *To Walter and Nela Edgar, For love of words and books and South Carolina.* It was through words that I first came to know Pat Conroy in 1976 when I read *The Great Santini.* While many readers focus on the dysfunction of the Conroy family, I was intrigued by his lyrical descriptions of the South Carolina lowcountry. The setting was not a mere backdrop—it was a critical piece of the story.

As a historian who studied, wrote, and taught about South Carolina, I was captivated. Conroy's words grabbed me. Here was a contemporary who truly understood the special, almost mystical, world of the lowcountry. And because he was a contemporary, I thought his work might be useful in my teaching. That led me to *The Water Is Wide*, which had been published four years earlier. Over the following years, each new Conroy book found a place on my bookshelf.

It was not until Pat found his home back in South Carolina, however, that our paths began to cross. And then he married Cassandra. I had just begun *Walter Edgar's Journal* on South Carolina Educational Radio when I received a copy of *The Sunday Wife.* After reading it I booked her for an interview, and she asked could she bring her husband along to listen in. The conversation the three of us had after taping the show lasted quite a while as she and I touted the beauty of L.A. (Lower Alabama)—especially its sugar-white sandy beaches. Pat countered every one of our comments

Portions of this essay were first delivered at a public memorial service on May 14, 2016, at Henry C. Chambers Waterfront Park, Beaufort, South Carolina.

with one about the lowcountry. That was October 10, 2002. After that date I knew that not only did Pat adore Sandra, but he also was truly in love with South Carolina.

The best way I know how to talk about Pat's love of the Carolina low-country is to let the man speak for himself. "My wound is geography," he wrote in the opening sentence to *Prince of Tides*. "It is also my anchorage, my port of call." *Prince of Tides* was Pat's fifth book, but it was fourth in what I would call Conroy's Lowcountry Chronicles. So let's start with *The Water Is Wide* and listen to the rhythm of his words as he captures the spirit and soul of the lowcountry.

> Yamacraw is an island off the South Carolina mainland not far from Savannah, Georgia. The island is fringed with the green, undulating marshes of the southern coast; shrimp boats ply the waters around her and fishermen cast their lines along her bountiful shores. Deer cut through her forests in small silent herds. The great southern oaks stand broodingly on her banks. The island and the waters around her teem with life. There is something eternal and indestructible about the tide-eroded shores and the dark, threatening silences of the swamps in the heart of the island.

In the second chronicle, *The Great Santini*, his focus is on Beaufort—the town he claimed as home and that came to claim him as its adopted son. The setting is early in the novel as Santini drives his family into Beaufort and to their new home.

> They had entered a neighborhood of splendid quiet, hushed gardens, and columned houses. The houses were not as spectacular as those that lined River Street, but many of them were older and more tastefully understated. The river had curved around to the boundary of this neighborhood. Four large houses sat at the farthest extremity of this point of land, each of them overlooking the water. Each house was almost hidden by huge oak trees that hovered over them.

The third volume of the lowcountry chronicles is *The Lords of Discipline*. From the prologue:

> My approach to Charleston is always silent and distracted, but I come under full sail, with hissing silk and memories a-wing above me in the shapes of

the birds I love best: old brown pelicans, great blue herons, cowbirds, falcons lost at sea, ospreys lean from dives, and eagles over schools of mullet. I am a lowcountry boy. My entrance to this marsh-haunted city is always filled with troubled meditations.

I've already mentioned the opening lines from *Prince of Tides*, but I think they bear repeating in context:

My wound is geography. It is also my anchorage, my port of call.

I grew up slowly beside the tides and marshes of Colleton; my arms were tawny and strong from working long days on the shrimp boat in the blazing Carolina heat. . . . I was born and raised on a Carolina sea island and I carried the sunshine of the low-country, inked in dark gold on my back and shoulders. As a boy, I was happy above the channels, navigating a small boat between the sandbars with their quiet nation of oysters exposed on the brown flats at the low watermark.

Beach Music is the fifth of the chronicles. The story often takes us far from the lowcountry, but the lowcountry is not forgotten. Returning to South Carolina, Jack McCall is driving to "Mepkin Abbey, a small city of prayer hidden deep in a semitropical forest thirty miles from Charleston, South Carolina. Its isolation was intentional." As McCall nears the monastery he spies a small red fox pup and its mother. "Wildness, I thought, that's what I've missed in Italy, that intimate connection with the inhuman and untamable." Shortly thereafter he leaves Waterford for the Isle of Orion.

The next morning I drove out in sweet sunshine, taking the two-lane road through the marshes and forests and over the tidal creeks that gave way to the Atlantic Ocean ahead. A black man was throwing his shrimp net from a bridge at low tide. It webbed out, spinning like a ballerina's skirt, a flawless circle of hemp, hitting the water and sinking rapidly to the bottom. I imagined its weights sinking to the silty floor, trapping every mullet, shrimp, or crab passing through that circle's arc, and wondered where my own cast net was, if I still had the patience to fill a beer cooler with shrimp when they were running strong and fast in the spring.

South of Broad, the sixth and final volume of Pat's Lowcountry Chronicles, ends in Charleston, a Charleston that would be battered by Hurricane Hugo.

I carry the delicate porcelain beauty of Charleston like the hinged shell of some soft-tissued mollusk. My soul is peninsula-shaped and sun-hardened and river-swollen. The high tides of the city flood my consciousness each day, subject to the whims and harmonies of full moons rising out of the Atlantic. I grow calm when I . . . hear the bells of St. Michael's calling cadence in the cicada-filled trees along Meeting Street. Deep in my bones, I knew early that I was one of those incorrigible creatures known as Charlestonians.

And after Hugo, Leo King reminisces about the Charleston of his youth, of his days as a paperboy:

I ride past concealed gardens flush with morning glories, ligustrum, white oleanders, and lavender azaleas galore. The morning birds sing a concerto for me in my swift flight beneath them. The forgotten music of a city awakening comes back to me. . . . It is Charleston. I hear the bells of St. Michael's ring out on the four corners of the law. It is Charleston, and it is mine. I am lucky enough a man that I can sing hymns of praise to it for the rest of my life.

There you have it—in six wonderful volumes—Pat Conroy's public confession of his love for the Carolina lowcountry. Now, Pat never grouped these six books together. Nor has any literary critic. That's my doing, and I am a historian. Historians are as familiar with annals and chronicles as others are with novels. While each one is independent, they are indelibly linked. That's my historical analysis.

I'd like to close by doing something that literary critics do all the time—regardless of whether they come from the Robert Penn Warren school of traditional critics or from today's deconstructionists. Literary critics like to put words into the mouths of authors, as in "he/she really meant to say this or that."

I am going to close with a slight paraphrase from Pat's sixth lowcountry chronicle, *South of Broad*, which we might imagine in Pat's voice: "It is the Carolina lowcounty, and it is mine. I am lucky enough a man that I can sing hymns of praise to it for the rest of my life." And Pat did, bless him. And we are the lucky ones because he did so.

A Lowcountry Love

~ MARY ALICE MONROE

Pat Conroy and I shared a love of the landscape of the low-lying coastal area of South Carolina we call the lowcountry. Over the years we've used the power of words to protect the sultry, winding creeks and rivers, the majestic and mercurial Atlantic Ocean, and all of the imperiled wildlife—sea turtles, dolphins, shorebirds, shellfish, and fish—that inhabit this watery home.

Pat's novel *Beach Music* especially speaks to me. In it, he wrote about the early days of the state's efforts to monitor the sea turtle population nesting on our beaches. I've been a member of the Island Turtle Team of Isle of Palms and Sullivan's Island for seventeen years. I didn't know my interest in these ancient mariners that shared the Earth with dinosaurs more than 210 million years ago would become a lifelong devotion. When I joined in 1999, the South Carolina Department of Natural Resources (SCDNR) managed the turtle teams. Every decision we make concerning discovering nests and eggs, moving nests or leaving them in situ, and emergence of the hatchlings is according to state and federal guidelines.

Back before SCDNR's presence on beaches in the mid-1980s, there were no guidelines—just a handful of dedicated women with a passion for log-gerheads doing what they thought best to protect them. These women were affectionately called "Turtle Ladies" by the community. Their hearts were in the right place, but with little knowledge they made what we now know were serious mistakes trying to help the hatchlings. I have a special fondness for these early turtle ladies. Most of them jumped on board with SCDNR to form official volunteer teams. My heroine in my novel *The Beach House*, Lovie Rutledge, was such a "turtle lady." Pat Conroy's "turtle lady" character in *Beach Music* was one of the few who resented what they saw as an intrusion. In the novel Conroy described the feud between the SCDNR agent, Jane Hartley, and the hero's mother, Lucy.

Fast-forward twenty years. I was serving on the board of the South Carolina Aquarium in Charleston, and we began a series of awards given out at our first Conservation Gala. That inaugural year we chose to give the new Legacy Award to Pat Conroy, who'd served on the aquarium's first board and whose words had inspired countless people around the world to discover the unparalleled beauty of the lowcountry, and in particular our marine life. That same year we gave the Achievement Award to Sally Murphy, the first head of the Marine Turtle Conservation Program and a legend in her time. Sally and Pat were both my friends, and I was the emcee of the gala. Amid great pomp I gave Pat his Legacy Award, and then I gave Sally her Achievement Award. While she stood by me I explained to the audience how Sally patrolled the beaches back in the day, then introduced her to Pat as the real-life Jane Hartley who had been vilified in *Beach Music*! Pat was stunned, and his face showed it. It was all in good fun, and we shared a laugh. Sally remains a huge fan of Pat's and more recently sat at a place of honor at his seventieth birthday celebration.

The lowcountry is really like a small town. Those of us who work together in different capacities—zoos, aquariums, bird sanctuaries, SCDNR agents, marine mammal protection, biologists, volunteers, and authors—know each other. We are comrades in arms fighting to protect this precious, unparalleled landscape that we share with countless fascinating creatures in sea, land, and air. With the continued development of our coastal lands and communities, state government and individuals must continue Pat's valiant fight as we work together to save what we love about the lowcountry. Pat Conroy had a lowcountry heart, and it beats still in the love he instilled in so many others of this place we call home.

One Day's Lesson

~ JOHN CONNOR CLEVELAND

Three-quarters of the way through Pat Conroy's *The Prince of Tides*, the narrator, Tom Wingo, describes the death of a relative, lamenting in the process an inability to fully articulate the loss. "The only word for goodness is goodness," he notes, "and it is not enough."

Ever since I learned of Conroy's death last month I've been thinking about that line and a day I spent with him in 2002.

For me, and for many growing up in South Carolina, Pat Conroy was a mythic figure: part documentarian, part poet laureate of the Palmetto State. Through his writing he was able to put into words what some of us innately understand, bound as we are by heat and history. He portrayed the South in full—all its contrasting mystery and ugliness, beauty and brine, laid bare—and did so in a way that made it feel accessible to outsiders and refreshing to those of us who live here.

In some ways, Pat Conroy put South Carolina back on the map: on best-seller lists and in Hollywood, but also in the minds of its inhabitants, sensitive as we are to decaying legacy and diminished status.

I met Pat through my mother, Kathleen Parker. A writer herself, she became acquainted with him after a random encounter in the late 1990s. Never lacking for congeniality, she returned from that occasion with a new best friend and a note addressed to me: "I met your charming mother, who tells me you want to be a writer. A little advice. Read everything, keep a journal and pay attention to the way people talk. Most importantly, marry someone just like your mama."

This essay was originally published in the *Weekly Standard*, April 25, 2016.

Four years later, I was seventeen years old, sullen, going through many of the growing pains familiar to the young and (creatively) restless. One day my mother—who is inclined toward "growing experiences" and was, perhaps, grateful for any chance to get me out of town and away from my friends—announced a day trip: "We're going to meet Pat Conroy," she told me. And soon enough we were in the car and headed from Columbia to Beaufort, the coastal antebellum gem that Conroy called home.

We met him at a little restaurant near the water where the purpose of the visit quickly revealed itself: my mother meant for me to spend the day with him, clearly in the hope that he could instill a little inspiration, if only by osmosis. I was game.

Conroy was exactly what you might expect him to be: warm, thoughtful, empathetic, with the right touch of Irish gregariousness. He was the kind of man attuned to whatever it is that sparks internal struggle, and he had no trouble relating to a skinny kid going through a hard time. As one critic wrote of *The Prince of Tides*: "The characters do too much, feel too much, suffer too much, eat too much, signify too much and above all talk too much." That was probably not far from Pat's own inner workings.

He suggested we take a drive, and off we went on a tour of Beaufort, a city of stately old mansions set against a rural backdrop no longer found amidst the gentrified grandeur of Charleston. As we drove, Pat peppered me with questions about myself, punctuated with his own stories and asides as we passed various landmarks from his childhood.

Occasionally we would stop outside a house or some particular place: "I put that dock in *The Prince of Tides*," he would say, or "that house is in *The Great Santini*."

At one point we pulled beside a white-columned building that had been a Union hospital during the Civil War; Pat told me the inside was covered in the patients' graffiti. The wounded and their guards, he explained, had taken to drawing on the walls to stave off boredom, and the markings from their lead pencils refused to fade over time.

At about two o'clock we stood in front of the grave of the Great Santini—Pat's father, Don Conroy, the subject of so much of his writing. Pat didn't say much, but I remember him speaking about his father's bravery, referring to himself as cowardly by comparison. Surely this wasn't true, I remember thinking; but it was a humanizing moment from a man whose rocky relationship with his father had given him so much to write.

Conroy was enamored of teachers and teaching, which he called "a heroic act," so it was fitting that, after meeting the man who had raised him, I met the man who had inspired him. His old high school English teacher Gene Norris turned out to be a delightful guy, mischievous and mustachioed, who talked about Pat's time in class and about Thomas Wolfe, another southern writer with a penchant for finding grandeur in the everyday. Clearly, the young Conroy had found genuine kinship in the classroom, which was probably what he meant to teach me.

It may well be outside my knowledge or ability to write a fitting eulogy for Pat Conroy, whose own gifts were unmatched. I know that he was a brilliant writer and that his words will surely find literary permanence—lead markings scrawled onto the southern soul. Beyond that, I can only say that he was kind to me and that he was a good man. It is not enough.

Knowing Pat through Jack

⌒ JONATHAN SANCHEZ

In 2003, while spending a summer in Orlando, I wrote a letter to Pat Conroy.

I was staying in College Park, at the Kerouac House, a little bungalow where Jack Kerouac had lived when *On the Road* came out and where he quickly wrote a follow-up novel, *The Dharma Bums*.

That same year, Conroy's *My Losing Season* came out, in which he wrote about spending fifth grade in Orlando. He said it was the happiest year of his nomadic childhood: climbing trees and eating grapefruit and making his first basketball team.

I'm not exactly sure why I wrote to Pat. It likely had to do with staying alone in Kerouac's house, dreaming grand dreams. I felt a sense of pride and stewardship, thought I could be some sort of literary go-between, squeeze myself between the shoulders of two giants.

They had some things in common. Both were athletes first. Kerouac went to Columbia on a football scholarship; Conroy was a point guard at The Citadel. Both were Catholic, both moved a lot.

They both wrote don't-look-back, maximalist prose—Kerouac on a type-writer, Pat on legal pads because his father had told him only girls took typing classes. They had unique voices that were muscular and sensitive and expansive. Their athleticism showed in their writing. They often tried to dazzle you. Sometimes, like aging ballplayers reliving past glories, they fell short.

Portions of this essay originally appeared in *Publishers Weekly*.

Jack was the liberal outsider voice of the Beats, the face of 1950s counterculture, but was also a red-blooded patriot. Pat was the liberal outsider voice of the New South—of a rarely acknowledged southern counterculture standing up to racism and the status quo—but was also a proud son of The Citadel.

I mailed my letter. I probably thought he would come right away and give a reading and I'd introduce him and my book would get published and we'd sit on his porch on Fripp Island and drink iced tea.

I did not get a response.

In September 2003 my writer's residency ended. I went back to Charleston. I worked part-time at a bookstore on King Street. A few years later, the owners wanted to retire and I bought them out.

In the fall of 2009, *South of Broad* was about to be published, Pat's first book in six years. I came home to find a message on voicemail.

"Hi, Jonathan, this is Pat Conroy. I'm sorry I'm such a disorganized mess, but I just came across the letter you wrote me from the Jack Kerouac House, and I just wanted to say thank you so much and if there's anything . . ."

I ended up getting to interview him for the *Charleston City Paper*, and I convinced him to come sign *South of Broad* at my store. Blue Bicycle Books would go on to host four book-release events with Pat over a six-year period. For a locally owned bookstore in downtown Charleston, I don't think I have to tell you how lucky that is. Pat Conroy was the most famous southern author of the last fifty years, and even though he only lived here in college, his Charleston association runs deep.

My relationship with Pat turned out to be less about the Beats and more about business. I sold his books. He may have appeared to be a charming, carefree raconteur, but he brought an industrious, entrepreneurial spirit to his career. Over forty-five years he managed to touch just about every aspect of the publishing world.

He started out self-published. Three years after graduating from The Citadel, Pat put together a collection of letters, stories, and drawings about Lt. Col. Thomas "The Boo" Courvoisie, the popular commandant of cadets. He drove around the South selling copies of *The Boo* out of his trunk.

"What a pathetic figure I must have been," he said, "going around begging bookstores to take my book."

I have to admit, if the next Pat Conroy walked in my door today with his first book, I don't know if I would take it. At Pat's first event at our bookstore, he signed a first edition of *The Boo* that later sold for $2,000.

When a publisher offered a $7,500 advance for his memoir about teaching children on Daufuskie Island, his first reaction was to turn it down, saying, "My last book cost me way less than that."

He was a book-signing beast. Note that I did not say book-signing machine. He was almost too personal for his own good, moved through the line slowly, spoke with everyone.

When Pat first came to our store for that *South of Broad* signing, he was still recovering from a stay in the ICU due to complications from diabetes. It was a cold, rainy day in December, and he arrived two hours early to sign stock, often interrupted by "close friends" who just had to say a quick hello. We learned our lesson in the future, cordoned him off, and guarded the door.

At 1:00 p.m. Pat went out to an unheated wedding tent in the parking lot and signed for seven hours. Some fans left crying, overcome with emotion, including those who had waited till the bitter end. Pat came back inside and finished signing stock, then hit the two-lane road for Beaufort on a rainy night.

"That's the second time this year I thought I was going to die, Jonathan," he later told me about the drive home.

Of course, before going to bed that night he likely read a few advance review copies by up-and-coming authors. He was a self-proclaimed "blurb slut." Even after his death, books are still coming out that Pat promoted. I know of one very successful southern author who asked for a blurb by offering sexual favors (in jest, we all hope). He blurbed her anyway; their relationship remained platonic.

He was nominated for an Oscar for best-adapted screenplay for *The Prince of Tides*. Five movies were based on Pat's books. Actors who portrayed Pat (or fictional characters based on him) include Jon Voight (*Conrack*), Michael O'Keefe (*The Great Santini*), David Keith (*The Lords of Discipline*), and Nick Nolte (*The Prince of Tides*).

All of his backlist, even *The Boo*, is still in print in hardback. The reprints are published by the Old New York Book Shop Press, a joint venture between Conroy and Cliff Graubart, his bookseller friend from Atlanta.

The big publishers missed the boat on this one, not recognizing Pat's singular presence as a southern writer. Southerners want *The Water Is Wide*—the original cover has a written transcript of Pat teaching the kids—up on the shelf next to their grandmother's *Gone with the Wind* and their mother's *To Kill a Mockingbird*.

Pat's writing is not for everyone. He has been called wordy, and a lot worse. His work is at times lovely and pastoral and elegiac, but it can also be weird, dark, modern, grotesque. People who don't live in the South will never really understand his full, complex appeal, or just how big he is here.

I've never met another writer who couldn't walk down the street without being recognized. That crushing level of attention, both positive and negative, was another thing he and Jack Kerouac shared.

That secluded summer in the Kerouac House, I read Jack's letters. The later ones were a little depressing for an aspiring writer. The years after 1957 and *On the Road* weren't pretty, as the sudden fame sent him on a twelve-year decline into drink and profligacy.

Pat's life was not without its rocky patches, but he was able to push through and control his own fate. He was a good businessman and partner.

At our last event with Pat, he and his biographer Catherine Seltzer gave a talk at a nearby venue, and then I led them by a back way to the bookstore. We turned a corner and came upon a party of groomsmen standing on a sidewalk putting on their tuxes.

They recognized Pat, he posed for pictures, and then I pulled him along as he wished the groom "great love." Of several regrets about Pat, one is that I was always pulling him along. I should have realized that a man who takes six years to respond to a letter is not going to be rushed, though he will come through.

Pat Conroy was a giant, a deeply generous person in so many ways, and we will miss his great love.

Free Uncontinental Breakfast

~ GEORGE SINGLETON

My first two encounters with Pat Conroy occurred, as I remember, over a fifteen-hour period, in an Atlanta hotel with a high atrium that served as the host of the Southeastern Independent Booksellers Association's annual conference. I stood at the bar waiting for a bourbon, and he sidled up and nodded to me. I introduced myself—he knew my name, which surprised and giddified me—and said, "I have to tell you this story. My mom and I watched the movie *The Great Santini* back in about 1980, on HBO. Both of us said, 'That's kind of like Dad.' My father was a rough, hard man at times."

I went on to tell Mr. Conroy that a couple weeks later the movie came on again. My father sat in the den watching it, then he barreled out of his rickety reclining chair. I said, "What's wrong?"

My father said, "I know what you're thinking!"

I said, "We didn't say anything, Dad."

"I know what y'all're thinking!" he said and limped—my father had fallen forty-five feet into the empty hold of a merchant ship some eighteen years earlier and undergone a number of fake hip installations and/or repossession/installations—somewhere toward the back of the house, bellowing along the way.

Mr. Conroy smiled and shook his head. He said, "Man, I'm sorry. And you loved him."

I about started crying. I said, "More than anything, though I didn't know it most of the time."

Now I need to jump ahead to the following day, a Sunday morning, at the same hotel. Ron Rash and I had driven to this book convention together, and I packed my bags upstairs so we could get out of there as quickly as possible. Neither Ron nor I felt comfortable in these situations. Ron called up and said, "Mr. Conroy's downstairs, and he wants to talk to you."

I lugged my duffel bag down to find Ron, Pat's stellar wife, Cassandra King, and Pat seated in the middle of a packed Sunday buffet-style restaurant. Pat held a copy of the *Atlanta Journal-Constitution*'s art section in his right hand, folded up. It just so happened—and I had known about it—that wonderful Teresa Weaver had written pretty much a full-page review of my collection *Why Dogs Chase Cars*. I'm talking a glowing review, one that publishers still glean quotes from for my subsequent books all these years later.

"Look at you, look at you!" Mr. Conroy bellowed. He waved the newspaper. "Mr. Big! Look at you, Mr. Big!" He had that gigantic Conroy smile plastered over his face, and he shook his head back and forth.

Cassandra laughed, said, "Paaaaaaaat," in diminuendo fashion. People turned their heads his way.

I said, "Good morning," to Cassandra and, "Hey, Mr. Conroy."

Ron Rash hadn't made it big-time at this point. He looked down at his pitiful plate of one biscuit with sawmill gravy. He wore a tie that his mother, Sue, had given to him for an Easter Sunday long ago.

"Yesterday you were shit on my shoe. And tomorrow you'll be shit on my shoe," Mr. Conroy laughed out.

"Paaaaaaaat!"

"But today you're Mr. Big. Way to go, George." He nodded up and down like a northern Louisiana oil rig.

I looked at Mr. Conroy, understood that he was flat-out messing with me—that he knew he could mess with me, which I admired mightily, and that I wouldn't be offended whatsoever—and I said, "So. Why're you at this conference, again? You pushing a cookbook or something?"

Cassandra laughed. Ron stared down at his sawmill gravy—I think he'd used his fork to write "Serena," in cursive, in the dregs. Mr. Conroy jutted out his free hand, his index finger pointed my way. He pulled his head back, smiled wider, and said, "You got me!"

I sat down and ordered a cup of coffee. Mr. Conroy said, "Tell me some more stories about your daddy."

And then we were attuned to one another.

To Know the Author and the Man

⌒ SANDRA BROWN

I'll never know what possessed the producer of that morning talk show to book me as a guest on the same day as Pat Conroy.

But that's how I came to meet him in the green room between his time in the makeup chair and mine. Just as we were being introduced, I was summoned to the lighted dressing table in the corner. I said to Pat, "Excuse me while I get fluffed up."

He laughed.

I fell in love.

At least that was the day I lost my heart to Pat Conroy, the individual. I, as millions of other readers, had been in love with his writing for years. He was a supernova in a literary galaxy far, far away from the one in which I orbited.

When I was introduced to him that morning in a Dallas TV studio, I'm amazed my star-struck self was able to speak at all, much less come up with something that amused him. Even more remarkable is that he treated me as a colleague, asking me about my tour and expressing genuine interest in the book I was promoting.

I never would have expected him to remember me from that brief chat.

Fast-forward several years. I was a featured speaker at a book fair in Florida. Following my program, a lovely blond lady came to my book-signing table and introduced herself as novelist Cassandra King. We talked shop for a few minutes, and then she moved on. The next person in my signing line asked me, "Did you know that's Pat Conroy's wife?"

I came out of my chair so fast I think I flipped it over. When I caught up with Cassandra, I babbled a lame apology for not knowing her and making the connection. She was gracious and sweet and said, "When I told Pat you were going to be here, he asked me to tell you hello. He remembers meeting you in Dallas."

We talked for several minutes and discovered we were "practically neighbors" in South Carolina, with them living in Beaufort and my husband, Michael, and I having a vacation house in Hilton Head. She gave me her card and made me promise to notify them next time we were there.

Several months later the four of us met for lunch. It was a genial occasion, the first of many more to follow. We were delighted and surprised to discover that we Browns shared another neighborhood with the Conroys in the mountains of North Carolina, where we spent time during the summer.

It was there that I introduced the Conroys to our son Ryan. He had come down from New York to spend a couple of weeks of concentrated writing in our "cabin in the woods." He was working on a novel about a high school football team who all drown when their rivals for the championship push their schoolbus into a flooding river. The players emerge from the mangled bus as zombies who are bent on playing and winning that final game—come hell or high water. So to speak.

As Ryan was synopsizing the plot to Pat and grousing about being stuck in the middle, Pat stopped him in mid-sentence. "What's at stake?" he asked. "What happens if they *lose* the game? Figure that out, and you've got your book."

Play Dead by Ryan Brown was published and received a starred review in *Publishers Weekly*. Ryan credits Pat for asking the all-important question that turned his idea into a story.

I was an eavesdropper on their conversation, but I learned the lesson, too. As I plot each book, I hear Pat asking, "What's at stake?"

Two thousand and eight marked the beginning of a new decade in my life. Michael thought that merited a very special celebration. He told me afterward that the surprise birthday party he hosted in my honor had taken months to plan. In secret, he'd invited family, lifelong friends, long-lost friends, colleagues, and writers whom he knew I held in high esteem—among them Pat.

A health issue prevented him from attending, but he sent a video greeting that was played during the event, and it made a greater impression than one from a president and first lady! In every circumstance he made an impact.

Pat loved to hold court and tell stories. No one in his company took exception if he dominated the conversation, because his oral storytelling was as riveting as his writing. He could be incredibly charming.

He was reputed to have a querulous and difficult side. I didn't know that Pat Conroy. The one I knew was fiercely loyal to people, places, and ideals, and when he felt passionately about something he could be gruff and opinionated. He gave no quarter during friendly arguments, which he usually won with sheer tenacity if not persuasion.

I was nervous around him only once, and that was when I cooked for him.

Pat loved food. He published a cookbook, and I am a card-carrying noncook. When I told him that, he chided me, saying that if I could read, I could cook. I didn't believe that then, and I still don't. That was one of those friendly arguments he won with tenacity. So, in a weak-minded moment, Michael and I invited Pat and Cassandra to dinner, and the menu was up to me!

I fell back on what I knew, the one thing I make that is sorta, kinda edible and even tasty: Texas chili. First, I had to get the all-clear from Cassandra. Did they have any dietary restrictions? Pat did, but she told me that he would love chili.

He arrived at our house, went straight to the kitchen stove, raised the lid on the chili pot, sniffed, and asked what was in it. I quoted what I'd once heard a cowboy say about chuck wagon chili. "If you can tell what's in it, it ain't did right."

Pat laughed and, as I recall, ate two servings. He might have had heartburn later, but he professed my chili to be delicious, the best he'd ever had. Possibly he was just a damn good liar, but I choose to believe he was exercising that incredible charm I referenced earlier.

He was at his charming best the last time I saw him.

In September 2015 I was invited to speak at a book fair in Winston-Salem. I didn't know that Pat and Cassandra were also featured authors until I arrived and saw their names on the roster. It had been a couple of years since I'd seen either of them, so I was excited over this unexpected crossing of paths.

When my program and book signing concluded, I was escorted to a lounge for the participating authors, where I was to wait for my ride to the airport. I walked into the authors' room and there sat Cassandra and Pat— who, not surprisingly, was holding court from the center chair of a conference table.

He, Cassandra, and I had an affectionate reunion, swapped updates on the events in our lives, and expressed deep regret that so much time had elapsed since we'd been together.

Then, for half an hour, I and the other writers gathered around the table were held in thrall. His anecdotes made us laugh. He talked wistfully about our shared love affair with writing and grumbled about the vagaries of the publishing industry. He didn't lecture with the lofty condescension of a know-it-all but addressed us as a foxhole comrade, an equal who had suffered the agony and experienced the ecstasy of our common undertaking.

No one who was in that room with him that day will ever forget those moments in time. We were graced with both his brilliance and his humanity.

My arranged transport arrived far too soon.

Pat, Cassandra, and I made promises to stay in touch and to get dates on the calendar when we were going to be in the same neck of the woods at the same time. To my everlasting regret, those promises went unfulfilled.

I hugged Cassandra, then turned to Pat to say good-bye, not knowing that it would be for the last time.

He placed his hands on my shoulders, kissed both my cheeks, and then, with that roguish Irish twinkle in his blue eyes, said, "You know I love you more than Michael does."

Pat Conroy, the author, left us an unmatched legacy of prose that molded our minds, fractured our hearts, and stroked our souls. Devoted readers who were fortunate enough to have met him or hear him speak will never forget the experience. They will boast of it whenever his name is mentioned. Long from now, writers on every level, from the struggling starter to the multi-best-seller, will continue to revere his work as a source of inspiration and enlightenment.

For having known Pat Conroy, the author and the man, my life was blessed.

A Name to Remember

～ NICOLE SEITZ

Growing up in the lowcountry, in my mind, Pat Conroy was the South's biggest celebrity. He'd been writing for decades and had probably met as many people as he had written words. Which is why I just knew he wouldn't remember me, and so I introduced myself to him every time I saw him. To me, it was presumptuous to believe the great Pat Conroy would remember my existence.

My first encounter with Pat was in 2006, just before my first novel came out, *The Spirit of Sweetgrass*. I'd sold that book in a two-book deal. I was on cloud nine but knew two things: one, I really didn't know how in the world I'd written that first novel, and two, I had no idea how to write a second. Having launched into the writing world quite accidentally, I decided there was much to learn. A trip to the annual South Carolina Book Festival in Columbia was in order. My book would not be out for a while, but I didn't care. I needed to be around other writers. Perhaps something would rub off.

On the two-hour drive from Charleston I talked with my mother on the phone. We discussed how her sister, my aunt Bonnie, would have loved to be going with me that day. How she would have loved to know that I was about to publish a book. My aunt had died of breast cancer at age forty-six about ten years earlier. She was an aspiring writer and artist, like me. We were kindred spirits in many ways. As I rolled down I-26, my mother told me about the time Pat Conroy walked into the little bookstore on Hilton Head Island, where I grew up, to do an impromptu book signing for *The Prince of Tides*. It was my aunt's favorite book, and he was her favorite author. There he was in front of her, but Aunt Bonnie froze up. Even with my mother's prodding she could barely get herself to stand in his presence.

My head swirled with my aunt's memory as I attended the book festival. I hid behind potted plants, only to be pulled out by a gregarious author, the late Richard "Dick" Côté, who told me graciously, "You're one of us now." I walked along the antiquarian section and suddenly came to an abrupt stop. There in front of me was an advance reading copy of *The Prince of Tides*, signed by Pat Conroy. It cost a gazillion dollars but I had to have it. In a surreal moment, I could see the three of us swirling together, Aunt Bonnie, Pat Conroy, and me. We connected with such intensity I decided to buy that book no matter the cost, even though I didn't have that sort of spending change.

It was worth every penny. Two weeks later, leafing through that book, I got an idea. I would write to Pat Conroy, the best-known author I could think of, asking him if he had any advice for a newbie. In the letter I told him the story about my aunt in the Island Bookseller.

Pat Conroy called me the very next day after receiving my note.

Words cannot explain what it felt like to hear Pat's voice in a message on the phone. To this day, I think that is still the highlight of my writing life. I panicked and got the entire family out of the house before gathering the courage to call him back. What I said was utterly cringe-worthy—"What's it like to be a writer?" and "How do you like being a writer?"—but he replied, "If you gotta do it, you gotta do it." Great wisdom I'd ponder and begin to understand over the years.

I remember Pat just wanted to talk about my aunt. He said he was working on a novel, and my letter played some magical part in whatever he was writing that day. I now know it was *South of Broad*. He said, "Your aunt would make a fascinating novel."

"You think so?" I asked. "There is a lot of anger there . . ." You see, my aunt didn't tell us she was sick until just before she died.

"Anger's good!" said Pat.

Anger's good. Two weeks after that phone call I was sitting at a playground with my two small children and the nannies of the wealthy families who lived nearby, wondering what in the world to write about for my second novel, which was now under deadline. I had an epiphany. Pat Conroy had told me what would make a great novel! I knew I'd be an idiot if I didn't see it through.

My second novel, *Trouble the Water*, was an imaginative retelling of my aunt's final year. *Library Journal* gave it a starred review and named it one of the Best Books of 2008. It would never have seen the light of day had it not been for Pat's gracious gift of encouraging a new writer. I've heard similar testimonies again and again. Half of what is written in the South may never have been if it weren't for Pat Conroy. He has been that influential in our literary community.

I finally met Pat in person in January 2010 in Jefferson, Texas, at the annual Pulpwood Queens Girlfriend Weekend, the biggest, zaniest book club gathering around. I got the chance to introduce myself to him. I explained who I was and how he blurbed my first book, *The Spirit of Sweetgrass*. He said he knew who I was.

But still I couldn't believe him.

Here was a man who stood in line to buy our books and have us sign them after each author got up to speak at Girlfriend Weekend. I could see with my own eyes his humility and lavish support of other authors, yet I still felt unworthy and forgettable. It's not how he made me feel, it's just the way I was inside, perhaps more like my aunt than I knew.

Fast-forward several years. I'd been writing my seventh novel, *The Cagemaker*, and had not yet found it a home. I remember pitching the idea to Jonathan Haupt, then publisher of usc Press, but it was about New Orleans, not South Carolina, so I thought it wouldn't have a chance. Jonathan explained that Pat Conroy, editor of the Story River Books imprint, was looking for southern—not just South Carolina—books and writers for Story River. Perhaps there was a chance. That was in May 2015.

Over the course of several months I went back and forth with Jonathan over my book, making substantive edits to get it in shape to present it to Pat and the editorial board. In November, I was at a book event on Hilton Head Island with Pat and a group of his Story River Books authors. He was magnanimous and had lines wound all around the place waiting for him. I needed to say something to him before I left. Finally I sensed my break, or perhaps forced it. I knelt down on the floor beside him. I introduced myself to him all over again, as I was known to do. He listened to my pitch with interest and told me to tell Jonathan to get the book to him ASAP. I remember saying, "I can't thank you enough," then scooting out of his way.

"For what?" he said. "I haven't done anything yet."

I turned back to him and said, "Trust me. You've already done more than you know."

These would be the last words I ever said to Pat Conroy.

Roundabout we go. I was back in Columbia on February 19, 2016, at the Deckle Edge Festival, the one that took the place of the South Carolina Book Festival. I was there promoting a book I'd compiled and edited for flood relief, *When You Pass through Waters: Words of Hope and Healing from Your Favorite Authors*. It had been a labor of love because all the proceeds went to charity. I stood at a reception face-to-face with Jonathan Haupt. We never discussed my novel, *The Cage-maker*, still under consideration at USC Press. All we could talk about was Pat's illness. I wanted to encourage him, to honor him, to show our collective love for him, so I suggested we pull a book together for him. "Everyone has a Pat story," we agreed as we took turns sharing ours. Jonathan said he'd been thinking about a book as well. Then we parted ways.

On March fourth I got an e-mail from Jonathan saying Story River Books would like to publish my novel. It was the news I'd been waiting almost a year to hear. Separately, he asked if I would agree to coedit with him an anthology of writers' reflections on Pat Conroy.

I read the note and then went downstairs to let it soak in. I'd write him in the morning, I thought. And then something came over me. No. I would write him tonight. Now. I accepted the offer with Story River Books three hours before Pat passed away.

I awoke the next morning to learn the news of Pat's death from the *Charleston Post and Courier*. I felt the blow deeply, that yin and yang of up and down, of gain and loss, of Aunt Bonnie, Pat Conroy, and me swirling wildly in my mind. Still, I have inadequate words for that moment.

I do know this. Even in death Pat is still graciously giving. I will spend the rest of my writer days trying to honor this man. It is with sincere regret that I didn't realize sooner that he was just a man and nothing as large as the pedestal I'd put him on. If I had figured this out sooner, I might have allowed myself into his orbit. But some people shine so brightly in this earthly life that it can be blinding.

Pat Conroy was no god. He was simply a man. A flawed, authentic, brilliantly talented man bestowed with gifts of the pen and the heart, both of which he used well. And in the end, it doesn't matter if he knew my name. Because I know his. And it's one I hope to help carry on.

He Was Mine, He Was All of Ours

~ SEAN A. SCAPELLATO

When I was sixteen years old, working as an emergency room tech at Piedmont Hospital in Atlanta, a nurse gave me my first Pat Conroy book, *The Lords of Discipline*. (Conroy said the opening is the single best line he'd written: "I wear the ring.") I read the five-hundred-page book in a weekend. Never before had a novel reached out and grabbed me by the throat like this one had. I had no idea words could make a person weep or laugh out loud or grow ruby faced with anger. That book started me on a bender that would include consuming every word Conroy ever published, like some crazy-eyed, starving beast.

In time, and to my lasting joy, I came to know the writer himself, both the man and the myth, and it changed my life. Of course, when you are a friend of Pat Conroy's you become a magnet for questions and favors from others. I have been asked dozens of times if I can get a book signed, have Pat attend a book club, invite him for a dinner, ask him to attend this fundraiser, to be a guest at this school. Years ago we were having lunch at Rue de Jean in Charleston, and three people interrupted our meal. Another time, I drove him to pick up his car from a dealership in Charleston, and the mechanic produced a copy of *Beach Music* for Pat to sign as he paid for the oil change.

From 2008 to 2009 I drove to Beaufort once a month to attend a writers group Pat had assembled—guys like Bernie Schein, Scott Graber, and John Warley. Theirs was a more intimate and seasoned friendship, and they did not idolize Pat the way I did. They harassed him, made fun of his "pompous, overblown prose." They ribbed him for his academic laziness and infamously poor military polish (Pat graduated The Citadel with the rank of private). Their jibes were classic locker-room bravado about masculinity, women, and religion. Pat gave it right back, with most of the return fire crosshaired on Bernie. I relished having a front row seat to the show, but perhaps what was most fascinating to me was that they hassled each other mercilessly in one breath and in the next loved as deeply as men who've fought in war alongside each other. And when it came to the writing, they remained in awe of their friend.

Each month we met in the second-floor conference room of Scott's law office—a postwar Victorian on the edge of the Point, Beaufort's famed historic district. We drank wine in ladder-backed chairs around an antique table amidst legal volumes and made the talk of writers by lamplight. Pat came sometimes. Sometimes he called to check in. We all talked through the chapters of stories and the psyches of those who peopled the pages. We deconstructed plots, offered advice, much of it anecdotal bits taken from Pat's career. Bernie led. Pat shared the struggles of his early career, when he could hardly give away his books. I absorbed it all like the good disciple I was. Nearly every meeting was filled with lightning wit and Bernie's wild (read: apocryphal) tales of sexual conquests and his demigod status among men. In the end, Scott, John, and Bernie all published the books we'd spent more than a year workshopping.

During this time I was also given the ethereal opportunity to help with Pat's novel-in-progress. Like us, he was trying to get a book finished, except his work came with the added pressure that he'd not published a novel in fourteen years. It was the big Charleston novel he'd been wanting to write since the '80s when Hurricane Hugo wrecked the Holy City. The book was expansive and risky, taking place in both Charleston and San Francisco, and Pat was nervous. I helped him with research, and as a favor to Sandra, his wonderfully talented wife (and fellow novelist), I typed the final third of the book with gusto. Pat's handwriting is small, cribbed, and inscrutably cursive. Deciphering it was an exercise in squinting and frustration. Where I could not make out a word, Sandra instructed me to bracket and guess.

Pat's manuscripts were never first drafts in the sense that most writers and readers imagine. His sentences contained polish, precision, brio. Large swaths of description that I transcribed in draft appeared virtually intact when the novel was published. Occasionally I would spot a factual error about Charleston, and I would make a note for Sandra and fix it. But the truth was that when Pat committed the story to the page, the sentences seemed to arrive fully formed like Athena bursting from Zeus's head—such rarefied air, this witnessing a Pat Conroy novel in the making.

The book took the country by storm once again, shooting straight to number one on the *New York Times* best-seller list, and I gratefully acted as Pat's body man for his marathon signing at Blue Bicycle Books in Charleston that December. I witnessed hundreds waiting their turn in the gray cold to hug him, shake his hand, have their photo taken with him, just like I'd done so long ago. He signed for more than eight hours into the evening without a break. Writers fawned. A few wept. Pat gave his soul to the people in that line. I had no way of knowing that this would be the final Pat Conroy novel in his lifetime.

Pat always said that Thomas Wolfe made him want to be a writer, that his English teacher Gene Norris and his mother turned him into one, and that the great Archibald Rutledge taught him how to *be* a writer. For me, Pat did all three. I think the reason so many people adored him has to do with the inarticulable sensation that his person was as large as his art. As people fell in love with Ben Meechum, Will McLean, Tom Wingo, Jack McCall, and Leo Bloom, they fell simultaneously in love with Pat, the writer and the man. As in most things, Pat did not disappoint.

Pat was my hero, my muse, my mentor. He pulled me out when I was too much inside my head. He propped me up when I was disenchanted with the craft. His passing creates a void as huge as the chasms left by the other greats of southern literature: Faulkner, O'Connor, Warren, Welty, Styron, and Lee. His legacy marks the South Carolina lowcountry the way Fitzgerald marked the Jazz Age. No writer shall ever describe marsh grass, the sunrise over the Atlantic, or the Spanish moss in a water oak and not evoke Pat's lyricism and rhythms.

Years ago when I took some time away from writing to go back to school, Pat would call every so often to see if I was still putting pen to paper. For years, the answer was no. I remember his face at a Story River Books event about a year before his death when I told him quietly I was writing again. He broke into a grin. "Good for you," he said. "The world needs to hear more of that marvelous prose style of yours. It's time to start calling yourself a writer again." Pat was like that—always the good teacher, always building up others and compelling us to march forth. Our last conversation on a late night in August was an offer for a book, my book, one that he wanted to publish because it was time for the world to know about me. I won't lie; I wept.

Wordsworth said, "To me the meanest flower that blows can give / Thoughts that do often lie too deep for tears." Pat's passing is a cruel taking, but for all of his journey, though the water may have been wide, his time here gave us the greatest gift of all—those spirit-filled words and a hope for what is beautiful. As I sit to write these words in sadness on the morning after his death, I feel his strength and his gentle prodding to keep pushing words around on the page. *Do it. Do it for the love of words and story*, I think he'd say.

All I know is that I loved him and I miss him terribly. What I wouldn't give for one more lunch, one more phone call, one more of those bear hugs. I will remember him the rest of my life, and I will keep trying to fail better. "Great love," he always said as his closing wish to any conversation or correspondence. To him, I whisper, "Good night, sweet prince" as "flights of angels sing thee to thy rest."

The Ring of Friendship

~ LYNN SELDON

My name is Lynn Seldon, and I wear *the* ring. It's not one of those diminutive rings from The Citadel. It's a substantial chunk of gold from the Virginia Military Institute (VMI).

I always loved comparing rings—and military school stories and nightmares—with Pat. We shared a love/hate relationship with our chosen colleges—especially our "initiation" rites as Citadel knobs and VMI rats—but we wore our rings with pride as part of a unique brotherhood.

I stand proudly in an overflowing platoon of people who were influenced by Pat's words on paper and in person. We first met in the fall of 2009, the year *South of Broad* was released. Fittingly enough, it was in Charleston, just north of Broad.

I'm a longtime travel journalist, and a close friend of mine in the tourism industry had called to say she thought she could coordinate a brief meeting with Pat when he was in town for a book signing at Blue Bicycle Books—a store he loved and where I'd eventually have my own signing. My friend arranged a call with Pat's wonderful wife, Sandra, who said he was free for a few minutes the next morning. I countered with an offer to let a VMI grad buy a Citadel grad some lunch.

After calling Dick Elliott—the (now former) owner of Slightly North of Broad—to see if we could reserve a table at the back of his beloved restaurant, I met Pat in the lobby of the Mills House for the short walk down Queen Street and up Broad to SNOB. During our stroll, Pat quizzed me about VMI, my life as a travel journalist, and my knowledge of Charleston. We stopped several times along the way to admire the architecture, including the renovated Dock Street Theatre, where he waxed poetic—of course—about his Holy City.

Sandra had told me that Pat had an hour or so for lunch, but that lunch—and subsequent pot of coffee back at the hotel—lasted the entire afternoon. Little did I know of the many meals and other confabs to come during the next all-too-short six-plus years.

I'd planned to "interview" Pat with pithy questions about what he'd order for his last meal (incredibly, he paired each dish with a specific wine), but the lunch turned into more of a conversation between seemingly long-time friends who had once served in the trenches of a military school. Pat ordered Frank Lee's famed shrimp and grits and, as he would do with me many times over many meals, happily shared his food.

As the restaurant emptied, Chef Lee came over to the table to introduce himself to Pat, as did Dick Elliott. It was the first time I'd seen Pat interact with "fans," and I've never forgotten his ability to completely engage with another person visually and verbally—from his piercing Citadel blue eyes to his oh-so-southern drawl.

Sometime during lunch, Pat wondered out loud why no one had written "The VMI Novel," as he had done for The Citadel with The Lords of Discipline. I'll never forget him looking me squarely in the eyes and saying, "I think you can do it, Lynn."

After lunch (I still have my scrawled and sauce-stained notes) we retraced our steps to the bar of the Mills House. Pat asked if I wanted to continue our chat over coffee. Duh.

We talked about life, writing, travel, and, specifically, his love of Charleston, Beaufort, and the lowcountry. He even brought up the VMI novel again before we finally parted and I made my way up Meeting Street in a daze.

The next time I saw Pat, it was in the pretty Shenandoah Valley town of Lexington, Virginia, where he was scheduled to speak at VMI. Pat came north with his friend and Citadel classmate, the novelist John Warley. (I loved A Southern Girl and now call John a friend as well.) We met for dinner at the classic Southern Inn on South Main Street along with their friend

Wyatt Durrette (VMI class of 1961). Pat and I both ordered shad roe, which was in season.

The next morning we headed up the hill to VMI, and Pat, as always, gave a great speech that was totally unrehearsed. Somehow I'd ended up sitting next to VMI's superintendent, Gen. Binford Peay, VMI class of 1962.

Pat began by saying he was wearing the "real" military school ring, holding his hand aloft, but he'd actually forgotten his Citadel ring and had borrowed John's just before his speech. After the laughter died down, Pat then pointed up to me and said, "There's a VMI graduate named Lynn Seldon that I'm trying to get to write a novel about VMI. I am as excited about that publication as I can be."

I can't remember much more of what he said that morning. I was too focused on him making my work on the novel so public. I wrote in between paying freelance assignments, lots of travel, and some monklike stays back at VMI's Moody Hall, where alumni can stay for free, and the book Pat referenced eventually saw the light of day about five years later.

One of those paying-gig assignments was a feature about Pat and Sandra for *Writer's Digest*. For the interview, Pat graciously invited my wife, Cele, and me down to their Fripp Island home. Of course they gave us a great interview that would eventually become a cover story, but the thing I remember most will always be heading back to their bedroom and adjacent library and writing room.

To say that Pat collected books is a vast understatement. As he outlined in *My Reading Life*, his lifelong love affair with books had led to a vast collection. The books would eventually be moved to their Beaufort home on bucolic Battery Creek, where I would spend many more memorable moments with Pat and Sandra.

During one of our subsequent phone calls Pat told me about his somewhat regular Thursday lunches with friends at Griffin Market in downtown Beaufort. "You should come," he said.

I'll never forget those lingering lunches with Pat and "the boys." He was typically joined by Citadel classmates John Warley and Scott Graber, best friend (and wonderful writer in his own right) Bernie Schein, artist Jonathan

Hannah (now Bernie's son-in-law), Aaron Schein (Bernie's brother), and occasional others. The concept of the University of South Carolina Press's Story River Books was hatched there when then–usc Press director extraordinaire Jonathan Haupt came for lunch.

During these lunches, tours of town with Pat (from the Great Santini's grave to the house where they filmed *The Prince of Tides*), and time back at Pat and Sandra's house, Pat never failed to ask about progress on my novel. Despite my plodding he was always encouraging.

In 2013, four years after we'd first met in Charleston, I placed a printout of what I thought was the completed manuscript on Pat's writing desk, ominously atop what appeared to be a first edition of Hemingway's *A Farewell to Arms*. I had titled my short novel *Of Rats & Rings*, at which Pat laughed, "Rat Seldon! Never name a novel after a rodent!" I quickly countered with Steinbeck's *Of Mice and Men*, but Pat would have none of it—and he was right, of course.

Just a few days later I received a call from Pat, which caller ID relayed as "Donald Conroy," and I briefly thought the Great Santini himself was somehow on the other end of the line. Paraphrasing what James Dickey had once told him, Pat started the phone call with, "I read your book, Bubba. Now the real work begins." He then proceeded to outline the problems with my plot succinctly and tell me how I might fix them. He also gave me the right title: *Virginia's Ring*.

It took another year and the real work—and bloodletting—that Pat suggested, but *Virginia's Ring* was released in 2014. The compelling cover art was completed by Pat's longtime cover artist, Wendell Minor. Pat graciously referred me to him, and Wendell (which, ironically, is also my given name) was kind enough to give me the "Pat Conroy rabbinical discount" for his wonderful work and time. Pat also graciously provided a short cover blurb ("a triumph and a tour de force") and a longer plug inside, which has surely led to more sales of *Virginia's Ring* than my mere words.

Virginia's Ring is a physical reminder of Pat's influence on my writing and life. But it's the memories I'll cherish more. The meals. The calls. The time with Pat and Sandra in Beaufort and beyond. I stand at attention in that overflowing platoon and salute Pat and everything he did for so many. After all, we wear the ring.

Pat's Gift

〜 MICHAEL MORRIS

Many years ago while driving underneath a canopy of live oaks in south Georgia, I received a call from my friend Janis Owens. Janis, Cassandra King, and I were scheduled to speak in Thomasville, Georgia. "We've got a slight change of plans," Janis said. "Cassandra is sick and can't make it." I expressed disappointment at missing the chance to visit with my Alabama friend. "But she's sending a replacement," Janis added. "Pat's coming."

For the rest of the drive to Thomasville my mind raced with questions to ask the man who spoke to my soul with *The Prince of Tides*, a novel I'd literally stumbled upon one summer in my hometown library. I'd met Pat before at his book signings. But it was just cocktail conversation, the same he graciously extended to the legions of fans standing in line to meet him. Now I'd have time to fill in that conversation for twenty-four hours under the same roof. As it turned out, we would be sharing a condominium in Thomasville. What if I made a damn fool out of myself, as I was prone to do with celebrities I adored? (If you don't believe me just ask Linda Gray of *Dallas* fame. But that's another story.)

Hollywood was on my mind. Right after Barbra Streisand turned *The Prince of Tides* into a movie, I read an article recounting how she invited Pat to her home for dinner. While discussing ideas for casting the movie, Barbra asked how he would feel if she were to play Lowenstein. Supposedly she then pressed a button and her wood-paneled wall became a movie screen. Barbra had already filmed a scene of her playing the role. It was all very dramatic, and I lapped up the details in the story. Decades after I'd read the piece, the details remained locked in my mind. I thought if there was a lull in the conversation I'd bring up that story.

As I walked into the condo with the same reverence I might a sanctuary, I peeked around the rooms, expecting the great Pat Conroy to burst forth with celebrity magnetism.

I saw a nondescript bag in the first bedroom and eased into the second one. While I was unpacking, the front door of the condo opened. I heard footsteps and then a booming voice, "Has the famous Michael Morris arrived?"

Stumbling out into the living room where he stood, I all but bowed. Pat said, "Now, I took the first bedroom I saw. If you want to switch . . ."

"No, no," I stammered.

"We have some time. Let's visit." He sat down on a white club chair and took off his baseball hat embroidered with the state flag of South Carolina.

All of my preplanned questions went by the wayside. He asked the questions, and they were all about *me*. Pat talked about my novels, which I was dumbfounded to discover he had read. He asked about my childhood and where I grew up. He was amused that I considered mullet a hometown delicacy, and later it would become a running joke. I carried on about how the setting and themes of *The Prince of Tides* spoke directly to me. Pat smiled and listened as if he hadn't heard the same thing a million times from other readers. And I found myself confessing hidden pieces of my life. The abuse in the novel was something I understood. "Most writers had shitty childhoods," he said. We never did get around to Barbra and her dinner. Somehow, nervous gossip no longer mattered.

During our panel the next day the room was packed. People were standing in the back, overflowing out into the hallway. Pat sat in the middle between Janis and me. The order was such that Janis answered questions first, then Pat, and then me. His answers were as rich and beautiful as his novels. I was entranced by his words, hanging onto them the same way the audience did. So mesmerized I was that my mind went blank. He passed the microphone to me, and I drawled out some ignoramus response. This went on for about four questions until finally, I leaned into the microphone and said, "Do y'all know how stupid I feel following this brilliant man?" At the next question, when it came Pat's turn he said nothing. Instead he slid the microphone over to me and squeezed my shoulder. The audience laughed, and the twinkle in his eye put me at ease.

It didn't take long to feel comfortable with this man who favored driving a white Oldsmobile instead of the 500 series BMW I'd imagined. After our time in Thomasville we went to visit Janis's cousin in Tallahassee. The four of us sat in her living room laughing and talking as if we were all family catching up at a reunion. "Let's keep in touch," he said as I started to leave. I thought he was just being polite. But keep in touch he did. His wisdom and encouragement were portioned out during evening phone calls.

When my cellphone happened to be turned off and I missed his call, I'd always find voicemail with the same message. "It's up to me to keep this *blankety-blank* friendship alive." After he died, I learned that Pat left that message for everyone. But he said it in such a way that I believed it was just for me.

Pat had no tolerance for pretension. It was one of his qualities I admired most. He loved to tell how a famous writer arrogantly snubbed him at a book convention. Whenever I encounter a big ego in the literary world, I think of that story. It makes me smile. Pat said he was weary of developing friendships with writers. "Our tribe isn't always kind to our own," he said. I like to think Pat's kindness covers the sins of those who are intoxicated by the fluff in their press kits. His open-heartedness and humility are examples to follow.

I also love Pat's take on book reviews and can still hear him telling me, "Ignore all reviews. The good ones inflate you and the bad ones deflate you. Besides, when we receive a good review we conclude the person must be an idiot for thinking our work is any good."

Call it a sixth sense or pure genius in reading people, but Pat always knew when my confidence was evaporating. When I first got to know Pat it had been five years since I had a novel come out. I was secretly questioning whether to keep writing. Without ever mentioning my dilemma, Pat picked up on it. He told me flat out, "Your confidence is shattered." While I was working on *Man in the Blue Moon*, his phone calls were frequent. He shared his insecurities about his own work, a declaration that astounded me and one I argued. But the next day, when I sat at my computer staring at the blank screen, I somehow felt empowered. If Pat Conroy could feel this way and produce masterpieces, then maybe it was okay for me to have doubts. I plowed on with the story.

Pat was coach and priest mixed together. (And I know he'd have a comment about being compared to a priest.) He had a way of making me open up and go deeper in my work and face my own demons. When I finished *Man in the Blue Moon* the phone calls became less frequent. I had stayed in the game and made the score.

A treasured possession is the blurb Pat provided for the novel. He didn't type, because his father thought only girls should learn the skill, but he managed to peck out the words that appear on the cover of *Man in the Blue Moon*. It was sent in an e-mail, all lowercase, with few periods and many typos. It's a work of art constructed with a sincere effort to help a fellow writer.

I am careful not to portray us as the best of friends, because above all I want to honor Pat by following his authenticity. But he came into my life when I was filled with self-doubt and hungry for encouragement. He guided me through a dark tunnel, and when I could see the light of day, he was off to help the next writer who needed him.

Recently, I was cleaning out voicemails on my cell phone and came across one from Pat. "It's up to me to keep this dying friendship alive." But that's not the case. My friendship, like the soul-gripping words he put to paper, will be eternal.

Somebody Else's Luck

~ KATHERINE CLARK

When I first met him, the man was already a myth. Once upon a time he had fought a racist white school board on behalf of poorly educated black students on a Gullah Sea Island. He had fought a chauvinistic and misogynistic military college on behalf of a female cadet who wanted to enter its all-male ranks. He had written powerful books that helped start national dialogues on topics that were once hushed up, like family abuse and dysfunction, mental illness, and the brutal excesses of macho military culture. Hollywood stars had portrayed him and his stories on the big screen. People waited hours in line to meet him, shake his hand, and thank him for helping them come to grips with their own problems. Even as he lived among us still, he already belonged to the realm of legend.

But when I actually met this legendary figure, he was dressed in what he called his "Mr. Hefty Bag" outfit: cheap khaki pants paired with an even cheaper cotton shirt with no collar or brand logo. His shoes were old and shapeless, often worn without socks, and looked like bedroom slippers. If he had to dress up for an occasion, he simply put a jacket on top of all this, which might or might not match the color of that day's cotton shirt.

I think this is one of many ways he fought against his fame and hid from celebrity. He did not want to walk the earth as a Famous Person. He wanted to be a man among men—and women. And most shocking of all—he wanted to be my friend.

When I interviewed Pat Conroy on the telephone for an author profile in 2009, we began a conversation that never ended. A publicist arranged this first phone call, but when the interview was over and the profile had run in the newspaper, Pat called me again. And again and again and again.

The friendship with Pat Conroy that developed over the telephone changed my life. Beginning when he was a schoolteacher on Daufuskie Island, Pat changed the lives of the people he encountered. He gave of himself to a heroic degree in the service of others, and often to the disservice of himself. In phone call after phone call, he gave of himself to me in the form of not just his stories, experiences, and opinions, but also his fears and his anxieties, which helped me understand, as his books did, too, that I was not alone in my own struggles and doubts. And when it came to my own life's issues, he gave me endless hours of advice, insight, encouragement, hope, and reassurance.

As the phone calls became years of friendship, I realized that Pat Conroy had given me something more than himself. He gave me myself. When we first started talking I was a despairing, unconfident writer whose career had stalled after two nonfiction books. I couldn't get traction with the fiction I'd always wanted to publish. Then Pat entered my life. He read my manuscripts. He told me he loved them. He helped me make them better and stronger. And then, when he founded the fiction imprint Story River Books at the University of South Carolina Press, he published my novels and wrote forewords for two of them.

Even that's not all. He went book touring with me. He appeared with me at panel discussions and readings. When I received a disappointing blurb from an author I admired (whom he jokingly called a heavenly body), he cheered me up with a parody of the blurb in this e-mail:

dear katherine,a new blurb just arrived from the desk of ██████████████ I think it will sell more books than the original blurb . . . . . . I have just read katherine clarks new work and after wading through its ponderous,paper wasting tome I think thati can actually claim that she has produced a book. also,upon,careful reflection,ican also say,quitedefinitively,I believe,thatit is written in english or somethingvery similar.to name things,she uses nouns. to move the book along,she employs verbs,and to desribe thing,she makes the brave choice by using adjectives.she writes about a very fat man that I would not choose to fuck.I would like to spend my valuable time fucking katherine clarks book with a blurb thatis as far removed from human praise as a skunks turd deposited in a dempster dumpsterlocated in an inuit outhouse near the arctic circle.she writes very many sentences that often turn into paragraphs that often become pages,then chapters,and finally turn into what looks and feels like a novel.but I do not wish to be quoted that she might have written a novel.I was moved to tears when I finished the book and used it to light my grill for a tasty meal of a first time novelist.katherine clark wonders at the injustice of my not being famous.I hear it makes pat conroy happier than anewly hatchedmaggot entering into thefeast of a human asshole for the first tasty bite.just passing along my read on one of the havenly bodies that populate your literary universe,great love,pat conroy

In his memoir *My Reading Life*, Pat tells the story of being taken as a high school student by his English teacher, Gene Norris, to visit South Carolina's poet laureate, Archibald Rutledge, at his family's home, Hampton Plantation. The senior poet gave the teenage Conroy a warm welcome along with a tour of his library, the house, and the extensive grounds, during which the two talked about literature. Afterward, when Gene Norris asked his student what he'd learned that day, Pat dutifully produced some nuggets from his discussion with Rutledge about literature. Gene corrected him. What you learned, he instructed, is how to conduct yourself with aspiring young authors if you ever become a famous author yourself. This is a lesson Pat Conroy did not forget when he did, in fact, become a famous writer. I am only one of the many, many beneficiaries of his generosity to aspiring younger writers.

In addition to publishing my novels, Pat's generosity to me included actually giving me a book, in the form of telephone conversations we recorded for his oral biography, *My Exaggerated Life*. In one of these interviews he told me he'd enjoyed an inordinate amount of luck in his literary career, and without that luck his career would never have gone as far as it did; he would never have known the level of success he'd experienced. Typically, Pat failed to mention the gifts he brought to the game—the prodigious talent and the powerful stories about taboo subjects. Instead he saw himself as the lucky one, and he sincerely believed he owed a debt to the universe for the luck he'd enjoyed. "I want to be somebody else's luck," he told me. "I want to be the luck that other writers need to get that first break, to get their start." Accordingly, he made liberal use of his name and fame in the service of many fledgling literary careers.

But Pat Conroy didn't just rejuvenate my career; he rejuvenated my spirit. I rediscovered faith in myself along with self-confidence. I regained hope in a professional future. I learned all over again how to laugh at life and was glad to be alive—in a world that had Pat Conroy in it. Above all, he showed me what it really means to be somebody. Pat Conroy was a real somebody not because of his literary achievements or his celebrity, but because of his humanity.

Now that I am living in a world without Pat Conroy, my life has changed again. My phone will never again ring with that beloved voice asking "How ya doing, kid?"—which had magical powers to heal whatever ailed me, gladden the heart, and lead the way forward through the gloom. But I keep that voice inside me and guard it like a precious flame. I also have a task, since Pat always waved away thanks and seemed uncomfortable with gratitude. "Just do it for someone else when you can, kid," he told me. "That's how you thank me." And I will do my best. Because my luck was in getting to know Pat Conroy, and for that I owe the universe a debt.

A Scene with Pat Conroy

~ SONNY BREWER

Not saying I will finish writing this scene from where I'm sitting, but let's get started.

In this chair.

At this table.

Almost the same time of day twenty-two months ago when I last saw Pat Conroy in this very same bookstore.

The sun is hard on the backs of the cars parked outside. A white glare comes off the windshield of the Buick in front of the picture window that announces in pale blue letters ten inches tall, INDEPENDENT BOOKSTORE for INDEPENDENT PEOPLE. Passersby on the sidewalk fronting Page and Palette in Fairhope, Alabama, have on shorts and summery-looking shirts and tops. I've got on sandals. It's the nineteenth of October, and there's been no frost on the pumpkins.

The ceiling fan overhead is pushing chilled indoor air down my collar, and my hands are getting cold. I could move to another table, but for this scene I need to sit right here where I sat that December. From this vantage point I can see the spot where they'd set up a table with Katherine Clark's books stacked high. "Meet the Author" was on a placard tilted beside one stack of *The Headmaster's Darlings*.

Faith Kaiser was seated opposite me, a little frown on her face. She and I had been working on her first novel. Like me, she got a later start at this book writing thing, both of us near sixty. I was not scowling, but I was bothered. It was my job as her editor to tell her where her story jumped the tracks and how to pry it back into place.

"Damn it, Faith. You have to dial back on the narration and write in scene."
She wasn't looking at me. She was watching something over my shoulder.
Her eyes went wide. Her mouth opened. "Look, Faith, maybe we should take
this to a more private spot. I need you to hear what I'm saying."

"There's Pat Conroy!" she said. She put her hands to her face, palms to
her cheeks.

I looked to my left, toward the picture window. I'd lost my writer to
another writer.

Faith dumped on me the contents of her entire mental hard drive under
the file name Pat Conroy. How much she adored his writing. How his books
had made that profound impact upon her. I could just imagine some reader
at a Q&A asking, "And what books steered the course of your own writing?"
That's what Faith would hear when her novel made it to the bookstores. If it
ever did. Her publisher wasn't going to put up with all this windy narration
in passive voice. She was wasting her money on me.

"Look, you want to meet Pat?" I could see him through the door opening between the Latte Da coffee shop and the bookstore proper. This side
was remodeled with new paint and fresh plaster that left some places with
exposed clay tile blocks from a hundred years ago. I watched as Pat walked
up to the table where Katherine's books waited for customers. He wore kha-
kis and a loose striped shirt. Pat's skin was always ruddy. It went well with
his white hair and good cheer. The bookstore that December was full of
warm air—thermostatically controlled, heat pump–delivered air. I wasn't
shivering in air-conditioned breezes as I am now, nearly two years later.

"Oh, my God!" said Faith.

"Can you stand and walk?" I told her to get up and let's grab him before
somebody else spotted him.

We walked up behind Pat, and I put my hand on his shoulder.

"Sonny!" Then a little something-something, a quick catching up. "Pat,
I want to introduce you to Faith Kaiser." He turned his big old smile on
this woman who might have otherwise puddled right there if Pat hadn't
engaged her immediately with questions. When Faith told her I was editing
her novel, he beamed.

"But I can't get her to write in scenes," I blurted.

"Oh, my, you've got to write in scenes, Faith!" He said some stuff about making talking pictures for the readers. Good stuff, well delivered with passion and grace. Pat could've been a teacher for much longer than the little time he put in before being fired. Thank God. What if he'd taught distracted youth instead of himself writing in scene?

"I'm going to give you an assignment, Faith. Homework. Go home and write this very scene we're now making. You and me and Sonny. Tell me how the bookstore smells. That coffee from the next room. Show the reader how the crowds aren't yet here for this wonderful book of Katherine's." And on, as he set the writing task clearly for this woman he did not know, but whom he embraced in a big, boisterous way. People were looking our way. Pat's voice carried. Faces were lighting up in recognition of THE Pat Conroy here within arm's reach.

Yep. Quick as that, we lost Pat to the room at large as he charmed all comers. He sincerely loved the people who drew up into his personal space. He loved beginning authors and wanted to give some helping advice. Or more. Katherine wasn't a newbie, but he'd written the foreword to her latest and was out on the bookstore trail to help her get it out to readers.

That's Pat.

It's also Pat that he bought a book from Heather Hickox, an employee of Page and Palette who worked on the night he introduced Katherine. She apologized to Pat that she wasn't a "real" writer like him. He told Heather he was on his fourth book before he called himself a writer. He made her blush when he asked her to please autograph *Goodnight Fairhope* for him.

I've got stories of how he helped me. How when I asked him, too near the deadline, would he contribute something to *Don't Quit Your Day Job*, and he told me he'd only had the one other brief job as public school teacher. Which we all know about. But he'd written something about that part of his life in *My Losing Season*, and that it was cut and in a trunk in his attic. I could have that. I said I'd take it.

When my fuzzy deadline had come and gone by three days and I didn't yet have the piece from Pat, I called him. No answer. So I called Sandra, his wife.

"Oh, he's been up late the last two nights working on something for you. He's working on it now." She told me I'd have it in a day or so. When it came—in plenty of time—I read it through tears. It hit my wife even harder. It was a powerful essay about working one summer as a census taker for his Catholic church when his mother refused to allow him to go to Mississippi to register black voters. When Pat set out to help somebody, he colored way outside the lines. His contribution to the anthology hummed like a high-voltage wire.

And Faith went home to revise her manuscript. She wrote some very good scenes, stringing them together with strong effect that drew her a nice review from *Kirkus* for her first novel, *Secrets of the Devil Vine*. And just as I am about to text her, sitting at this table where we sat December 3, 2015, with the sweet smell of coffee and cream tempting me, a text appears from Faith. She wants to tell me her book has just been released and is on the shelf. I walk through the door past where she stood and met Pat Conroy. I take her book in my hand and shiver at this uncanny timing.

Faith didn't do her homework.

I just did it for her. Didn't move from this place. Tried making a scene here in this corner coffee shop—of me and Pat and Faith—just as he asked.

I wish Pat were here to grade me. He'd be easy with me.

That's So Conroy

~ MARGARET EVANS

In the days immediately following Pat Conroy's death, I couldn't write a word. It happened on a Friday night, and by Saturday morning long, comprehensive tributes were appearing in publications as nearby as the *Beaufort Gazette*, as far-flung as the *New York Times*, and everywhere in between.

Lowcountry Weekly was scheduled to go to print the following Monday morning. I'd already written my column—some trifle, or so it now seemed, about the Donald Trump phenomenon—but there was still time to bump it for a Conroy homage.

And I couldn't write a word.

Apparently, I was in that stage of grief known as "lame." To my everlasting shame, we went with Trump. The Wednesday after the Friday we lost the great Pat Conroy, I gave my column space to Donald Trump.

Pat would have gotten a great kick out of that. It's just *so Conroy*.

"So Conroy" is an expression some of us who knew him have been using for a while now. It's a wide net of a catchphrase. It typically means something like "perversely hilarious" or "ridiculously tragicomic." But "so Conroy" can also describe a certain operatic grandiosity—equal parts agony and ecstasy—with which events often unfolded around the man . . . and everyone in his charmed/cursed radius.

For instance, when Pat's dear colleague and protégé Jonathan Haupt, then with USC Press, spent more than a year meticulously planning a glorious

Portions of this essay originally appeared in the Beaufort, South Carolina, *Lowcountry Weekly*, March 23, 2016.

three-day celebration of Pat's life and legacy—the Pat Conroy at 70 literary festival—it was only natural that Jonathan's mother-in-law would die unexpectedly during this illustrious event. Because . . . that's so Conroy.

When Pat's best friend, Bernie Schein, and his wife, Martha, planned their dream trip to Italy, long before Pat had a clue he was sick, they should have predicted that Pat would be lingering on his deathbed the day they were supposed to leave. Because that, too, is so Conroy.

And as Pat lingered on that deathbed, tenderly arranged in front of a large window so he'd have a view of his beloved Battery Creek—where the sun sets golden over the marsh and egrets rise up like spirits on the wind—we should all have known the Conroys' septic tank would burst and that the only view out that window would be a giant backhoe digging an enormous, gravelike hole in his backyard.

So, *so* Conroy . . .

If I sound flip and irreverent, I learned from the master. I debated the appropriateness of the preceding paragraphs, then I remembered who I was writing about. This is the man who penned the funniest funeral scene I've ever read about his own *brother's* funeral—the one who jumped off a building to his untimely death.

For Pat Conroy, tragedy and comedy were faithful companions, yin and yang, Siamese twins impossible to separate, conceived in love and born of a painful labor. And nothing was sacred.

Except everything.

So those of us who have lost him—and that's all of us, really—are left laughing through our tears as we remember him. And those of us who write—and there are many, many writers in Conroy's wide circle—we're left wondering what we can possibly say about this man for whom so many rivers of ink have already been spilled, and who was himself the king of spilled ink.

Almost everything you ever wanted to know about Pat Conroy he told you himself. You know about his tortured childhood in the house of Santini, about his harrowing days at The Citadel among the Lords of Discipline. You know he was fired by the school board for teaching poor black island children that the water (and the world) is wide. You know he loved basketball and books, cooking and beach music. He told you all of this.

And then he died, and journalists all over the country told you more.

I've been trying to think of things *I* could tell you, little things you might not know about Pat Conroy. Since I went to work for him (for the second time) about three years ago, I'd been writing about him on my blog occasionally, so I went there to review.

Did you know Pat had lately become enamored of fantasy fiction? He was fanatical about George R. R. Martin's *Song of Ice and Fire* series, and he compared Martin to Shakespeare. He had also discovered C. S. Lewis late in life and was so enthusiastic about *him* and his friendship with Tolkien that he ran the idea by me, about a year ago, of getting a group together to travel to an Inklings weekend in Black Mountain, North Carolina. How I wish we'd done it.

You might not know that Pat was very interested in God. Though he didn't go to church much, he still considered himself a Catholic, and he wrestled mightily. During our chats about the Inklings, he once told me he wished he had a writers' group like that of his own. "Wouldn't it be great?" he said. "For those guys, the question of God was always on the table. Maybe you struggled with the idea of God. Maybe you rejected it altogether. But the question was always on the table. It mattered, and it mattered a lot. So many writers I know today don't even address the question. They're not even God-curious. I still think that's the difference between a great writer and a merely good writer. Great writers—whether they're believers or not—are God-haunted."

Pat Conroy was God-haunted. Maybe you didn't know.

Unlike most people I know, Pat loved to talk on the phone. His favorite time to call, and he called *lots* of folks, was late at night. If you missed that call, you'd end up with voicemail beginning, "Clearly it's up to Conroy to keep this dying [expletive] friendship alive . . ." If you were lucky enough to answer, you'd end up in a rollicking conversation ranging from the sublime to the ridiculous to a high-school-level gossip session. I'll never forget the time he called me right after the 2010 Beaufort International Film Festival. I was idling in the school pickup line that Monday afternoon, waiting for my daughter, when my cell phone buzzed. "Just wanted to dish about the film festival," Pat said. He'd had such a great time, couldn't believe "our little Beaufort" had pulled it off, gushed on and on about how beautiful Blythe Danner still was.

Like most men, he loved beautiful women. But he was always courtly about it. Never roguish. His wife, Cassandra King, is one of the most beautiful women you'll ever meet, and he was devoted.

I saw Pat's friend, poet and novelist Ellen Malphrus, the other day, and we discussed the fact that Pat doesn't really seem gone to us. "It's not like we can't still talk to him or hear his voice," she said. And she's right. He left himself to us. In so many words.

And I, for one, feel Pat Conroy all around me as spring unfurls here in his cherished lowcountry. While out walking in the Cypress Wetlands last week—thinking about Pat and how he adored this season—a cardinal zoomed across my path at warp speed, eye level, so close to my face I felt the wind on my cheek and heard its *whoosh*. His feathers may even have brushed my sunglasses; I'm still not sure. It was all so swift and sudden, so frightening and wondrous, I was left shaking as I watched the red bird disappear into the rookery.

They say a cardinal encounter is a visitation from a loved one who has passed. Leave it to the son of Santini to go all "fighter pilot" on me.

That's so Conroy.

Missing Conroy

〰 RON RASH

One thing I learned early on about Pat was that any story I told he would top. I suspect that if I'd said my grandmother had been eaten by a grizzly bear Pat would have had a grandmother eaten by a *Tyrannosaurus rex.*

My favorite example took place one night when we were eating dinner. The subject of dispiriting book signings came up, and I told Pat that I'd endured the worst such signing ever. "Let's hear it," Pat said, so I told about an event years earlier when I'd done a reading and signing at a small library in South Carolina. Books would be available for sale, my host assured me. The books were indeed there, but the audience was not. Three people showed up: the person who'd invited me, a friend of his who promptly fell asleep, and a grim-faced nun who appeared to have come solely as an act of penance. After my event, I dutifully went pen in hand to the signing table. None of the three came near the table.

"Zero books sold," I told Pat. "Zero. No one even picked one up to pretend they might buy it. They didn't even *touch* a book. It doesn't get worse than that."

Pat looked at me, a twinkle in his eyes.

"Oh, no, no, no," Pat said in his inimitable way. "I can top that."

"How do you top *zero* books sold?" I asked.

"I'll tell you how," Pat answered and began a story about a book signing soon after self-publishing *The Boo.*

The signing was in a chain bookstore. He'd been given a chair and a small table on which he placed copies of the book. He sat and waited for custom-ers to come his way. As the two-hour signing was about to expire Pat still hadn't sold a book. Few people had even made eye contact. But then an elderly man did. He came over and spent the next few minutes talking to Pat, finally picking up the book to peruse it. After a while longer he decided to purchase a copy, but only if Pat would personalize the book for him. So Pat asked the man's name, wrote the name and a few words, then signed and dated it.

The man thanked him and was about to go pay for the book. Then, according to Pat, the man took one step toward the checkout counter, fell to the floor, and died.

"That's not zero," Pat said, since the book could not be either sold or resold. "That's minus one, Rash."

I miss those stories, just as I miss our conversations about books and any other topic that came up, because Pat could make anything interesting. I miss his great heart, which was filled with courage, generosity, and loyalty. I miss his teasing, as when he told a reporter that my wife, Ann, was a recovering meth addict and that I'd never owned a pair of shoes until I was in high school. I miss his jokingly referring to me as Mr. Big and himself as Mr. Small. But what I find myself missing most is that booming voice. Whether arriving on a late-night phone call or at a dinner or across a hotel lobby, it announced that Conroy was with me, and the world was suddenly more alive, and better.

Perhaps my favorite moment in all of Pat's work is in *Beach Music* when Jack and Shylah are dancing in a beach house about to crash into the sea. So much is revealed about Shyla and Jack, foreshadowing their whole relationship. But it recently occurred to me that the scene is a metaphor for Pat's life and writing. The trauma of his childhood and adolescence could easily have sent him into the abyss. I know that writing about issues evoking his past trauma could be cathartic for Pat, but there was also peril in descending into that past. Blending memory and art was a dangerous dance too.

Jack and Shyla risked their lives to create something beautiful in that tottering beach house, and so did Pat as he took what might have destroyed him and made it beautiful and true; unlike Jack and Shyla's dance, his art will endure. But the man himself will be greatly missed; his friendship was one of the great blessings of my life.

Remembering the Storyteller

~ TERESA K. WEAVER

A couple of years ago I asked Pat Conroy how he had managed to become so much more prolific as he got older. "Teresa, I'm dying!" was his answer. He was smiling when he said it, and I know he meant he was dying in that way that we are all dying, slowly and inevitably. Still, I wish it wasn't such a vivid memory.

As the book editor at the *Atlanta Journal-Constitution* and then at *Atlanta* magazine, I interviewed Pat many times over the course of twenty years. Always, he was the ideal subject—open and unguarded, hilarious and heartbreaking, respectful and utterly irreverent. But my most indelible memories are not so much about things he said as about how people responded to him. He connected with his readers in an extraordinary way. They didn't just adore his books; they adored him.

People bought tickets, lined up for hours, whatever it took to hear him talk about his books, his famously dysfunctional childhood, and his near-desperate love of reading. Afterward they would stand in line for a few hours more to get a book signed. He would stay until the last book was signed, which always took a while because he wanted to chat with each and every person in line. "So, where's your family from?"

In May 2014 I was in Columbia, South Carolina, to see Pat donate his papers to the University of South Carolina, my alma mater. When he spotted me as he walked into the room, he did a double take and came over to ask, "What are you doing here?"

I said, sort of flippantly, "This is a big deal. Where else would I be?" To my astonishment, he got a little choked up and wrapped me in a big, unexpected bear hug.

Pat was such an outsize personality that it was easy to forget what a gentle soul he could be.

At the South Carolina Book Festival in 2014 Pat tripped on a tricky top step while going onstage and landed hard on his already-bad knees. A collective gasp went up in the audience, and you could practically feel hundreds of hands reaching out to lift him, to steady him, to make sure he was okay. That generosity and goodwill pervaded every gathering of his readers.

In the fall of 2015 I felt compelled to go to Pat Conroy at 70, the literary festival celebrating Pat in his adopted hometown of Beaufort. I had no idea that the first festival bearing his name would also be the last one of his lifetime.

On a day trip to Daufuskie Island during that festival, my sister and I met Sallie Ann Robinson, a celebrated Gullah chef and cookbook author who was one of the children Pat taught in a two-room schoolhouse and immortalized in *The Water Is Wide*. When asked, "What did Pat Conroy teach you?" Sallie Ann took a long, long minute to find the right words. With a catch in her voice, she finally said, "Pat Conroy opened up the whole world to us."

Some literary critics dismissed him quickly and easily as "a storyteller"—a not-so-subtle insinuation that somebody so popular could not possibly be a serious writer. Wisely, Pat continued to delight his readers and exasperate the critics. He was a storyteller and a generous man, and that is a gracious plenty.

Coinblaze and Starwater in the Letters of Pat Conroy

~ CATHERINE SELTZER

The first time I visited the home of Pat Conroy and Cassandra King in Beaufort, Pat gave me "the tour." It was something he did regularly—I think he recognized the unseemly curiosity that overcame most of us as soon as we hit the doorstep, and he graciously sought to satisfy our nosiness (and, really, preserve our dignity) by offering to show us around. I was in town to interview Pat for a book about his work, and while I came armed with a stack of questions about his writing process, the tour provided its own answers.

We started in Pat's office, with its massive desk looking out over the star-tling beauty of Battery Creek, and then headed into the library, a large room he had converted by filling it with rows of tightly packed shelves. Just inside the door, a woven basket held a set of handwritten manuscript pages wait-ing to be retrieved and typed. It was thrilling, honestly, an intimate glimpse into his writing life, but I like to think I kept some semblance of cool until Pat gestured to a box of his journals in a corner and said, almost casually, "You're welcome to use these if you think they might be helpful."

Despite his tone that day, Pat knew the significance of the gift he was offer-ing: if getting to peek into his office was a chance to imagine how he wrote, the journals—and later, the letters and manuscripts to which he also granted me access—offered a chance to witness his development as a writer with an immediacy that was almost electric. Pat knew the excitement of this expe-rience. He was fascinated by writers and writing, and his library included any number of writers' memoirs, published journals, and, of special interest to him, letters. Pat once claimed, "No one loves to read the letters of writers

I admire more than I do," and he often found things in writers' letters that spoke to him as much as their work did. For instance, he observed (in a 2014 letter of his own), "Flannery O'Connor's letters compose one of her finest works and demonstrate a part of her soul that not only sustains but enhances her work." We glimpse this part of Pat through his letters, too.

Pat wrote letters irregularly—"My best letters vanished into thin air with my love of the telephone," he had confessed to me—but he wrote them with a devotion to the form. Pat even toyed with incorporating letters into his own work: in his early years as a writer he and his sister Carol embarked on a (short-lived) manuscript project comprised of letters to one another, and later he briefly flirted with the idea of an epistolary novel. Certainly, many of his public letters—those written to newspaper editors in cities across the country in protest of acts of racism, anti-Semitism, or just general idiocy—have become legendary.

Pat's private letters are among his most compelling, though. Some of my favorites are those written while he was at The Citadel, despite their occasionally overblown, earnest rhetoric. (When I would mention these to Pat during our interviews, he would groan melodramatically.) What seems so remarkable about these letters is that Pat was dedicated to translating his experiences and seeking a distinct voice for doing so. Take for example a series of letters from June 1964 in which Pat wrote of his time as a census taker for a Catholic outreach program. He had committed to living in the basement of a church in Omaha, Nebraska, near where his family was stationed, and surveying the poor white, African American, and Native American members of the community about their needs. In an early letter his tone was sanguine, and he reported looking forward to his first day, one that would surely be "the day of embarkation, the day of departure from my sheltered past." Just days later that departure was real rather than imagined, and Pat sought to capture the world he encountered through a new lens: "The people are becoming symbolic with the broken window, the gloomy passage, and the naked bulb. . . . There is a darkness and the lingering shadow, the empty can of beans, the gray phantom rat, the scrap of food consumed by hordes of roaches, the man with the black teeth, the woman with the purple leg, the woman who tells you without emotion that she knows she's dying, and the whole black epic of another city, in another world, in another time." Pat would later reflect on the experience from the perspective of a mature novelist in the 2010 essay "Deacon Summer," but there is an immediacy, an ambition in these letters, composed when he was just eighteen, that is equally transfixing.

Pat's fascination with language, evident in all of his early letters, sometimes became its subject as well. I love this passage from a letter he wrote to his sister Carol in 1977 as part of their epistolary manuscript:

> When I was in the Dominican Republic, I had a wonderful talk [with Arturo, a linguist.] [H]e admitted that he never read a novel with pleasure because it offered him few surprises. No matter how bizarre the plot, there was always an inevitability, a tedious predictability to the destinies of imaginary characters. But then he said something extraordinary. When he opened up a dictionary, no matter what the language, he was constantly astonished at the history of words, their sources and derivation, their changes, their distortions, their monstrous clowning, their veers curves leaps and pirouettes as they rolled off the tongues of men and women through the centuries. A peasant can change a language. Wouldn't you love to invent new words? [F]ull of coinblaze and starwater. Arturo was telling me that the history of words gripped him more than the history of men. He reads dictionaries—German, Arabic, French, Spanish, Russian—a prisoner of words, a fool for the rapture of the language.

Pat could be describing himself in this last line, of course. To read these letters is to see a writer not only practicing his craft but also reveling in language in its purest form.

When I began work on a full biography of Pat, he wrote letters in addition to our twice-weekly phone interviews. In them, he wrote about writing— the frustration and doubt involved in starting a new novel, the deep satisfaction when "the juices stirred"—but I learned as much about his approach to writing in the fact of the letters themselves. He wrote them, I believe, to hold himself accountable in ways that our interviews didn't always do. Ever self-aware, Pat repeatedly cautioned that as much as he was committed to the accuracy of the biography, in our interviews he might "game the system," slipping behind the comfortable mask afforded a charming conversationalist, "part of the packaging and one that you're aware of."

Writing demanded a different kind of discipline. He noted, "Writing a letter has always derived from the same source as my fiction. . . . [W]hen I find myself writing on a piece of paper, whether I'm recommending someone for a Guggenheim or making out a grocery list or writing down a recipe or writing a chapter to a novel, I find myself locked into an act of high seriousness. Even when I write one of my bonobo-like e-mails, because I'm writing, I've got to throw a piece of myself into the action." Writing could never be casual in the way that speaking could: it demanded his best effort, and it demanded adherence to truth. Pat often told audiences that the "secret" to great writing is to "go deeper," and reading his letters is a chance to witness Pat burrow past easy narratives in search of a harder truth.

Pat pushed me to hold myself to a similar standard: "I want you to think hard, write hard, and be far better than even you believe yourself to be," he wrote. This echoes the advice he gave regularly to writers, but it seems especially powerful because my topic was Pat himself. When he urged me to "go deeper," he was inviting me to challenge his understanding of himself, even as he was sharing it with me. "Tell the truth," he wrote in a letter about the biography, "and hold nothing back. If I stand for anything, it is that. If I didn't believe that was a fact my whole writing life was based on, then I've chosen the wrong profession and you are wasting your time."

Pat understood that "truth" is a slippery concept. He mused in another letter that "the whole word embraces a country of the arbitrary, an impossible end zone," and he worried that he didn't always confront the truth as directly as he felt he should. But Pat also believed in its power unreservedly, a faith that strikes me as almost impossibly brave.

Pat spoke often of the importance of circles in his work, and he began to anticipate the ways in which experiences, images, and ideas would loop back upon one another. I was thinking about this essay and Pat's letters when I witnessed my own Conroyian circle on a visit to his gravesite in the small oak-shaded cemetery maintained by historic Brick Baptist Church on a St. Helena Island back road. Pat had long paid tribute at the gravesites of writers who meant most to him: he left flowers on Thomas Wolfe's grave whenever he was in Asheville, and he wrote in a letter to me that "the cemeteries of Paris were like being given a house key to the heart of French literature.

Westminster Abbey seems holy in a way that has nothing to do with God." So my heart filled when I entered the cemetery and saw that Pat's readers had been making their own pilgrimages. His headstone was surrounded by containers of flowers, small tokens, coins, and the inevitable bottle-tops. What struck me most, though, were the letters. On that day there were a few short notes of gratitude posted for others to read and, among them, a thick, sealed envelope propped carefully against the headstone, where, seemingly in both invitation and answer, Pat's distinctive signature is engraved. I'm not sure of the letter's author or its content, but I feel certain it was written for the satisfaction of writing to express some essential truth, of "throwing oneself into the action." I can think of no more perfect tribute.

A Circle Lit in Holy Light

~ BREN McCLAIN

Picture a circle, one lit in light. Even holy light. That's the shape of my relationship with Pat Conroy.

It begins in July 1995 in Charleston, South Carolina, at one of Pat Conroy's landmark signing events, He sits at a table, and fans snake long, left and right, around any nook and cranny that will oblige them. I am one of those fans, and in my hand I carry his latest work, *Beach Music*. The space in front of me opens up, and there he sits with rosy cheeks and twinkling eyes, and I give him my copy and say something in a voice so tentative I don't know how he hears me. "Mr. Conroy," I say, "I'm writing a novel, too."

"Oh, yeah?"

I want to take my words back. How dare I say such in the presence of a master?

"You need all the advantages you can get," he says. He takes a piece of green paper beside him and begins to write something on it.

I hold my breath.

He writes the name of his agent, her agency, and street address. "Say Pat Conroy recommended she look at your manuscript."

My eyes mist over.

He signs my book, and I bow toward him. In my car, I peep at the inscription. "To Brenda McClain, I hope to read your novel one day. Pat Conroy."

I finish that novel, but I do not contact his agent. I feel too little.

~

Fast-forward to 2008. I have written a second novel, one that I hoped would honor motherhood, but I have failed. The novel is no good, so I put it up. Then early one morning I visit my daddy's farm in Anderson, South Carolina, and I see what I need to "fix" the story. I'm drawn to the pasture, to a corner where a barbed-wire fence holds back a gathering of mama cows whose calves were taken from them the day before and placed in a corral some thirty yards away. Their sounds back and forth are guttural, primal. In front of me stands the centerpiece for the story I've been trying to tell. I make a promise to the mama cow in the deep corner position. I toss out 99 percent of novel two and write a third one, naming it *One Good Mama Bone*. Along the way, I must admit I have moments where I doubt the wisdom of writing a novel with a cow so prominent. Let's face it—cows are not the most popular animals. I think, *Bren, maybe you should change it to a horse.*

But I don't. I made a promise to the cow in the deep corner, who would become my Mama Red in the novel. I will later buy her from my daddy for $1,000 to prevent her from going to slaughter.

It takes a long while to find a publisher for *One Good Mama Bone*, but when I do, our circle continues. None other than Pat Conroy himself offers me a contract with his original fiction imprint, Story River Books. To think that he read my words, read about Sarah Creamer and Mama Red and the Dobbins family and Ike Thrasher—that knocks me out. That he actually wants to publish my words makes me fall to my knees in gratitude. In reverence.

~

Now it's late October 2015 in Beaufort, South Carolina, Pat Conroy's hometown. It Pat's seventieth birthday celebration, the whole town one big party. The festivities kick off and—you guessed it—I'm in another one of his landmark signing lines. This time for Catherine Seltzer's *Understanding Pat Conroy*. My hands are sweating, my neck is splotchy, and I am talking a mile a minute. I know this because I am in line with two friends, who tell me to calm down. They know what I plan to do once the space opens up in front of me.

The space opens up. I hand him the book, already turned to the signing page, where a sticky note bearing my name, "Bren," awaits him. This is the festival's effort to try to speed things along.

He begins to write. I say, "Mr. Conroy, I want to thank you for publishing me. I'm one of your Story River writers." My voice is wobbly.

He looks up, his eyes twinkling. "What's your last name?"

"McClain."

He shakes his head. "I don't remember your name. What's the title of your book?"

"*One Good Mama Bone.*"

His flings open his arm wide and yells, "The cow!"

Of all that he could have said about the story, he chose the cow. *The cow.* I am crying now, and it's one of those ugly cries where your tears let loose. Freed.

He inscribes my book, lifts it my way. I extend my hand to shake his. He takes my hand and kisses it.

Inside my book he has written, "To Bren, The marvelous writer who now is part of Story River history. Pat Conroy."

So, Pat and me, and the circle I was telling you about. It's lit. Holy light.

Great Love and a Poet's Heart

~ MARJORY WENTWORTH

Pat Conroy was always bigger than life, and this quality made him seem indestructible to everyone who knew him. He was a giant of a man in all ways, and I consider myself one of the lucky ones who circled in his orbit.

It is no exaggeration to state that when we moved to Charleston in 1989 for my husband's job, the only thing I knew about this place was what I had read in Pat's novels—particularly *The Prince of Tides*. The sense of place is so palpable in Pat's work; I could smell the pluff mud rising off the pages of my paperback. I knew of Pat's love of poetry before I met him. He has a poet's heart. Attention to the specifics of details and images permeates his writing and creates a sense of place that is intoxicating. In fact, Pat studied poetry with the late James Dickey and for a time was quite serious about becoming a poet.

I admire everything about Pat's writing. His sentences are dazzling and exquisitely crafted, and his language choices are exact, like a poet's. So when I began to write poems inspired by the lowcountry landscape, I looked to his work to discover how to do it. I even used a line from *The Prince of Tides* as an epigraph for a pivotal poem I wrote about all that we had lost and experienced during Hurricane Hugo: "My wound is geography." The wound he referred to was tied to his difficult youth and his abusive father. But his themes about surviving a dysfunctional childhood gave me the confidence to write about subjects I had shied away from in my own work, like my mother's rape and other personal difficulties. Pat talked about how excruciating it was for him to experience the psychic pain required to write what he committed to the page, and there's a deep courage at the root of his art that I greatly admire.

It takes a certain strength to step out of your life and embrace another's, or in a larger way a group of people. And nowhere is Pat's big heart more evident than in his early years teaching on Daufuskie Island and his gorgeous book *The Water Is Wide*. This experience entered my consciousness and helped me understand that to be in this place and *not* write about the African American experience is to not really be here at all.

Our introduction, however, was not auspicious. When our mutual friend Dottie Frank introduced me to Pat, she said, "This is my poet friend Marjory I told you about, the one whose cousin hit Stephen King with a car." (This cousin was a distant one, connected to me through the marriage of one of my mother's many sisters.) Pat, of course, was a friend of Stephen King's, and yet he was still nice to me.

Pat and Cassandra have been kind and supportive at every stage of my writing life here. I am so grateful. They served on the Advisory Board of LILA (Lowountry Initiative for the Literary Arts), an organization I cofounded. They were always generous and donated signed books whenever requested. If I was in Beaufort doing a reading or event, one or both of them was invariably there. Pat, of course, was a self-proclaimed blurb slut! And he would never write anything negative about another writer. His generous spirit set a tone that trickled down the writing ranks. If the greatest among us can give endorsements, then each of us can do the same. His approach to such things reminded everyone to be supportive of one another.

Pat didn't send me many e-mails, but when he did they mattered so much. I always got such a kick out of his e-mail address: atticus@____. His notes were always about my writing or some literary accomplishment and were filled with over-the-top comments that brought tears to my eyes: "I read your new edition of collected poems yesterday and the lowcountry can thank the gods that your life brought you to Charleston." When I was inducted into the South Carolina Academy of Authors he sent a note describing how much it meant to him when he was selected, since he was a military brat and could never quite say where home was. He reminded me that I was "an immigrant from New England" and suggested, "Let them carve that on your tombstone, girl." He referred to me as "his" poet laureate, which of course meant the world to me. He believed in me and supported me as a writer, and it meant more to me than I can say. Pat signed his e-mails "Great Love," and that is what he brought to this place, his writing, his friends and family, and the world. Great love.

I loved his sense of humor; he had nicknames for everyone. Dottie Frank was the *Dotted One*, his wife, Cassandra, was the *Dragon Lady*, his friend John Warley was *Lord John*. But, no one brought out Pat's zany sense of humor more than his friend Bernie Schein. They were like a *Saturday Night Live* skit. Years after *The Prince of Tides* was filmed here, I heard the infamous stories about Bernie calling Pat whenever a book came out and imitating a famous movie star or director such as Robert Redford who expressed a desire to make the book into a film. So when Barbra Streisand actually did phone Pat to see about optioning the book, he thought it was Bernie and hung up on her. I can still remember the great South Carolina film commissioner Isabelle Hill standing in our kitchen asking us if we knew anything about Pat Conroy. What was his problem? Why wouldn't he answer Barbra Streisand's phone calls? Little did I know.

I regret that I never got to say good-bye to Pat properly and tell him how much he meant to me, but I think he knew. I know how hard he fought to stay alive. I know he was still working on a manuscript. I know that Cassandra never left his side, and that he was surrounded by the great love of family and friends.

My mother entered hospice care on March 2 of this year, and she passed away soon after that. I will always associate these two losses in my life. Pat died on March 4, but that week in the midst of Pat's funeral and all the arrangements, Bernie's dear daughter Maggie Schein called and texted and checked on me. Pat's brother Tim sent me text messages with a line from a favorite poem almost every day, and Cassandra sent us a box of fruit. In the throes of their grief, those closest to Pat sent their love to me and my family. Every day I felt that big Conroy heart was still beating in the world. It always will be.

Sublimely Conroy

~ PATTI CALLAHAN HENRY

Sometimes we ask words to bear the burdens that only our hearts can carry. And so we give up because we can't find what we need inside our language. But Pat Conroy never gave up. He dug and he excavated and he found both the words and the stories to share with us. He might have done it at great cost to his own soul, but always at great gain for ours.

Madeline L'Engle says that the author and the reader "know" each other because they meet on a bridge of words. It was on that bridge where I found Pat Conroy, long before we met each other in the world. Of course his real-life friendship was richer and stronger than the bridge of words, but the words came first.

I came to Pat first as a reader falling in love with his rich prose, then as a writer with a desire to learn. In his writing he taught me to pay attention to the details: the way the sunlight fell on the marsh or an emotion bubbled up from the subconscious.

But what Pat taught me as a friend and as a writer far surpasses any writer technique. What I learned from his life and friendship was a kind of theology: *Stories and Life are both marvelous and dreadful.* I can't, as a reader or a writer or a human being, shy away from the broken world. I wanted everything to be so "nice," but Pat said, "Well tough, it isn't all so nice."

With Pat there can be no dualism, no either/or. No good/bad. No right/ wrong. It's all there together—the noble, the cowardly, the awful, the shining. As it must be in both our writing and our lives.

Portions of this essay were first delivered at a public memorial service on May 14, 2016, at Henry C. Chambers Waterfront Park, Beaufort, South Carolina.

He knew how to write a line that reverberated like a tuning fork in our souls. He once wrote an essay about how often he'd moved around as a child of a Marine and that he'd never had a hometown until he chose Beaufort. But instead of stating the facts he wrote, "I never spent a single day in a hometown." And because I have the same feeling of dislocation—having moved many times—I thought, "*Exactly!*" I wanted to call the man who wrote those words, but that was when I didn't know him except as a photo on a book jacket.

To become friends with someone after being a fan is at first an odd thing, a little bumpy. Can we be a friend *and* a fan? How is it to get past the image and come to know the person as who they are beyond the words they write? Because in many ways, aren't we the words we write? I don't know any other profession that is as close to the cuff, as bone to marrow of who we are, as writing is.

And especially someone who writes about family and struggle as Pat did. We can come to believe we know him. But it's not true. We can't be friends with an image. But we can be friends with the complicated, empathetic, gregarious, vulnerable, funny, and sharp-witted man. The man who would call when he found out I was sick and say, "I hear you're catching hell in Alabama." We can be friends with a man who loves his wife as a best friend.

But as special as he made me feel, I wasn't the only one. Pat and I weren't lifelong friends, except on my end. We were newly minted friends just finding our way. And like all of his friends, I'd get that call: "I'm the one who has to keep this dying friendship alive." I wish I'd kept every one of those voicemails on my phone. I knew it was a line he used, just a little jab to make me call him back, because there was no way I'd ever let that friendship die. If I'd had it in my power, there's no way I would have let him die.

He was that way with loads of writers, because he was more than a friend, he was a mentor. He didn't want to just bask in his own light, he wanted our light to join his. He bought our books; he remembered our names; and then he went and helped start a publishing imprint of his own—Story River Books—to help us put more stories into the world.

Offhandedly we talk of Pat's writing and we use the word "beautiful." And by God, it is. But if he taught me anything, he taught me the use of the just-right word, and we'd have to go past "beautiful" to describe him and his stories, we'd have to go all the way to the word "sublime."

And here's the difference.

"Sublime" means of "outstanding spiritual, intellectual, or moral worth; something that is set or raised aloft, high up, something inspiring awe and veneration." The sublime is intensified by darkness and takes a certain pleasure in that absence of light.

And honestly, I can't think of a better word to describe his work.

So while we take the opportunity to memorialize and mourn Donald Patrick Conroy, and we take his great love, friendship, stories, and mentorship into the world, let's not do so merely beautifully, let's do it sublimely—with outstanding spiritual, intellectual, and moral worth, taking a certain pleasure in the absence of light, just like the man himself.

Catering the Funeral of Beaufort's Favorite Eulogist

~ DEBBI COVINGTON

> A recipe is a story that ends with a good meal.
> —Pat Conroy, *The Pat Conroy Cookbook*

My first encounter with Pat Conroy was at a funeral. It was to be the first of many times we would see one another at funerals—Pat as eulogist and me as caterer.

Pat had come home to Beaufort to give the eulogy for Morgan Randel, a beloved Presbyterian, former school superintendent, and the father of Pat's childhood best friend, Randy (whose tragic death Pat described in *The Water Is Wide* and his cookbook). I was in my twenties then and working as the church secretary for First Presbyterian Church. As usual, I was in the kitchen with the women of the church helping prepare food for the reception that followed the worship service. At first, I was a little too timid to approach Pat. I'd never been formally introduced to him, and he didn't know me from Adam's housecat. Still, I found the courage to march straight up to him and offer him a meatball—my recipe. The rest is history.

Over the years, I'd run into Pat in the grocery store and, of course, at quite a few more funerals (where he was often the eulogist). He would always smile that big Pat Conroy smile of his. When I was at last introduced to Pat, he told me he already knew who I was. He knew all about my catering business and my *Lowcountry Weekly* food columns. I was totally in awe!

In February 2015, South Carolina–born actress Andie MacDowell was selected to receive the Spirit and Pride of South Carolina Award at the Beaufort International Film Festival. Pat was the presenter. I catered the pre–awards ceremony party at the Cuthbert House Inn. That night, I gave both Pat and Andie copies of my cookbook. Pat made me inscribe the book to him. Again I was flattered. I catered the cocktail hour preceding the awards ceremony the next night as well. Near the end of the hour, when guests were being seated, Pat was waiting for me in the corner near the auditorium entrance. He called me over to him and told me that he had read my cookbook from cover to cover the night before. I could feel the blood rushing to my cheeks.

We talked about some of the recipes, and he told me the ones that he wanted to try and asked a few questions about ingredients and techniques. Then he asked, "Do you plan to write another cookbook? When you do, let me know and I'll pen something for you." I was over the moon!

Time passed quickly. That summer I had the honor of catering a tapas party for Pat and Mina Saklyama to celebrate the anniversary of the fitness center they opened together, Mina and Conroy. I was doubly honored to cater the opening reception for Pat's seventieth birthday celebration, the Conroy at 70 festival, in October 2015. The last time I saw Pat was at that festival. I had taken a plate of food to his signing table, where he was autographing books for fans in a line that seemed to be a block long. He nodded and gave that big Pat Conroy smile one last time. It was at the awards reception for the Beaufort International Film Festival the following February that I learned Pat was ill.

Donald Patrick Conroy left us on March 4, 2016. When I got the phone call from his family asking me to cater his funeral reception, I had Pat's cookbook in my lap and just happened to be reading the chapter "Why Dying Down South Is More Fun." It seemed like fate or serendipity. Pat, whom I had seen for years most often at funerals, had already planned his own funeral reception menu for me, right there in his cookbook.

I show people that I care about them through food, and four of Pat's lines from that chapter really hit home for me because of that: "Cooking food for a grieving family and their friends is still one of the classiest ways to send a love note that I can think of."

"Pickled Shrimp is my answer to death in Georgia. In South Carolina, I generally respond with a shy and unexpected gift of Dunbar Macaroni."

"I cannot think of ham without thinking of Southern funerals."

And most important, "When I die, I fully expect all the shrimp in Beaufort to be pickled that day."

Following Pat's lead, I created a menu that represented both Pat Conroy and South Carolina, including pickled shrimp and Dunbar macaroni (from Pat's cookbook, with my own variations), and ham and Swiss poppy-seed rolls, which have been served at so many Beaufort funerals that they're sometimes called "funeral sandwiches."

Maybe not all of the shrimp in Beaufort was pickled that day, but I can promise that close to fifty pounds were. If only Pat had been there to enjoy them.

Good-bye, our dear Mr. Conroy. You will be missed. Beaufort—and Beaufort funerals—will never be the same without you.

PICKLED SHRIMP

(from *The Pat Conroy Cookbook: Recipes and Stories of my Life* by Pat Conroy)

1 cup thinly sliced yellow onion
4 bay leaves, crushed
1 (2-ounce) bottle capers, drained and coarsely chopped
¼ cup fresh lemon juice
1 cup cider vinegar
½ cup olive oil
1 teaspoon minced fresh garlic
1 teaspoon coarse or kosher salt
1 teaspoon celery seeds
1 teaspoon red pepper flakes
2 pounds large (21–25 count) shrimp, peeled and deveined

Mix all ingredients except shrimp in a large heatproof glass or ceramic bowl. In a medium stockpot over high heat, bring 4 quarts abundantly salted water to a rolling boil. Add the shrimp and cook until just pink, about 2 minutes. (The shrimp will continue to "cook" in the marinade.) Drain and immediately transfer to the marinade. Bring to room temperature, cover tightly, and marinate overnight in refrigerator. Transfer shrimp and marinade to a glass serving compote or bowl. Serve chilled.

Riding the Literary Thermals with Pat Conroy

~ JOHN LANE

Employing the metaphor of a literary thermal assumes a great deal of a casual reader, who must accept a few things: that literature may be seen as a landscape, a sacred topos, a mystical terrain with irregular topography; and that there are currents flowing upon this metaphoric land, winds and updrafts, air heated and cooled by the sun. And that on those cultural updrafts life has granted some lucky writers the gift of a glide upward with what looks like little effort. I've thought about this metaphor often since Pat Conroy died. For six months in 2015 I got to ride the literary thermals with him after he chose my first novel, *Fate Moreland's Widow*, as the sixth book in his Story River Books southern fiction imprint.

I am a literary bird—poet, essayist, fiction writer—and Pat Conroy is a literary bird as well, but what sort of literary birds are we? Conroy was a bird of great wingspan. Eagle? Hawk? Roseate spoonbill? Sandhill crane? Whatever Pat Conroy is, he spent years riding literary thermals high and catching the big view, soaring upward on culture's warm blasts, then soaring outward for miles. Conroy was like a literary hawk who swoops in and devours literary immortality, swallowing it whole. He was voracious in that way like a bird of prey. And like a rare bird, people gasped sometimes when they spotted him.

It's too soon to know for sure whether Conroy achieved that immortality he sought chasing his hero, Thomas Wolfe, though it looks good—millions of books sold, tens of thousands of Facebook friends, five movies, a literary center. And me? I'm still flitting about at sixty-one, more like a yellow-throated warbler, a grosbeak, or maybe a water ouzel—abundant but dramatic, mostly happy to fly no higher than the tallest oaks.

Throughout the spring, summer, and early fall of 2015 I appeared on stage with Conroy six times, each time with the types of crowds only Pat Conroy can draw in the heart of Conroy country—Charleston, Greenville, Winston-Salem, and twice in Decatur. "Chattooga man," Conroy always said when he greeted me, referring to the nonfiction book I'd written about the famous *Deliverance* river and James Dickey's relationship to it. These appearances with Conroy were Q&A panels with other Story River authors. Conroy was always the animated moderator—telling Pat Conroy stories but mostly asking us about the nuances of our own work and listening attentively to our answers, which sometime went on longer than they should.

Conroy's commitment to Story River Books was hard to believe; the editorial work was something the most famous novelist in the South didn't have to do. He was still soaring when he died. *Fate Moreland's Widow* came out from Story River in March 2015. On my novel's back cover Conroy contributed a generous blurb, and soon after its publication he wrote about the book several times on his Facebook page—each posting beginning "Hey out there," his signature callout to rally his 50,000-plus online friends to whatever literary weather had his attention at the moment. Thanks to Pat, my Amazon numbers redlined for a few days, my readership as measured by BookScan went up by hundreds, and several book clubs outside my usual writerly range map (South Carolina and a little beyond) assigned the novel to their members.

At times the events that spring, summer, and fall turned into a literary Magical Mystery Tour—like the time the woman stood up in the Decatur First Baptist Church, where three hundred had turned out in the rain, and testified that she would only come out in such a downpour for two southern cultural icons—George Jones and Pat Conroy. Or the time later in the spring at Furman University when we all arrived early for a cocktail party with some of the university's big donors. As we sipped our champagne a fan took snapshots through the closed glass doors of Conroy circulating inside. I like to think I photo-bombed some of her images.

At the Decatur event in May I arrived about 4:00 p.m. and met novelist Bernie Schein for a drink in the lobby of the hotel. I'd met him at the South Carolina Book Festival only a few days before. I enjoyed the talk—his Story River novel *Famous All over Town* had been the fourth in the series—and he'd also been Pat Conroy's best friend since high school. Talkative and jovial, Bernie was having the time of his life on the Magical Mystery Tour. Story River had published Bernie's daughter Maggie's *Lost Cantos of the Ouroboros Caves* as well, and she was there for the panel too. We decided we'd all meet in the lobby to go over to the event space, a nearby Baptist church, at 6:30.

A huge thunderstorm blew in that spring evening right when we left the hotel for the event. Those with a literary imagination might see this storm as ominous in retrospect, foreshadowing Pat Conroy's illness and death only ten months in the future, but I like to remember it as a perfect literary back-drop for the spectacle of the Magical Mystery Tour.

Rain fell in buckets as we drove several blocks to the church. "Pat Conroy and Friends" the church marquee announced—like a rock concert or a revival. In the car the Schein family verbally sparred good-naturedly as we looked for a parking place close to the entrance. It's what they do in their family. Growing up a southerner, I'd always done my best to avoid conflicts, even good-natured conflicts of a family type, so I listened in fasci-nation as the banter moved back and forth between them. I'd soon discover, event after event, that the same banter was natural for Bernie, Maggie, and Conroy. They'd been at it for decades.

We had trouble finding a parking place. The lot was full, and we were all very excited—what a literary crowd! Turned out when we got inside, Pat Conroy and friends had the sanctuary, but there was also a full Monday night Baptist prayer supper going on in the cavernous fellowship hall.

We all gathered in an impromptu "green room" behind the sanctuary almost filled with curious Pat Conroy devotees and the curious about the new Story River imprint he was editing. We waited for Conroy to arrive. Genius fiction writer Mary Hood, whose novella *Seam Busters* followed *Fate Moreland's Widow* in the Story River lineup, had settled in a comfort-able chair long before we arrived. With her long gray hair and metal cane she looked strangely distinguished and mystical, like the Pythia at Delphi waiting for the next question.

Conroy soon arrived, and things picked up after he greeted everyone. The joking began between Conroy and Bernie, but there was also a sign that Conroy held Mary Hood and her fiction in high reverence. He kneeled down, leaned close, and talked privately with her for a long moment.

The Magical Mystery Tour went on about 7:15 with about three hundred in the sanctuary. The weirdest thing for me was the three Baptist church jumbotrons projecting our faces to the multitudes as we spoke. Conroy asked us each a couple of questions. The first question of the night was for Mary Hood, and she set a high bar. "What do you think when people compare you to the great southern storyteller Flannery O'Connor?" Hood spiraled into a sort of literary trance response. She intoned in vivid literary incantations a brilliant lit crit stream of conscious about O'Connor, her life, and her work. It went on for ten minutes. Then at the end, she brought the house down when she asked, "Oh, what was the question?"

I learned riding the literary thermals with Pat Conroy—the short skyward spiral of the book tour—that Pat Conroy is a generous man, and his friends are generous to him in return. I learned that Conroy's world pulls together more straws than a lowcountry sweetgrass basket. That he loves the lowcountry in general, and Beaufort in particular. That literary friendship is a powerful thing and needs always to be cultivated. In nine years I will be seventy. Like a stone dropped in a pond, my ripples radiate outward. After thirty-five years my literary circles are still widening. I'm now proud to count Pat Conroy among those I've followed on my flight.

At the end of that evening in Decatur I reached a deeper insight into Pat Conroy. I saw another side of him as we all sat late in the hotel bar and ate Japanese food. I saw how loyal Conroy was to his friends and his family. He was very funny, as everyone knows, but he was also very vulnerable. Twice he leaned over to me that night to offer a personal comment. The first time he said, "I want you to remember how much I love your novel," and the second time he said in his usual undercutting humor, "I also want you to take more time answering those questions. You can go long. It's OK. And you know, I wanted to tell those people how much of a better paddler you were than James Dickey."

The World Is Wider Than the Water It Holds

〜 ANTHONY GROOMS

My introduction to Pat Conroy was by way of Jon Voight, the six-foot-two leading man who played him in *Conrack*, the movie version of *The Water Is Wide*. Familiar with Voight from his roles in *Midnight Cowboy* and *Deliverance*, I nonetheless made him the face of Pat Conroy. Even after I had seen pictures of Conroy, with his round face, button nose, and broad smile (a grown-up Irish cherub), it was still the visage of Voight that I conjured when I thought of Pat Conroy.

The film attracted me, in large part, because of Voight's portrayal of Conroy as a charming, enterprising, and heretical white schoolteacher in an all-black elementary school in 1969 South Carolina. I don't remember exactly when I first saw the film, which debuted in 1974, but it impressed me as being in the tradition of schoolhouse films I admired such as *To Sir, with Love* and *Up the Down Staircase*. Had I been more sophisticated, I might have dismissed it as a typical race redemption film in which a white teacher plays hero on the issue of black civil rights. Frankly, in those days, the idea of the white hero appealed to me. I had attended a nearly all-white elementary school in rural Virginia during the early days of the Freedom of Choice plan, a ploy meant to divert full integration of the schools, and it was just the kind of teacher that Voight portrayed, a young, progressive white, who offered me solace, protection, and a sense of worth as I struggled, my parents pushing me, out of the humiliating quagmire of Jim Crow. In my view, there were too few white heroes.

Reflecting now, as a middle-aged man, I admire *Conrack* less, seeing the film as having created an idolatrous character and a story that promotes a facile version of race redemption. It is, sadly, the best Hollywood could and will do. But the film is not the book. Conrack is not Conroy.

When, at last, I came to *The Water Is Wide*, I realized that *Conrack* was a jaggedly sketched version of Pat Conroy's complex and deeply moving portrait of the people of Daufuskie Island, of the Beaufort County school system, and—most important—of himself. *The Water Is Wide* is among the most affecting and rawly honest books written about race relations in the South—and Conroy's white hero is as full of doubt and self-effacement as he is full of passion and self-righteousness. In fact, Conroy lambastes his own do-gooder impulses and is as nearly cynical about the do-gooder as Mark Twain in *Huckleberry Finn*.

My first school, though larger than the Daufuskie Island schoolhouse, was much on par with it for its lack of resources. But whereas Daufuskie, or Yamacraw as it is called in the memoir, had a rudimentary library donated by what Conroy calls "earnest ladies and pious men," Ferncliff Elementary had only a shelf in the teacher's closet with two incomplete sets of thirty-year-old encyclopedias. Between the two sets, the alphabet was covered. As with Yamacraw, there was a Mrs. Brown, too, the self-hating and child-humiliating black principal. But she was not my teacher. My teacher was Mrs. Johnson, a gangly, mustachioed woman who wobbled about in kitten heels and seemed perpetually bent by the weight of a carpetbag of a purse. She was a local woman, a friend of my grandmother's, and nearly as stealthy in her teaching as the young Conroy was. When she taught from the state-required Virginia history book, she let us read about happy slaves and dependent colored people. Then she told stories about Frederick Douglass, W. E. B. Du Bois, and local blacks of note: John Mercer Langston and her favorite, Maggie Walker, the first black woman to own a bank. In Mrs. Johnson's class we sang the national anthem and then we sang the Negro national anthem. When the all-white, nearly all-male school board members made their annual twenty-minute visit to the school, we students never mentioned Langston or Walker, but stiffly reported on other locals, Thomas Jefferson and Patrick Henry. Oh, Mrs. Johnson made good use of those encyclopedias!

My situation was as perilous as many black children's, but it was never as hopeless as that of Prophet, Anna, Big C, and the other Yamacraw children.

My parents, both grotesquely undereducated by the state of Virginia, none-theless saw education as the Underground Railroad for their children. When the county offered Freedom of Choice, my parents enrolled me and my sister into the white elementary school, which had a small but well-stocked library and a part-time librarian. But Freedom of Choice was nei-ther free nor easy for us, and especially not for my parents. Many decades later, my father told me how members of his own family opposed his send-ing us to the school, mostly out of fear for us but also because it looked like "Rob is acting uppity." He told me a prominent white man offered to pay his taxes for a year if he would withdraw us from the school. Luckily, my father worked in a neighboring county and had some economic buffer. My mother worked for a factory, a much-needed employer in the county and owned by a northern company, and so her job was safe, too.

Unlike *Conrack*, *The Water Is Wide* is a race conversion narrative, not a race redemption narrative. In it, Conroy admits to his own hateful attitude toward blacks as a teenager. He tells how he happened upon the Greensboro Woolworth's sit-in—and how witnessing it and realizing what it was did nothing to change his perspective on civil rights for blacks. There is no aha moment in which he realizes the wrong of segregation, but rather he is guided by a progressive teacher and liberal friends, and by his experi-ences with his black high school students, who vent their anger on him in response to Martin Luther King's murder. Still, it is the delusion of saving the world and the appeal of having a job away from administrative supervi-sion as much as anything that brings him to the black schoolhouse. Once on Yamacraw, once he meets his students, the process of his conversion begins in earnest. He begins to know his students as individuals and to understand the legacy of the deprivation that imprisons them. He begins to understand his own white privilege and to reckon with it. Heroes of redemption narra-tives rarely reckon with their own privilege.

Importantly, Conroy uses his race and class privilege for the betterment of his students. This is the privilege of access—access to the superintendent who sees Conroy as a younger, albeit misguided, version of himself; access to materials from the school board; and access to a network of white friends who prevail upon their white neighbors to host the black children. But resources are not the most important aspect of Conroy's privilege; rather it is knowledge of and a perspective on the world that people of his race and class take for granted—travel to Europe—celebration of holidays—appreciation of the fine arts. His is a perspective on the bigness of the world and the assumption that it is here to explore. In effect, the greatest of all white privilege, a privilege not generously given to blacks during Jim Crow, is the privilege to dream. Conroy inspires his students to dream, to question, to be curious. He teaches them the name of the ocean they live beside and encourages them to imagine what lies beyond it. They begin to understand something of the big, wide world. This is the teacher's gift to students, but as evident in the portrayal of Mrs. Brown, not a gift that black teachers were often allowed to give during the Jim Crow years.

Huston Diehl began her teaching career in my county in 1970, the year Pat Conroy was fired from the Daufuskie Island school. She wrote about her experiences as a white teacher in an all-black elementary school in a memoir she entitled *Dream Not of Other Worlds*. She taught my cousin. The title of the book, she said, reflected the low expectations that the white community held for the black students. But more than that, these were low expectations that were aggressively reinforced by the deprivation of resources and enforced by law in an attempt to exert economic and political control on the black community. In spite of the horrendous physical violence engendered by Jim Crow, the suppression of intellect was the worst violence of all because it stunted and dehumanized generations of blacks, and its legacy lives with us today. The few of us who escaped, though not without wounds, did so because of persistent parents and visionary teachers like Johnson, Diehl, and Conroy.

The Water Is Wide is not solely focused on the schoolchildren, however. Conroy luxuriates in what I think is at his core, a gregarious personality. He melds with all people. He seeks conversations—some uncomfortable, some rebuffed. He revels in the stories of the natural raconteurs he encounters. As a writer, he captured these stories and the voices that told them with aplomb. He is also blessed with a nearly supernatural insight, able to see strengths, vulnerabilities, sincerities, and hypocrisies—and most importantly able to touch on the ironies of the human disposition—the black schoolteacher who loathes blacks, the white racist who is an essential resource for the black community, the white who speaks derogatorily about blacks as a whole but respects us as individuals. And he does not spare himself this gaze, critiquing his own shortcomings and successes. The South that Conroy writes about is the South I know—with eddies and tides and marshes and currents as complex as any coastal river. This is the complexity I hope to achieve in my own writing.

It was not until a few months before he died that I met Pat Conroy in person. I was meeting a writer who shared Pat Conroy's agent, and so had entrée to the table where Conroy and a group were dining in a restaurant. I introduced myself to Conroy, and he warmly greeted me. I went around the table introducing myself to others and fell into conversation with someone I knew from years before. As I talked, I felt an arm slip into the crook of my elbow, and Pat's smiling, cherubic face came close to mine as he pressed into me, teasingly, and pulled me warmly, charmingly into the sway of his current. Great teachers have that way.

On the Wings of the Incoming Tide

〜 ELLEN MALPHRUS

Serendipity. That's what Conroy always called it, the Dickey/deer story of how our trajectories collided in the Blue Hill, Maine, pharmacy where he was collecting his wits after he and Sandra had struck a deer (the first of his life) just minutes before—and where I'd stopped off for film en route to the tip of Canada on a two-pronged quest to photograph puffins and savor the perfect lobster roll. We began singing the praises of James Dickey, revered mentor to us both, made a lunch date to talk about him more, and never really shut up talking about him—or so our spouses say.

That was the long-ago summer the four of us—Pat, Sandra, my husband, Andy, and I fortified our friendships in cottages by the sea (turned out we were nearly neighbors). When we stopped in to bid them adieu on the way back to Carolina (with the Chaisson dory Andy and his comrades had crafted at the Wooden Boat School tied atop the Tahoe) Conroy had packed us a resplendent smorgasbord of a picnic, including those cool clamp-top Grolsch beers, that we enjoyed with glee as we descended the eastern seaboard. Because he's Conroy. Because he took the time.

That was also the summer that, after cajoling me into a writing sample by asking that I jot down what it was like to have been in so many of Dickey's classes, Conroy began gently encouraging me to complete the manuscript that became *Untying the Moon*. As I dawdled, his nudges turned to nags—then full-blown pestering—over lunches and porch talks and late-night phone calls. Thank heaven for it, or the novel still might not be in a form

Portions of this essay originally appeared in *Shrimp, Collards, and Grits* magazine, June 2017.

that holds together when you pick it up and shake it. And when the time came for my book launch this past October—a lovely moss-draped, blue-skied garden party at the Heyward House in Bluffton—hundreds of people showed up, and surely not just for Ellen Malphrus. They showed up because my buddy, my brother-in-Dickey, was at my side signing the foreword he'd written for my book. Because he's Conroy. Because he took the time.

And then time blinked, a mere two months. "Malphrus, I'm a trouper." That's what he said when he loaded up to leave E. Shaver Bookseller in Savannah after our December 10 book signing—the one that turned out to be his last. Just the day before, he and I had given a presentation (okay, sat on a stage and cut the fool) then signed books for the Women's Association of Hilton Head Island (WAHHI)—nearly five hundred women (plus Pat and Andy). He was weary and not exactly feeling his best, and I was giving him a sisterly "talking to" about pushing himself too hard. That's when he said it: "Don't worry about me, Malphrus, I'm a trouper." Yes, indeed.

In another blink of time, concern about his feeling poorly turned into a bedside vigil with his cherished family and friends. Days of bolstering, with stories and poetry and songs and prayers and kind gestures by the boatload. And it was no damned pity party, I can tell you that. Conroy wouldn't have it. When the septic tank guys dug a hole in the lawn, across which Pat gazed toward the abiding river, a hole big enough for us all to have jumped in if we'd opted for mass suicide, we laughed. And when the day bed, upon which folks who'd come to say a final farewell could sit, collapsed (not once but twice), we laughed. And when, in the lingering last hours, the cloth that had been draped across a lamp to make the room more tranquil caught fire, we laughed. And when rainwater filled my forgotten convertible, we laughed. Of course we laughed. It's classic Conroy.

As the moment came and Pat crossed over, I took leave of the bedside where his family had so graciously offered me a place, walked out to the dock, lay down on the splintered boards, and opened the floodgates of my tears. As they filled Battery Creek I looked up into the totally cloud-blocked sky, and while I watched, the patch just overhead the House of Conroy opened to a starry ring of sky. A perfect circle of love.

The day after Pat's burial on St. Helena Island, on the salt marsh island retreat where I'd gone for solace, a deer came crashing through the dry palmetto fronds while I was in a sunset river trance and put me in mind of Dickey's "The Starry Place between the Antlers," where he writes of his fascination with and yearning to see deer swimming. A blessing of our barrier island is that I know well that "starry place between the antlers," having beheld deer swim forth and back to the mainland for years. Never, though, had one come bounding right past me, close enough for each of us to bear witness of the other. With it came another full circle—to Conroy's Maine deer story. Magic happens around rivers. Serendipity. Chance. A dispatch from Dickey. Call it what you will.

The final inscription Conroy wrote to me is dated October 26, 2015. His seventieth birthday. His last. It reads: "To Ellen Malphrus, The great poet and writer who came to me by magic over the body of a slain deer and the memory of James Dickey—and whose friendship turned into something far more than that—something rare and large and unkillable. I love you. Pat Conroy."

Full circle. Within it, friendship does not die. Love is unkillable. Art is everlasting. And yes, there are angels. I have known them to ride on the wings of the incoming tides—maybe even swim them.

The week before Conroy's seventieth birthday gala, he and I sat down for a filmed interview. One of the things we talked about was what he has tried to do with his life and with his work. In closing he said to me, "It's the voyage out that is important." Pat is on a different voyage now, and the vessel he has built is not only made with his writing—which would keep it afloat forever—but is also built with his generosity of spirit, his kindness, his compassion, his insistence to stick up for little guy, his commitment to try to help heal those who are hurt. It is also built with his love for his sweet Sandra, his children and grandchildren, his sisters and brothers, his friends, and his readers. It's a vessel sturdy enough to weather the ages. The ripple behind it will fan from his beloved lowcountry rivers out to sea, and we will feel the beauty of that gentle wake each time the tide rolls out and in again.

Until Then

Of Pat Conroy, our sweet Prince of Words
I can only say this:
If ever a man went to his grave knowing he was loved, it is this man.
He who lashed himself to the mast and rode out the telling of the tale with a
Blistering insistence on truth.
The truth that was in him.
That was his to tell.

Can only say this:
Here was a man who, again and again, re-wove a net ever-shredded by
    shark's teeth,
And with it cast for words-on-troubled-waters and tamed them into
    dolphin whispers.
Waters where we can all dive and come up refreshed.
Salt crusted, but enriched.

Can only say this:
By the time of his Story Rivered burst into three score and ten—
Packed to the hilt with promise and peace—
He, who feared love could last only as long as a sucker punch to the heart,
Had come to know better.
Had come to feel the floodgates open.
Because of you.
Because of us.

And, finally, can say only this:
Would that we all could face eternity in the
Steadfast embrace of such familial fidelity,
Then turn to cross over,
With the delicate kiss of Cassandra soft upon our brow.

Hold fast the light, sweet Prince, our beloved,
When the time comes, and we row out to meet you
In the heron-hush of eventide.

The Extended Hand

~ MARK POWELL

I came to know Pat Conroy through his work: it is, of course, the truest way to know a writer. One's innermost isn't spilled out in online posts or interviews. The world is glossed with ephemera as gauzily insubstantial as fog, and as useless. But one's innermost, the product of years of focused obsessive work, can be a lifeline if read by the right person in the right moment. I was that right person in that right moment, and Pat's work came to me as exactly that: an extended hand.

I read *The Lords of Discipline* riding back and forth to away basketball games my junior year of high school in Walhalla, South Carolina. A senior had given it to me—he was headed to the Air Force Academy after graduation—tossing it my way and saying only, "I think you'll get it." I did get it, whatever *it* was. More important, I think it got me. I was a not quite bookish kid living a very unbookish life. But after reading Pat Conroy the first time I began to understand there was a larger world I could read my way into, and it was like discovering water at the same moment you realize you are dying of thirst.

Like Pat, I wound up at The Citadel, an English major and an athlete—I ran cross-country and track. And like Pat, I think, I was restless without ever knowing exactly why. But I knew where to look for answers. Over the next four years I read my way through all of Pat's books, along with Faulkner and O'Connor and McCarthy, and I felt initiated into a larger world, one new to me but completely familiar. Which is, I think, a way of saying I came home through the work of Pat and a few others.

I also fell in love. Nothing calls like to like as powerfully as books—there is, perhaps, no stronger attractor—so in hindsight I shouldn't have been surprised when during my knob year I received a letter from a girl with whom I'd gone to high school. She had just read *The Lords of Discipline*, and she hoped I was okay. She hoped—and I used the line later in my fourth novel, *The Sheltering*, the novel for which Pat wrote an introduction with all his trademark generosity and eloquence—she hoped I hadn't turned mean. Probably nothing in life has kept me from "turning mean" more than that letter. We married a few years later, and as I write this we are days away from our seventeenth anniversary. We have two children, and together we have read all of Pat's books, not only because they are beautiful, which they certainly are, but because they are part of the fabric out of which we have made our life.

When I met Pat years later I experienced a sort of existential stage fright. It's dangerous to meet your heroes. We were at the Decatur Book Festival, and *The Sheltering* had just been released. I remember walking through the Georgia heat to the restaurant where we were to have dinner, excited, grateful, and more than a little nervous. Fortunately, Pat turned out to be as much a gentlemen in life as he is on the page. He turned out, in fact, to be one of the kindest human beings I've ever had the good fortune to meet.

Reading Pat, and later knowing him, has been a life-class not only in how to write but how to live. To be loyal, to be honest, to be kind. To love the South while refusing to accept its failings and shortcomings. To pay forward what cannot possibly be paid back. To write about your family, to love your family. To look directly at all the world's horror, to face it honestly, but never to turn mean. That's what knowing Pat and reading Pat taught me, and is teaching me still.

He Kept His Word for the Sake of Ours

∿ MARY HOOD

Pat Conroy and I met several times over the years in rooms crowded with authors and readers. The first time, Pat gave the keynote at the American Booksellers Association in New Orleans. It was the year *The Prince of Tides* came out, the book not yet fully edited, and still, uncorrected advance reading copies were being handed out by the hundreds. The kind of writer I am—dreading missteps, needing all the help I can get with typos, grammar, and the fine points—thought the typos alone would make him suicidal. I started praying for him right then in that vast hall where he would be speaking in a matter of moments. I thought Pat would look devastated. He looked and sounded great, and said his wife had told him he had slept "like a valise." He shared and made us laugh and then he read and made us cry. I was just a face in the crowd, two more hands among thousands applauding, applauding. I was praying, too. I prayed for him to live out his life and die of natural causes. Has anyone ever died of typos? He didn't.

This brash and good and burdened young man—with his heart full of words and the chaos of hope and stammering, shimmering inchoate ambition—stood confessing how he had gotten off a California tour bus with the other brochure wavers, snapshot and star stalkers in Hollywood, and made a decision. No matter how he got to where he was going, or if he was never to get there but only to be under way, he knelt—he told us—on some celebrity's emerald turf and pounded it with his fist and cried from the depths of his soul his dare and prayer to Santini and highest heaven: "As God is my witness, I will not be a weenie!"

His personal devastations and humane expectations, his setbacks, his glorious, furious attempts on goal, his raising of banners and rallying cries on the battlefields of his life, his fulminating emotions—on the page or from the podium or into plain air—could show up on weather radar, his cyclonic heartbreaks breaking ours. His amazing good cheer rallied us toward joy. His testimony opened eyes and dialog around home fires, in hunting camps, on seagoing ferries, in schoolrooms, in boardrooms. In tea rooms. In hospices. Between bunks at camp. Between bombs in war. When readers talked about Pat Conroy, they were finding a way to talk about themselves. His was not the only family story he was telling. He bore the honorable firstborn's burden of leading the way and staying in sight, close enough for reaching back.

So now we have come to the moment I enter his story river. I am so glad he chose my stories to be published by Story River Books. Glad I had finally finished them. We never corresponded directly during the editing; he made editorial suggestions through Jonathan Haupt. One was that Pat wished for a little bit more at the very ending of my novella "Seam Busters." I hoped I could find something. I went looking, and it found me. I had trusted Pat's instincts and found the words he wanted. It made the story stronger, and it proved again what I believe about good editing: it is a gift from God.

Pat geared down like a determined farmer who has laid a mortgage on his very soul for the making of this crop; every word, phrase, sentence, page counted. His, always. And now with Story River, ours. He aimed his roaring combine into the southern fields of grit lit and drove hard, back and forth but always forward, like a storm was coming and deep chill, and he would rescue us all; he would not lose us, neither bloom nor seed. Thanks to him, we have been gathered safe into shelter, but he, the master of the harvest, had no time to linger. He raised the hurrah, hugged everybody in sight, and strode on to wider fields.

The last time I saw Pat Conroy on planet earth was in 2015 at the Decatur Book Festival, months from his seventieth birthday. We were in a vast chamber—there were columns and marble—in the old Decatur Courthouse, high up. I sat between Pam Durban on my right and Pat Conroy on my left. The tables were shoved together, so Pam and I were at one table, Pat at the next.

There was a slight fault, a gap, but not a significant one, between the tables, but an elbow might have got caught in it, if one leaned. Neither Pat nor I leaned. The room was filled with Pat's fans, standing along the walls, sitting on the floor, in every aisle leaving hardly room for a fire marshal's boot to dare a step.

There were microphones on the table, but mine drooped, and when it came my turn to read, I had my book to hold, a copy new enough it tried to shut. I had the listless microphone to fiddle with. I felt overwhelmed and, suddenly, sad and weary. My eyes stung. I remembered the words I had written in my Writer's Companion pocket notebook, along with my New Year's Resolutions. "Never say maybe when you mean NO." I suddenly wished I was anywhere but there, a feeling I often get in large crowds, and especially when the microphone is aimed, more or less, my way. Suddenly the perky green-and-turquoise bow I had tied onto my ponytail did not feel perky enough to banner me on . . . and besides, it was behind me, so of no use unless I tossed my head. I am not a head tosser.

No time to bolt. Intro over, applause done, I was "on."

I dealt with the stiff new spine on the book, I dealt with the crowd and saying thank you for inviting me and opening words and setting up my reading, and thanks again to the crowd. When I began to read, the thing just went on and on. It felt as if years had passed, and there I was, still on that paragraph. I felt the vibrations and trembling of tense muscles, holding still, because as my mom had said—more than once—good posture takes off ten pounds, and on the edge of my chair, heels on the floor, at least everything was balanced, but when it came time to turn that page?

There was really nothing I could do to stop my mind from running along on its own and seeking, like a wren in a parlor, the way out. Thoughts of flights of all types, even as I read the words in front of me. Inside my skull the enviable little free bird I had been watching fly out and back, hawking insects in the treetops outside the windows while Pam Durban's beautiful voice was reading of winter coming on. The advice of Thoreau uselessly reminding me, "We live in a world owls inhabit."

My elevator fantasies are *not* the same sort Erica Jong got famous for. I am always—on airplanes, in elevators, PTA meetings, crowded parlors, movie houses—seeking exit, fresh air, and gone. Long gone. The trembling of my whole self was not just strain from holding still and keeping on. It was fear I wouldn't. It was fear because I knew I could so easily, even at that moment, give up being a writer, fling the book down, and run off. I had run off. Often. I was coming to the bottom of the page.

And then, on my left periphery, a slight motion.

A giant paw moved slowly over to my side of the gap between the tables.

It was Pat Conroy's strong and steady right hand, and it clamped the left edge of my book like something you buy from Levenger's, a reader's tool to make things easy, and make you feel like royalty. When I turned the page, he lifted pressure slightly, took the turned page under his care, and held steady.

On behalf of literature in general and southern storytelling in particular, Pat Conroy made promises to readers, to everyone he chose for his Story River imprint, flagrant, vast, princely promises costly to his own work and rest. Story River Books was his avowed creation. He gave his word and he kept his word, for ours.

We have his own words about how indefatigably he loved stories and how words enchanted him. He became their wizard and devotee. We have his own testimony about how much sentences mattered, and how they can, flung from beyond sight, reel out like lifelines shot from some steady and distant deck or tower and gather us safely home.

Afterword
Shared Blessings, Shared Sorrows

~ CASSANDRA KING CONROY

Although no afterword is needed to complete this heartwarming collection of writers' tributes to Pat, I appreciate the opportunity to express my gratitude to Nicole and Jonathan and the contributors for such a treasured gift. Reading the essays, having Pat come to life through these remembrances, was bittersweet for me, of course. At times it was too much, hurt too much, and I had to put them aside until I pulled myself together. I could see him too clearly, could hear him speak the words exactly as he'd said them. I saw the twinkle in his bright blue eyes and the impish look I knew only too well. Although the remembrances bear a common theme—meeting Pat, being influenced by him—each is filtered through the writer's personal reflections, so each offers a unique perspective. In that way, every one of these essays cheered me. And every one of them broke my heart.

If Pat were here, he'd be overwhelmed by the many expressions of true and deep affection that this collection reveals. I doubt that he, the master of words, would know how to say how much it meant to him, however. Oh, sure; he'd be profuse in his thanks and gratitude—over the top, even—but those of us who knew Pat best would be able to see him struggle to cover up how moved he was, as we'd seen him do many times before. Inevitably he'd end up making a joke of it. It was the way he masked feelings too deep to express. It was as much a part of who he was as the mischievous twinkle in his eyes.

As couples are prone to do, Pat and I grew morbid in our old age. We talked about our demise, as our grandparents before us had done. Maybe it's nature's way of easing us into the inevitable, but by the time Pat and I reached our sixties we were playing the game. Hard to imagine, Pat said to me, but someday soon, one of us will be left without the other. Then the other will have to carry on, to face the cruel world all alone. "That's going to be tough," I said with a grimace. "Yeah," Pat agreed. Then he thought a minute and said, "I'll sure miss you, girl."

The truth is, neither of us could ever talk about anything serious. It was one of the things that had brought us together. At one point in our courtship Pat said to me in utter exasperation, "I never thought I'd meet my match. You're worse at expressing your feelings than I am." It sounded ludicrous. Pat, the writer known for baring his soul and spilling his guts on every page he wrote, worried about expressing himself? But he did worry, a lot, that he, the wordsmith, could never adequately convey his love for those closest to him. It was the legacy left by a father who'd been incapable of expressing tender feelings, who went to his grave without doing so. It always tormented Pat that he might do the same.

There was some truth to it, some cause for his concern. One of my most treasured voicemails from him early in our courtship remains one of the funniest and most poignant. He left it when I was teaching a night class, and though he claimed to have forgotten I was in class, I wonder. If I had answered, I doubt he would have revealed as much. In it he said how much he'd enjoyed our previous weekend together, how much fun he had. "I can't tell you how much it meant to me," he said. There was a long pause, then he added, "Matter of fact, I can't tell you how I feel about you. If I do, I'll be too embarrassed to ever talk to you again."

So the wordsmith felt more comfortable showing his affection in other ways. He was doomed to make a joke of strong feelings. Mostly it came out as good-natured ribbing, but I'm sure he inadvertently hurt some feelings, too. A friend once told me that she couldn't stand to be around Pat and Bernie together because of the way they put each other down. I was surprised, because the "Pat and Bernie Show" was a prized comedy routine that everyone seemed to enjoy. But if you didn't know their bantering masked a deep affection that neither could comfortably express otherwise, then the barbs were definitely wince-worthy. Pat always knew when he went too far, and he fretted about it afterward. He might have had thick skin, and expected the same of you, but he also had a tender heart. He couldn't stand to see anyone hurt.

That was the complexity of the man I loved, and as exasperating as it could be, it also tickled me more than anything. One time he was fretting that he'd been too hard in teasing my youngest son, Jake, who was an easy target. Jake, the self-proclaimed wild man, a surfer dude from California, a jokester himself, loved the banter with Pat. If you could dish it out to Pat, you better be prepared to take it as well. It was Jake's sensitive, artsy side that Pat worried about. After a visit from Jake, Pat wondered aloud if he'd gone too far teasing him about his hippy-dippy image. I scoffed and assured him that Jake was fine, but frowning, Pat wasn't sure. He wanted Jake to understand that he adored him, and that's why he loved teasing him. Finally he placed the call. "Hey, sorry-ass stepson!" Pat called out cheerfully into Jake's answering machine. "Hope you made it back home okay. Your mama and I enjoyed your visit. Tell that nice girlfriend of yours that she has the worst taste imaginable in men. I hope she'll come to her senses and kick your worthless ass out. Great love, son, and come back to see us." When he hung up smiling, pleased with himself for making amends, I rolled my eyes.

No one was spared, but thankfully, his grandkids got him, their beloved Poppy, and saw through his gruffness. "Beat it, kids," he'd roar at them when they burst into his room to say hello. "I'm not your typical warm and fuzzy grandfatherly type. Tell your mamas that I don't want to hear about every second of your precious little lives. I don't give a shit what you made on your report card, and no, I'm not coming to speak to your school, either." They'd run out hooting and hollering to tell their mamas about Poppy saying bad words again. The girls would confront their dad, hands on hips, as the kids peered around their skirts gleefully. "I can't help it, girls," he'd say, deadpan. "I don't like grandchildren. Wish I did, but I just don't." Unappeased, the girls would scowl, but the kids howled with pleasure.

Not everyone got Pat, of course. I've had almost as many people, on hearing Pat was my husband, express concern for me as those who expressed awe or envy. "Bless your heart, honey," one woman whispered as she gave me a sympathetic hug early in my marriage to Pat. "How do you live with such a tortured soul?" I looked at her in disbelief. "*Pat*? Naw, he's a sweetheart. A big old teddy bear, really."

Her expression said, *It's worse than I thought. Poor thing's obviously in denial. Anyone with a lick of sense can tell that Pat Conroy is a modern-day Heathcliff, dark and scowling and perpetually tormented.* Pat roared with laughter when I told him the story later. "Thanks for not telling her the truth," he said, "about what an asshole I really am."

"You would've done the same for me," I said drily. At least he looked abashed, considering what he would've told the poor woman if it had been the other way around. His usual response when someone asked him about my writing was to say that his wife wrote pornography while he wrote only Christian fiction. He once announced to a packed audience at the Miami Book Festival that I was the author (then unknown) of *Fifty Shades of Grey*. Next to him on stage, I snorted. "You wish," I said. Oh, Pat.

And I'm doing it, too, of course. I have to try and cover up my emotions on reading these beautifully moving stories by keeping it light and playful, by sharing some funny little anecdotes of my own about Pat. I can't let everyone know how much these recollections mean to me, how I'll treasure them always. Words are so inadequate, and they're hard for all of us. They can't even begin to express our shared sorrow over the loss of this magnificent, irreplaceable man, or the void he left in our lives that will never be filled. They can't possibly make his readers see the Pat we knew, the wonderfully warm, funny, irascible, generous man we loved so much. Or, you know what? Maybe I'm wrong. Maybe that's what we just did, and we did it in a way that Pat would approve of. It was his way, the way we writers have shared our great love for him through this collection, and have tried to express an inexpressible grief. We did it the only way it could be done, through the magic of story.

Acknowledgments

We, the editors, are grateful for this opportunity to honor the legacy of our mentor and friend, Pat Conroy, with this labor of love. Recruiting, organizing, and editing the essays of a phenomenal group of nearly seventy authors over many months was a joy of discovery and revelation that readers will now get to experience as we have. Our work was made both possible and enriched by the efforts of many: the supportive board of directors and volunteers of the Pat Conroy Literary Center, our literary agent MacKenzie Fraser-Bub, our families, and, of course, Cassandra King Conroy, whose support of this anthology from the beginning filled our sails. To the pantheon of writers who graciously offered their recollections and time, it was a surreal and wonderful blessing to read your work in advance and do our part to give form and purpose to our collective mosaic. To each person and organization who granted use of the volume's photographs, and to the stellar publishing team at the University of Georgia Press—including Lisa Bayer, Jordan Stepp, Jon Davies, Steven Wallace, Jason Bennett, Katherine La Mantia, Alison Low, and Mindy Conner—we extend our sincere gratitude. And to the incomparable subject of our book, the larger-than-life Pat Conroy, no thanks can ever be enough.

Contributors

DOTTIE ASHLEY served as writer and critic covering the local performing arts and Broadway for the *State* newspaper in Columbia, South Carolina, and the *Charleston Post and Courier* for nearly forty years. She was selected by the United States Information Agency as one of twenty dance writers and critics to participate in a Russian cultural exchange program in 1990. She was also selected in 1981 to spend a month at the Eugene O'Neill Theatre Center in Waterford, Connecticut, where she and nine other theater writers saw a staged reading of a new play each night and submitted reviews to be critiqued by a master critic. Ashley is the only newspaper dance critic to twice win a fellowship sponsored by the American Dance Festival and is the only newspaper arts writer to be honored by the South Carolina Arts Commission with the prestigious Elizabeth O'Neill Verner Award.

WILLIAM A. BALK JR., veteran bookseller and master gardener, writes for WeeklyHubris.com. Balk serves on the board of directors of South Carolina Humanities and on the advisory council of the Pat Conroy Literary Center, where he is the volunteer coordinator.

RICK BRAGG is the Pulitzer Prize–winning author of *All Over but the Shoutin'*, *Ava's Man*, *The Prince of Frogtown*, and *The Best Cook in the World*. Bragg, who has written for numerous magazines, including *Sports Illustrated* and *Food & Wine*, was a newspaper reporter for two decades, covering high school football for the *Jacksonville News* and, among other topics, Islamic fundamentalism for the *New York Times*. He has won more than fifty significant writing awards in books and journalism, including, twice, the American Society of Newspaper Editors Distinguished Writing Award. A graduate of Jacksonville State University, Bragg was a Nieman Fellow at Harvard University. Bragg is currently Professor of Writing in the Journalism Department at the University of Alabama.

SONNY BREWER is the author of four novels, including *The Poet of Tolstoy Park*, *A Sound like Thunder*, and *The Widow and the Tree*. He also edits an anthology series, *Stories from the Blue Moon Café*. Brewer founded Over the Transom Bookstore in Fairhope and its annual literary conference, Southern Writers Reading. He is also founder of the nonprofit Fairhope Center for Writing Arts.

SANDRA BROWN is the author of more than sixty *New York Times* best sellers, including *Mean Streak*, *Deadline*, *Low Pressure*, *Lethal*, *Rainwater*, *Tough Customer*, *Smash Cut*, *Smoke Screen*, and *Play Dirty*. More than eighty million copies of her books are in print worldwide, and her work has been translated into thirty-four languages.

JONATHAN CARROLL is an American fiction writer primarily known for novels that may be labeled magic realism, slipstream, or contemporary fantasy. He has lived in Austria since the 1970s. Carroll's short story "Friend's Best Man" won the World Fantasy Award. His novel *Outside the Dog Museum* won the British Fantasy Award, and his collection of short stories won the Bram Stoker Award. The short story "Uh-Oh City" won the French Grand Prix de l'Imaginaire. His short story "Home on the Rain" was chosen as one of the best stories of the year by the Pushcart Prize committee. Carroll has been a runner-up for other World Fantasy Awards, the Hugo, and British Fantasy Awards.

RYDER CARROLL is a digital product designer and the inventor of the Bullet Journal® method. He has had the privilege of working with such companies as Adidas, American Express, Cisco, IBM, Macy's, and HP. He has been featured by the *New York Times*, *LA Times*, Fast Company, Bloomberg, Lifehacker, and Mashable. He recently gave a TEDx talk at Yale on intentionality.

MARK CHILDRESS is the author of seven novels: *Georgia Bottoms*, *One Mississippi*, *Gone for Good*, *Crazy in Alabama*, *Tender*, *V for Victor*, and *A World Made of Fire*. He is a native of Alabama and currently lives in Key West, Florida.

KATHERINE CLARK is the coauthor of the oral biographies *Motherwit: An Alabama Midwife's Story*, with Onnie Lee Logan, and *Milking the Moon: A Southerner's Story of Life on this Planet*, a finalist for a National Book Critics Circle award, coauthored with Eugene Walter. Clark is the author of the four-volume Mountain Brook series of novels published by the University of South Carolina Press's Story River Books, beginning with *The Headmaster's Darlings*, winner of the 2015 Willie Morris Award for Southern Fiction. Her most recent publication is *My Exaggerated Life*, an oral biography of the late Pat Conroy. She lives on the Gulf Coast.

JOHN CONNOR CLEVELAND is a writer and policy and communications professional in South Carolina.

CASSANDRA KING CONROY is the award-winning author of five novels, a book of nonfiction, numerous short stories, essays, and magazine articles, most recently in *Coastal Living* and *Southern Living*. Her *New York Times* and *USA Today* best-selling second novel, *The Sunday Wife*, was a *People* magazine Page-Turner, a South Carolina's Readers Circle choice, and one of Book Sense's top reading group selections. Also a *New York Times* and *USA Today* best seller, *The Same Sweet Girls* was a number-one Book Sense selection on release. Both novels were nominated for Southern Independent Booksellers Alliance's Book of the Year. *Moonrise* was a SIBA Okra Pick and best seller, as was *The Same Sweet Girls Guide to Life: Advice from a Failed Southern Belle*. Recently honored as a 2017 Alabama Humanities Foundation Fellow, Conroy is currently working on a memoir about life with her late husband, Pat Conroy.

MELISSA CONROY is the author and illustrator of *The Lowcountry Coloring Book*. She is also the author of two children's books: *Poppy's Pants*, which she illustrated, and *Grandma Is an Author*, both winners of the Pulpwood Queens Children's Book of the Year. She is a graduate of the Rhode Island School of Design, the University of Georgia, and Philadelphia University, where she teaches textile design. Conroy lives in Philadelphia with her husband and two children.

TIM CONROY is a former special education teacher and school administrator. His first book of poetry, *Theologies of Terrain* (2017), was edited by Poet Laureate of Columbia, South Carolina, Ed Madden and published in Muddy Ford Press's Laureate Series. A founding board member of the Pat Conroy Literary Center, established in his brother's honor, Conroy lives and writes in Columbia.

DEBBI COVINGTON is an award-winning chef, caterer, and writer. A food columnist for Beaufort, South Carolina's, *Lowcountry Weekly*, Covington is the author of the cookbooks *Celebrate Everything!* (Gold Medal Winner of the Benjamin Franklin Award), *Dining under the Carolina Moon*, and, most recently, *Celebrate Beaufort*. She has been featured as a "Master of Entertaining" in *Southern Living* magazine, and her recipes have been published in multiple cookbooks, including *Southern Living's Best Kept Secrets of the South's Best Cooks* and *The Best of The Best of South Carolina*.

NATHALIE DUPREE is the author of fourteen cookbooks that have sold more than half a million copies. She has hosted more than three hundred national and international cooking shows on PBS, the Food Network, and the Learning Channel. She has also written for many magazines and newspapers, including a column for the *Atlanta Journal-Constitution* on food and relationships that Peter Boyer called "unique in American Journalism today" in an article in *Vanity Fair* magazine. She has appeared many times on the *Today Show* and *Good Morning America*. Dupree has won wide recognition for her work, including four James Beard Awards, nomination to the James Beard Foundation's Who's Who in American Cooking, and numerous others. She is best known for her approachability and her understanding of southern cooking, having started the New Southern Cooking movement now found in many restaurants throughout the United States. She has been chef of restaurants in Majorca, Spain; Social Circle, Georgia; and Richmond, Virginia. For ten years she directed the Rich's Cooking School in Atlanta, where she stopped counting at 10,000 students. She has been the president of the Atlanta chapter of the International Women's Forum, founder and past president of IACP (International Association of Culinary Professionals), founder and board member of Southern Foodways, and founder and copresident of two chapters of Les Dames d'Escoffier, by whom she was awarded the honor of "Grande Dame." She was the founding president of the Charleston Wine and Food Festival. She was named the 2013 Woman of the Year by the French Master Chefs of America and in 2018 was inducted into the South Carolina Academy of Authors' the Palmetto State's literary hall of fame.

WALTER EDGAR, South Carolina's preeminent historian, is the Neuffer Professor of Southern Studies Emeritus and Distinguished Professor of History Emeritus at the University of South Carolina. The host of the popular SC-ETV Radio program *Walter Edgar's Journal*, Edgar is the author of the landmark *South Carolina: A History* and editor of the *South Carolina Encyclopedia* and *Conversations with the Conroys: Interviews with Pat Conroy and His Family*. His numerous awards and honors include the South Carolina Order of the Palmetto, the South Carolina Governor's Award in the Humanities, and induction into the South Carolina Hall of Fame.

STEPHANIE AUSTIN EDWARDS, a former dancer and costumer, is a novelist, writing teacher, and author consultant. Her twenty-two-year career in theater began in San Diego and moved her to New York City. She worked on Broadway and in film and on television with such talents as Liza Minnelli, Michael Jackson, Lauren Bacall, Woody Allen, Martin Scorsese, Hal Prince, Stephen Sondheim, Bill

Cosby, and Michael Bennett. Later, she returned to her roots in the South Carolina lowcountry where she now facilitates writers' groups, teaches writing workshops, and volunteers at the Pat Conroy Literary Center. Her debut novel, *What We Set in Motion*, won a Best Submission Award at the Atlanta Writer's Club Conference.

MARGARET EVANS is the editor and publisher of *Lowcountry Weekly*, where she pens her South Carolina Press Association Award–winning column *Rants & Raves*. Her articles and essays have appeared in publications throughout the South, most recently *State of the Heart: South Carolina Writers on the Places They Love*, volume 2, and *Southbound* magazine. She is the former editor of *Beaufort* magazine and former assistant to Pat Conroy. Evans lives in Beaufort with her husband, Jeff, and daughter, Amelia. She is a proud member of the Pat Conroy Literary Center's advisory council.

NIKKY FINNEY is the John H. Bennett Jr. Endowed Professor of Creative Writing and Southern Letters and a professor of African American Studies at the University of South Carolina. She is the author of the poetry collections *On Wings Made of Gauze*, *RICE*, *The World Is Round*, and *Head Off & Split*, which was awarded the 2011 National Book Award for Poetry. Finney was inducted into the South Carolina Academy of Authors in 2013..

CONNIE MAY FOWLER is the author of seven books—six critically praised novels and one memoir. Her novels include *How Clarissa Burden Learned to Fly*, *Sugar Cage*, *River of Hidden Dreams*, *The Problem with Murmur Lee*, *Remembering Blue*—recipient of the Chautauqua South Literary Award—and *Before Women Had Wings*—recipient of the 1996 Southern Book Critics Circle Award and the Francis Buck Award from the League of American Pen Women. Three of her novels have been Dublin International Literary Award nominees. Fowler adapted *Before Women Had Wings* for Oprah Winfrey. The result was an Emmy-winning film starring Ms. Winfrey and Ellen Barkin. In 2002 she published *When Katie Wakes*, a memoir that explores her descent into and escape from an abusive relationship. She teaches at the Vermont College of Fine Arts low residency creative writing MFA program and directs the college's VCFA Novel Retreat. Fowler, along with her husband, Bill Hinson, is founder and director of the newly minted Yucatan Writing Conference.

JONATHAN GALASSI, president and former publisher of Farrar, Straus and Giroux, is an accomplished veteran of the publishing world, the setting of his recently published first novel, *Muse*. In 2008 he received the Maxwell E. Perkins Award, which recognizes an editor, publisher, or agent who "has discovered, nurtured, and championed writers of fiction in the United States." Galassi is also the author of three collections of poetry—*Morning Run, North Street*, and *Left-Handed*—as well as translations of the Italian poets Eugenio Montale and Giacomo Leopardi. A former Guggenheim Fellow and poetry editor of the *Paris Review*, he also writes for the *New York Review of Books* and other publications.

JUDY GOLDMAN's *Together: Memoir of a Marriage and a Medical Mishap* is forthcoming from Nan A. Talese/Doubleday. Goldman is the author of two novels—*Early Leaving* and *The Slow Way Back*—a finalist for SIBA's Novel of the Year, and winner of the Sir Walter Raleigh Fiction Award and the Mary Ruffin Poole Award for First Fiction. Her memoir, *Losing My Sister*, was a finalist for both SIBA's Memoir of the Year and *ForeWord Review*'s Memoir of the Year. She is also the author of two books of poetry, *Holding Back Winter* and *Wanting to Know the End*, winner of the Gerald Cable Poetry Prize, Roanoke-Chowan Prize, Zoe Kincaid Brockman Prize, and Oscar Arnold Young Prize. She received the Hobson Award for Distinguished Achievement in Arts and Letters and the Fortner Writer and Community Award for "outstanding generosity to other writers and the larger community." Goldman lives in Charlotte, North Carolina.

SCOTT GRABER lives and writes in Beaufort, South Carolina, with his wife, the artist Susan Graber. A Citadel classmate and longtime friend of Pat Conroy's, Graber is the author of the novels *Malachi* and *Ten Days in Brazzaville* and is also an attorney.

CLIFF GRAUBART was born and raised in New York City. He attended the University of Toledo and is a graduate of Georgia State University. He boxed in the Golden Gloves, sold furs in Manhattan in his father's store, and once parachuted out of a perfectly good airplane in celebration of his fortieth birthday—all material for his short stories, which have appeared in the *Atlanta Journal* magazine, *GOODlife* magazine, *Atlanta* magazine, and the *Atlanta Gazette*. Graubart is owner of the Old New York Book Shop in Atlanta, where he lives with his wife, Cynthia, and their two children. He is the author of *The Curious Vision of Sammy Levitt and Other Stories*.

CYNTHIA GRAUBART, a former producer for the Food Network, is coauthor, with Nathalie Dupree, of *Mastering the Art of Southern Cooking*, which won a James Beard Book Award for American Cooking. Among Graubart's other books are *Slow Cooking for Two*, *Sunday Suppers*, and *Chicken* in the Savor the South series.

ANTHONY GROOMS's latest novel, *The Vain Conversation*, was selected by Pat Conroy for his Story River Books imprint for publication in spring 2018. Like much of Grooms's fiction, *The Vain Conversation* explores the complexity of race relations in the South during the Jim Crow years. His novel *Bombingham*, set against the civil rights movement, is often taught in high schools and colleges. It was a *Washington Post* notable book and was chosen as a citywide common read for Washington, D.C. His collection of short stories, *Trouble No More*, likewise has been widely adopted by teachers. Grooms has twice won the Lillian Smith Prize for Fiction and was a finalist for the Hurston-Wright Foundation Award. He holds fellowships from Yaddo, Bread Loaf, the National Endowment for the Arts, and Fulbright.

JONATHAN HAUPT is the executive director of the Pat Conroy Literary Center, the founding director of the annual Pat Conroy Literary Festival, and the former director of the University of South Carolina Press. He serves on the boards of the South Carolina Academy of Authors and the Friends of South Carolina Libraries and on the advisory board of the South Carolina Humanities and the affiliates steering committee of the American Writers Museum. Haupt's book reviews and author interviews have appeared in the *Charleston Post and Courier*; *Lowcountry Weekly*; *Fall Lines*; *Shrimp, Collards & Grits* magazine; and the Conroy Center's *Porch Talk* blog. He lives with his wife, Lorene, and their pack of rescued pets in Beaufort, South Carolina.

ALEXIA JONES HELSLEY is an American archivist and historian who currently serves as senior instructor of history and university archivist at the University of South Carolina Aiken. She is the author of several nonfiction books, including *Beaufort, South Carolina: A History*; *Wicked Beaufort*; *Hidden History of Greenville County, SC*; *A Guide to Historic Beaufort*; *Columbia, South Carolina: History*; *Wicked Edisto: The Dark Side of Eden*; and *A History of North Carolina Wine*. In addition, she is a contributor to *South Carolina Women: Their Lives and Times*, volume 1, and the *South Carolina Encyclopedia*. Helsley also chairs the Old Exchange Commission and is a member of the Beaufort High School Hall of Fame on the board of the South Carolina Historical Association. She is the recipient of the 2006 Governor's Archives Award, USCA's first part-time teaching award, and the Bobby Gilmer Moss Research Award (SCDAR).

PATTI CALLAHAN HENRY is a *New York Times* best-selling author of more than a dozen novels, including her most recent, *Becoming Mrs. Lewis* and *The Bookshop at Water's End*. A finalist in the Townsend Prize for Fiction, an Indie Next Pick and Okra pick, and a multiple nominee for the Southern Independent Booksellers

Alliance (SIBA) Novel of the Year, she now lives in both Mountain Brook, Alabama, and Bluffton, South Carolina, with her husband.

MARY HOOD is the author of the novel *Familiar Heat* and three short story collections: *How Far She Went* (winner of the Flannery O'Connor Award for Short Fiction and the Southern Review/LSU Short Fiction Award), *And Venus Is Blue* (winner of the Lillian Smith Award, the Townsend Prize for Fiction, and the Dixie Council of Authors and Journalists Author of the Year Award), and *A Clear View of the Southern Sky* (winner of the Townsend Prize for Fiction and, for its author, Georgia Author of the Year for Short Stories). Hood's work has also been honored with the Whiting Writers' Award, the Robert Penn Warren Award, and a Pushcart Prize. A 2014 inductee into the Georgia Writers Hall of Fame, Hood lives and writes in Commerce, Georgia.

JOSEPHINE HUMPHREYS is the Charleston-born author of four novels: *Dreams of Sleep*, winner of the PEN/Hemingway award for best first novel of 1984; *Rich in Love*, a *New York Times* Notable Book of the Year, with a movie version starring Albert Finney and Jill Clayburgh; *The Fireman's Fair*, also a *New York Times* Notable Book; and *Nowhere Else on Earth*, winner of the Southern Book Award. A graduate of Duke University, Humphreys studied fiction writing with Reynolds Price and William Blackburn and has won a Guggenheim Fellowship, the Lyndhurst Prize, and a literature award from the American Academy of Arts and Letters. She worked closely with Ruthie Bolton, author of *GAL, a True Life*, and wrote the introduction of that best-selling memoir. She has been inducted into the South Carolina Academy of Authors and the Fellowship of Southern Writers. She and her husband, Tom Hutcheson, live on Sullivan's Island and Johns Island.

JANIS IAN, a Grammy Award–winning songwriter, singer, and author, took the stage at age fifteen with a revolutionary song about interracial relationships, "Society's Child." It was 1966, and the nation responded with both hostility and accolades. The song rose to number one, and Janis was caught in the maelstrom of a divided country. Terrified by the hatred directed at her, she left the music industry, only to return a few years later with the worldwide hit "At Seventeen." In addition to being a songwriter, singer, and musician, Ian is a columnist and author. Her works include science fiction, poetry, magazine articles, and opinion columns, as well as her top-selling autobiography, *Society's Child*.

TERRY KAY is the author of seventeen published books. Three of his novels have been produced as Hallmark Hall of Fame movies—*To Dance with the White Dog*,

The Runaway, and *The Valley of Light*. His books have been published in more than twenty foreign languages, with *To Dance with the White Dog* selling two million copies in Japan. Kay is an essayist and regional Emmy-winning screenwriter as well as a novelist, and his work has appeared in numerous magazines and anthologies. A 2006 inductee into the Georgia Writers Hall of Fame and a 2009 recipient of the Governor's Award in the Humanities, Kay was further honored in 2015 by the Atlanta Writers Club's designation of its annual fiction award as the Terry Kay Prize for Fiction. In 2011 Kay was presented the Lifetime Achievement Award by the Georgia Writers Association. He has received the Georgia Author of the Year award four times and in 2004 was presented with the Townsend Prize. In 2006 he received the Appalachian Heritage Writer's Award from Shepherd University. In 2007 he received the Brooke Baker Award from Dunwoody Library honoring his career as a writer and the Stanley W. Lindberg Award given for an individual's significant contribution to the preservation and celebration of Georgia's literary heritage. A native of Hart County, Georgia, Kay and his wife now reside in Athens, Georgia.

JOHN LANE is a professor of English and environmental studies at Wofford College and director of the college's Goodall Environmental Studies Center. Lane is the author of a dozen books of poetry and prose, including six published by the University of Georgia Press, most recently *Coyote Settles the South*. Lane's book *Abandoned Quarry: New & Selected Poems*, includes much of his poetry published over the past thirty years plus a selection of new poems. His newest book of poems, *Anthropocene Blues*, was published in 2017. Lane's first novel, *Fate Moreland's Widow*, was published by Story River Books in early 2015. He has won numerous awards, including the 2001 Phillip D. Reed Memorial Award for Outstanding Writing on the Southern Environment by the Southern Environmental Law Center. In 2011 he won the Glenna Luschei Prairie Schooner Award, and in 2012 *Abandoned Quarry* won the SIBA (Southern Independent Booksellers Alliance) Poetry Book of the Year prize. In 2014 Lane was inducted into the South Carolina Academy of Authors. He and his wife, Betsy Teter, are among the cofounders of Spartanburg's Hub City Writers Project.

DAVID LAUDERDALE is a columnist and senior editor for the *Hilton Head Island Packet* and the *Beaufort Gazette*.

ELLEN MALPHRUS, the author of the novel *Untying the Moon*, lives and writes in her native Carolina lowcountry and southwest Montana. Her fiction, poetry, and essays have appeared in *Southern Literary Journal*, *Review of Contemporary Fiction*,

William and Mary Review, Georgia Poetry Review, Haight Ashbury Literary Journal, Savannah Literary Journal, Yemassee Literary Journal, and the anthology *Essence of Beaufort and the Lowcountry.* Malphrus is the deputy director of the Pat Conroy Literary Festival and an adviser to the Pat Conroy Literary Center. A student of James Dickey, she is writer-in-residence and professor of English at the University of South Carolina Beaufort.

ANDY MARLETTE is a political cartoonist and columnist for the *Pensacola News Journal.*

BREN MCCLAIN is the author of *One Good Mama Bone,* a novel published by Pat Conroy's Story River Books. The novel was long-listed for the 2018 Crook's Corner Book Prize, received a starred review in *Booklist,* was named a 2017 winter Okra pick by the Southern Independent Booksellers Alliance, and selected as the 2018 Pulpwood Queens Book of the Year. McClain is a two-time winner of the South Carolina Fiction Project and the recipient of the 2005 Fiction Fellowship from the South Carolina Arts Commission. She is at work on her next novel, *Took,* which received the gold medal for the 2016 William Faulkner–William Wisdom Novel-in-Progress.

TERESA MILLER founded the Oklahoma Center for Poets and Writers in 1994 and served as its director until her retirement in 2015. In addition to directing the center, Miller taught creative writing at Oklahoma State University and is the executive producer and host of the television interview program *Writing Out Loud.* A former editor for the University of Oklahoma Press, Miller is the author of the memoir *Means of Transit* and the novels *Remnants of Glory* and *Family Correspondence.*

WENDELL MINOR is nationally known for the artwork he has created for more than fifty award-winning children's books. His many collaborators include Jean Craighead George, Robert Burleigh, Buzz Aldrin, Tony Johnston, Mary Higgins Clark, and his wife, Florence. Minor is also the cover artist and designer of more than two thousand books for such authors as Pat Conroy, David McCullough, Fannie Flagg, and Nathaniel Philbrick among many others. His portrait of Harry S. Truman for the cover of David McCullough's book is in the permanent collection of the National Portrait Gallery in Washington, D.C. In 2013 Wendell and Florence Minor were given the New England Independent Booksellers Association (NEIBA) President's Award for lifetime achievement in arts and letters.

MARY ALICE MONROE is the *New York Times* best-selling author of twenty novels and two children's books. Her awards include the South Carolina Book

Festival Award for Excellence in Writing, the Southwest Florida Book Festival Distinguished Author Award, South Carolina Center for the Book's Award for Writing, the RT Lifetime Achievement Award, and the International Book Award for Green Fiction. In 2018 Monroe was inducted into the South Carolina Literary Hall of Fame. Her two children's books received several awards, including the ASPCA Henry Bergh award. Monroe's novel *The Beach House* was made into a Hallmark film starring Andie MacDowell. Her new novel, *Beach House Reunion*, was released in May 2018. Monroe serves on the board of the South Carolina Aquarium and the Leatherback Trust.

MICHAEL MORRIS is the award-winning author of *A Place Called Wiregrass*. His second novel, *Slow Way Home*, was named one of the best novels of the year by the *Atlanta Journal-Constitution* and the *St. Louis Post-Dispatch*. *Publishers Weekly* ranked his latest novel, *Man in the Blue Moon*, among the best books of 2012. A finalist for the Southern Book Critics Circle Award, Michael is a graduate of Auburn University and holds an MFA in creative writing from Spalding University.

KATHY L. MURPHY is the author of *The Pulpwood Queens' Tiara-Wearing, Book-Sharing Guide to Life*, a licensed cosmetologist, and the founder of the Pulpwood Queens and Timber Guys Book Club. She earned her BFA in art at the University of Texas at Tyler. Her colossally successful author events have attracted national attention and media, including features on ABC TV's *Good Morning America* and in *Newsweek*, the *Wall Street Journal*, and the *LA Times*. Her Pulpwood Queens Book Club started in her beauty salon/bookstore and has grown into the country's largest "meeting and discussing" book club, with more than 725 chapters nationwide and in 15 foreign countries. Each January, the Pulpwood Queens gather for the "Girlfriend Weekend," an event celebrating books and authors that brings hundreds of women from all over the country to East Texas.

MICHAEL O'KEEFE was nominated for the Academy Award for Best Supporting Actor and the Golden Globe Award for New Star of the Year for his portrayal of Ben Meechum in the film adaptation of Pat Conroy's *The Great Santini*. An actor, writer, director, and producer, O'Keefe has appeared in the films *Michael Clayton*, *Frozen River*, *Ironweed*, and *Caddyshack*; and in the television series *The West Wing*, *Law and Order*, *House, M.D.*, *Homeland*, *Blue Bloods*, and many others. O'Keefe holds an MFA in creative writing from Bennington College. A poet and songwriter, he is the author of the poetry collection *Swimming from under My Father*. O'Keefe is married to the actress Emily Donahoe.

STEVE ONEY is the author of *A Man's World: Portraits*, a collection of articles from his forty years of writing for *Esquire, GQ, Playboy*, the *New York Times Magazine*, and others. His first book, *And the Dead Shall Rise: The Murder of Mary Phagan and the Lynching of Leo Frank*, won the American Bar Association's Silver Gavel Award for best work on the nation's legal system and the National Jewish Book Award for history. Early in his career Oney was a staff writer at the *Atlanta Journal-Constitution* magazine. More recently he worked as a senior editor at *Los Angeles* magazine. His stories have been anthologized in *The Best American Sports Writing, 2006*, and *The Best American Magazine Writing, 2008*. Oney was educated at the University of Georgia and at Harvard, where he was a Nieman Fellow. He lives in Los Angeles with his wife, designer Madeline Stuart, and is at work on a book about National Public Radio for Simon & Schuster.

KATHLEEN PARKER, a South Carolina native, is a Pulitzer Prize–winning journalist for the *Washington Post*. Her twice-weekly columns on politics and culture are syndicated in more than four hundred media outlets.

MARK POWELL is the author of five novels, including *The Sheltering*, published by Story River Books, and *Small Treasons*, published by Gallery/Simon & Schuster. Powell has received fellowships from the National Endowment for the Arts, the Breadloaf, and Sewanee Writers' Conference, and was a Fulbright Fellow to Slovakia. He has also received the Chaffin Award for contributions to Appalachian literature. He holds degrees from Yale Divinity School, the University of South Carolina, and The Citadel. He lives in the mountains of North Carolina and teaches at Appalachian State University.

RON RASH is the author of the 2009 PEN/Faulkner Finalist and *New York Times* best-selling novel *Serena* as well as three other prize-winning novels—*One Foot in Eden, Saints at the River*, and *The World Made Straight*—three collections of poems; and four collections of stories, among them *Burning Bright*, which won the 2010 Frank O'Connor International Short Story Award, and *Chemistry and Other Stories*, which was a finalist for the 2007 PEN/Faulkner Award. Twice the recipient of the O. Henry Prize, he teaches at Western Carolina University.

SALLIE ANN ROBINSON is a cookbook author, celebrity chef, and cultural historian. A native of Daufuskie Island, South Carolina, she is noted for her knowledge of Gullah traditions and history. While she is an author in her own right, Robinson's literary debut actually came as the character named Ethel in Pat Conroy's classic memoir, *The Water Is Wide*. She was among the students Conroy taught on

Daufuskie Island and maintained a friendship with him as an adult. Robinson's published works have been acclaimed for her mixture of authentic Gullah recipes, home remedies, folklore, memoir, and documentation of the Gullah dialect spoken by island natives. They include *Gullah Home Cooking the Daufuskie Way* and *Cooking the Gullah Way, Morning, Noon, and Night.*

LAWRENCE S. ROWLAND is distinguished professor emeritus of history at the University of South Carolina at Beaufort and past president of the South Carolina Historical Society. He is the coauthor of the three-volume *History of Beaufort County.* Rowland lives on Dataw Island, South Carolina, with his wife.

JONATHAN SANCHEZ is a writer and the owner of an independent bookstore, Blue Bicycle Books, in Charleston, South Carolina. He is the author of the short-story collection *Bandit,* a two-time winner in the South Carolina Fiction Project, and a former writer-in-residence at the Kerouac House in Orlando. He is the founder of the Write of Summer camp for kids; the Poets in the Schools program at Burke High School; and YALLFest, Charleston's Young Adult Book Festival. Sanchez lives in Charleston with his wife, Lauren, and their two children.

ALEX SANDERS is the former chief judge of the South Carolina Court of Appeals and has served as the president of the College of Charleston and the Charleston School of Law. He is the coauthor of three books and numerous articles for law journals and regional publications.

VALERIE SAYERS is the author of six novels, including her most recent, *The Powers,* which contemplates baseball, pacifism, and acts of witness in parallel narratives of prose and photography. Her novels *Who Do You Love* and *Brain Fever* were named *New York Times* Notable Books of the Year. The film *Due East* is based on her novels *Due East* and *How I Got Him Back.* Sayers's stories, essays, and reviews have appeared in such publications as the *New York Times, Washington Post, Commonweal, Zoetrope, Ploughshares, Image, Witness,* and *Prairie Schooner;* and have been cited in *Best American Short Stories* and *Best American Essays.* Her literary prizes include a National Endowment for the Arts literature fellowship and two Pushcart Prizes for fiction. In 2018 she was inducted into the South Carolina Academy of Authors—joining her Beaufort High School psychology teacher Pat Conroy. Sayers serves on the board of directors of the Pat Conroy Literary Center.

SEAN A. SCAPELLATO is a writer of fiction and essays, a former creative writing teacher at Charleston County School of the Arts, and is now a lawyer in Charleston, South Carolina.

BERNIE SCHEIN, retired educator and Beaufort native, is the author of *Famous All Over Town: A Novel* published by USC Press's Story River Books. Schein is also the author of *If Holden Caulfield Were in My Classroom: Inspiring Love, Creativity, and Intelligence in Middle School Kids* and, with his wife, Martha Schein, coauthor of *Open Classrooms in the Middle School.* He holds an Ed.M. from Harvard University with an emphasis in educational psychology. A forty-year veteran of middle school instruction and administration, Schein has served as the principal of schools in Mississippi and South Carolina and helped found the independent Paideia School in Atlanta, where he was honored as Atlanta's District Teacher of the Year in 1978. His stories and essays have appeared in *Atlanta* magazine, *Atlanta Weekly, Beaufort Gazette, Creative Loafing, Lowcountry Weekly,* and the *Mississippi Educational Advance,* and he has been interviewed on National Public Radio. Schein's memoir of his lifelong friendship with Pat Conroy, *Santini's Hero,* is forthcoming.

MAGGIE SCHEIN, research director of the Humanities and Liberal Arts Assessment Lab at Harvard University and Research Fellow at The Citadel, holds a Ph.D. in ethics from the University of Chicago's Committee on Social Thought. An admirer of Taoist texts, philosophies, and practices, as well as the works of naturalists and Native American storytellers, Schein brings a wealth of complementary and conflicting perspectives to her imaginative, lyrical fiction. She is the author of *Lost Cantos of the Ouroboros Caves,* an expanded edition of which was published by Story River Books and includes illustrations by Jonathan Hannah and a foreword by Schein's godfather, Pat Conroy.

NICOLE SEITZ is the author of seven novels, the editor of *When You Pass through Waters: Words of Hope and Healing from Your Favorite Authors,* and coeditor of *Our Prince of Scribes: Writers Remember Pat Conroy.* Her flood anthology was a nominee for the SIBA *Death of Santini* Nonfiction Prize. Her novels, including *The Spirit of Sweetgrass, Trouble the Water, A Hundred Years of Happiness, Saving Cicadas, The Inheritance of Beauty, Beyond Molasses Creek,* and most recently *The Cage-maker,* have received starred reviews, been chosen as books of the month, and been put on "best of" lists for Books-a-Million, the Pulpwood Queens Book Club, IndieNEXT List, *Southern Living, Deep South Magazine, Romantic Times,* and *Library Journal.* Her novels have been nominated for the Southern Independent Booksellers Alliance Award. Seitz's short fiction, essays, and articles have appeared in numerous publications and anthologies. She holds a BA in journalism from the University of North Carolina at Chapel Hill and a BFA in illustration from Savannah

College of Art and Design. Seitz is working on her next novel in Charleston, South Carolina, where she lives with her husband, Brian, and their two children.

LYNN SELDON, a VMI graduate, is a longtime travel journalist. He has written more than a thousand magazine features and has published six books on travel. His first novel was *Virginia's Ring*; his second novel, *Carolina's Ring*, will be published in 2018. With his wife and fellow travel writer, Cele, he is coauthor of the guidebook *100 Things to Do in Charleston before You Die*.

CATHERINE SELTZER, the author of the scholarly monograph *Understanding Pat Conroy* and a forthcoming trade biography of Conroy, is an associate professor of English and women's studies at Southern Illinois University at Edwardsville. She is also the author of *Elizabeth Spencer's Complicated Cartographies: Reimagining Home, the South, and Southern Literary Production*.

ANNE RIVERS SIDDONS is the best-selling author of eighteen novels including *Burnt Mountain, Off Season, Sweetwater Creek, Islands, Nora Nora, Low Country, Up Island, Fault Lines, Downtown, Hill Towns, Colony, Outer Banks, King's Oak, Peachtree Road, Homeplace, Fox's Earth, The House Next Door*, and *Heartbreak Hotel*. She is also the author of a work of nonfiction, *John Chancellor Makes Me Cry*. She splits her time between her homes in Charleston, South Carolina, and Brooklin, Maine.

GEORGE SINGLETON has published two novels, a book of advice, and seven collections of stories, which include *The Half-Mammals of Dixie* and *Calloustown*. He was raised in Greenwood, South Carolina, and educated at Furman University and the University of North Carolina at Greensboro. Singleton has published more than three hundred short stories in the *Atlantic Monthly, Harper's*, the *Georgia Review, One Story, Playboy, Subtropics*, the *Southern Review*, and elsewhere. He has been awarded a Pushcart Prize, the Corrington Award, the Hillsdale Award, and a Guggenheim fellowship. He was inducted into the South Carolina Acdemy of Authors and the Fellowship of Southern Writers. Singleton teaches at Wofford College.

BARBRA STREISAND, singer, songwriter, actress, and filmmaker, has sold more than 68.5 million albums in the United States and more than 145 million records worldwide over a career spanning six decades. Her many honors include two Academy Awards, ten Grammy Awards (including Lifetime Achievement and the Grammy Legend Award), five Emmy Awards, a Tony Award, an American Film Institute Award, a Kennedy Center Honors Prize, four Peabody Awards, the Presidential Medal of Freedom, and nine Golden Globes.

WILLIAM WALSH is the director of the Etowah Valley Writing Program at Reinhardt University and a southern narrative poet in the tradition of James Dickey, David Bottoms, and Fred Chappell. He is a three-time finalist for his novels in the Pirate's Alley William Faulkner Writing Competition. Walsh is the author of seven books; his most recent collection of poems is *Lost in the White Ruins*. His work has appeared in *Five Points, Flannery O'Connor Review, Georgia Review, Kenyon Review, Michigan Quarterly Review, North American Review, Poetry Daily, Poets & Writers, Rattle, Shenandoah,* and *Valparaiso Poetry Review.*

JOHN WARLEY, a native South Carolinian, is a graduate of The Citadel and the University of Virginia School of Law. Now a full-time writer, he divides his time between Beaufort, South Carolina, and San Miguel de Allende, Mexico. He is the author of the novels *Bethesda's Child, The Moralist, The Moralist II,* and *A Southern Girl* (the first Story River Book), and the nonfiction book *Stand Forever, Yielding Never: The Citadel in the 21st Century.* He also wrote "The Citadel at War," a narrative history of the college etched into the granite walls of The Citadel War Memorial, which opened to the public in October 2017.

ASHLEY WARLICK is the author of four novels—*The Arrangement, Seek the Living, The Summer after June,* and *The Distance from the Heart of Things.* Her work has appeared in *Redbook,* the *Oxford American, McSweeney's,* and *Garden and Gun,* among others. The youngest recipient of the Houghton Mifflin Literary Fellowship, she has also received a fellowship from the National Endowment for the Arts. She teaches fiction in the MFA program at Queens University in Charlotte, North Carolina. She is also the buyer at M. Judson Booksellers and Storytellers in Greenville, South Carolina, where she lives with her family.

TERESA K. WEAVER, a former board member of the National Book Critics Circle, served as the longtime book editor for the *Atlanta Journal-Constitution* and *Atlanta* magazine. She is the former editorial director for Habitat for Humanity International and is now a development writer for CARE, a global antipoverty non-profit based in Atlanta.

MARJORY WENTWORTH's poems have been nominated for the Pushcart Prize five times. Her books of poetry include *Noticing Eden, Despite Gravity, The Endless Repetition of an Ordinary Miracle,* and *New and Selected Poems.* She is the cowriter with Juan Mendez of *Taking a Stand: The Evolution of Human Rights,* coeditor with Kwame Dawes of *Seeking, Poetry and Prose Inspired by the Art of Jonathan Green,* and the author of the prize-winning children's story *Shackles*. Her most recent collaborations include *We Are Charleston: Tragedy and Triumph at Mother Emanuel*, with Herb Frazier and Dr. Bernard Powers, and *Out of Wonder: Poems Celebrating Poets* with Kwame Alexander and Chris Colderly (2017). Wentworth taught at the Art Institute of Charleston. She is the cofounder and former president of the Lowcountry Initiative for the Literary Arts and the poetry editor for *Charleston Currents*. Her work is included in the South Carolina Poetry Archives at Furman University, and she is the Poet Laureate of South Carolina.